Praise for N

One of the most compelling recovery stories I've read. *Naked In Public* is a powerful and inspiring story that speaks to the courage that underlies recovery from childhood sexual abuse, sexual shame and sex addiction. In this memoir, Staci Sprout truly "leads with vulnerability."

~ Claudia Black, Ph.D., author of
Intimate Treason and "It Could Never Happen to Me!"
Children of Alcoholics: As Youngsters – Adolescents - Adults

◊ ◊ ◊

With this work, Staci Sprout has provided a much-needed voice for female sex addicts, who far too often are shamed into silence. Her highly personalized account of sexual addiction and the process of recovery is incredibly powerful. Sex addicts of both genders will easily identify with her story. Most importantly, Staci provides a clear example of how sex addicts, especially female sex addicts, can and do heal from this debilitating disorder. Family members of sex addicts and those who treat sex addicts will also benefit from reading this book. Highly recommended!

~ Robert Weiss LCSW, CSAT-S, author of
Always Turned On: Sex Addiction in the Digital Age,
Cruise Control: Understanding Sex Addiction in Gay Men, and
Sex Addiction 101: A Basic Guide to Healing from
Sex, Porn, and Love Addiction

◊ ◊ ◊

Staci Sprout has captured the journey of a woman dealing with sex-love-relationship addiction. Her vulnerability, authenticity, and incredible imagery will touch you deeply.

~ Richard Blankenship, LPC, CCPS, CCSAS, author of
Spouses of Sex Addicts: Hope for the Journey

Naked In Public is a story that weaves together the varied and subtle strands of memory and experience that shape the development of an addict. It provides both an inspiration and a template for decoding what is most formative in our childhood, and what is most influential in finding the way out.

~ Linda Hatch, PhD, CSAT, author of
Relationships in Recovery: a Guide for
Sex Addicts who are Starting Over

◇ ◇ ◇

A page-turning, honest pilgrimage through sexual addiction to recovery. Not your typical memoir; this book reads more like a whodunit.

~ Joe Guppy, author of
My Fluorescent God: a psychotherapist confronts
his most challenging case—his own

◇ ◇ ◇

A wonderful account that will offer encouragement and insight for any person struggling with addictions, and a beautiful helping guide for the person who loves an addict. An instant recovery classic.

~ Mari A. Lee, LMFT, CSAT-S, author of,
Facing Heartbreak: Steps to Recovery for
Partners of Sex Addicts

◇ ◇ ◇

An engaging, heart-centered read. Honest and gritty. I highly recommend it!

~ Renee S. Katz, Ph.D, CSAT, author of
When Professionals Weep

naked in public

A Memoir of Recovery From Sex Addiction and

Other Temporary Insanities

naked in public

A Memoir of Recovery From Sex Addiction and Other Temporary Insanities

Staci Sprout

RECONTEXT MEDIA

RECONTEXT MEDIA

Publishing And Promoting High Candor Stories About Overcoming Adversity

Published by Recontext Media, LLC,
1800 Westlake Avenue North, Suite 102,
Seattle, WA 98109, U.S.A.

LIBRARY PUBLICATION DATA
Sprout, Staci.
Naked in public: a memoir of recovery from sex addiction and other
temporary insanities /Staci Sprout (v.1.0)—First Edition.
p. cm.
ISBN: 978-0-9962668-1-9 (paperback)
ISBN: 978-0-9962668-0-2 (ebook)
1. Sprout, Staci—Memoir. 2. Addiction recovery. 3. Sex addiction.
I. Title.

Credits:
Interior design and production by J. L. Saloff, www.saloff.com
Front cover design by Svetlana Uscumlic, summart9@gmail.com
Copy editing by Lea Galanter, www.leagalanter.com

Disclaimer

HONESTY IS ONE OF MY CORE VALUES. I have done my best to re-create events, locales, and conversations from personal documentation and memory, and I believe this book is an accurate recounting of my experiences in fact and, when the details were a bit fuzzy, in spirit.

However, sex is a highly personal matter. To protect the privacy of individuals mentioned in this book, I have changed names and identifying details. I respect all the individuals I chose to include in this story, regardless of the nature of our past relationship. I have included only people and experiences that seemed to significantly carry forth the story I felt deeply called to tell; one I felt could be helpful to others.

I also chose to slightly composite my therapy work, except for Margaret and Garlough, who are described as I experienced them. I saw many therapists over the years from whom I learned much, but consolidated what was said, and when. I did my best to portray accurate transformational moments in therapy as I experienced them.

When I first became serious about writing this memoir, I hired a writing coach, the warm and talented M.J. Schwader (www.inspiredlifepublications.com). M.J. asked me what kind of story I wanted to write: informational, inspirational, or transformational. I said all three, but if I had to choose, I'd go for transformational. This book is intended to shake things up, in a positive way, for the purpose of sexual healing and evolution. However, it is not intended as a substitute for the advice of physicians, psychotherapists, or other professionals. Neither the author nor the publisher shall be liable for any emotional, psychological, physical, sexual, financial, or other kind of damages.

And finally, I am not a formal representative for any professional or volunteer group, 12-Step fellowship, or other organization, nor am I receiving financial or any other incentives to be a spokesperson for any outside organization, regardless of affiliation status or membership, present or past. Out of respect for the traditions of 12-Step programs, I did not use the actual names of any specific fellowships I attended as an adult. I did disclose my mother's membership in Alcoholics Anonymous, with her permission, because it was a central influence on my life and story. I did so with a firm belief that 1) what I wrote was accurate, and 2) I do not believe this record of my experiences will prove harmful to the mighty mothership of Alcoholics Anonymous, to whom I will be forever grateful for my family's recovery.

This book is dedicated to everyone who has been sexually neglected*
and abused, and especially those who became sexually addicted.
May we all find our way to the healing, freedom, and true sexual
sacredness that is our birthright.

This story is also dedicated to the beloved fellowships of 12-Step
recovery, where I have consistently received kindness and compassion at the precise times I felt least worthy of it.

---

*"*Sexual neglect* is the failure to teach children about sexuality, leaving them at the
mercy of playmates, media, their own imagination and other potentially dubious
sources to learn about what sexuality is and how it applies to their experience and
relationships. Sexual neglect includes not teaching children basic information about
the emotional, physical, mental and spiritual aspects of sexuality, and how these
aspects change throughout the life and relationship cycle. It includes the absence
of appropriate supervision at various developmental levels of the children involved.
Sexual neglect also involves not providing facts about diverse sexual orientations,
sexual boundaries, risks, and dangers of certain sexual choices and behaviors. As
children reach appropriate maturity levels, sexual neglect includes lack of information about sexual abuse and pornography in society, and lack of education about how
to handle potentially sexually abusive situations." Staci Sprout, "Sexual Ethics: Beyond
the Basics" (presentation, Shepherd's Counseling Services, Seattle, WA, Feb. 8, 2013).

Table of Contents

Contents

Contents

Preface

THIS IS A STORY ABOUT SEX ADDICTION AND RECOVERY. It's also a story of healing from sexual neglect and abuse through experiences of emotional and sexual awakening. For a big part of this journey, the main character (who happens to be me) doesn't even know she's asleep.

In my current life, I work as a licensed therapist, helping people who feel powerless over sex addiction. I'm a recovered sex addict, and I use what I learned, along with my training, to support my clients on their own quests for healing. Though I don't claim to be perfect, I'm grateful to say that fourteen years after walking into my first 12-Step support meeting for sex addiction, I have over eleven years of continuous sexual sobriety. I no longer struggle with the obsessions or compulsive behaviors I wrote about in this memoir. Although revisiting them to create it was painful at times, it was also profoundly healing.

This memoir is my response to the question "What does recovery from sex addiction look like?" In this book I share the good, the bad, and some of the ugly of my story. I've done my best not to be overly graphic, but I've tried to put the same raw candor that has been so transformative for me onto every page. Because sex in various forms is a part of this story, some content may be intense and objectionable to some people. I'm willing to risk it, because sexual secrecy and shame contribute to the toxicity of sex addiction, and I believe honesty and openness are a big part of its antidote.

If you are reading this book, it probably means you are curious about sex addiction, and you are courageous. This is not an easy topic to face, because even the words "sex addiction" can be deeply upsetting for many people. As you will see in this story, they were overwhelming to me when I first heard them, even though I was addicted to sex at the time, and didn't know it! No matter what inspired you to pick up this book, you may identify with some parts of the story from your own experience, which may trigger painful feelings. Please read with care at a pace that works for you, and seek support if you need it.

If you think you or someone you love might have a problem with sex addiction, I've included a ten-question self-assessment in Appendix A, "Am I a Sex Addict?" Nothing in this book is intended as medical advice, but taking the test can be one way to begin to explore whether or not sex is out of control in your life. If so, contact information is provided for multiple 12-Step fellowships and more in the Resources section at the end of this book. There are many ways to get in trouble sexually in today's world, but I believe it is the best time in human history to find effective help to get out of it. As Brené Brown, one of my favorite paradigm-shifters, says, "Vulnerability is not weakness." It is a sign of strength to ask for help!

If someone had given me that self-assessment test fourteen years ago (and I'd been truthful with my answers), I would have aced it. I was addicted, and it took me a long time to learn that sex is not a pharmaceutical. Back then, I didn't understand that I'd survived a painful childhood, and I didn't know how to grieve the overwhelming losses I'd endured as a result. I couldn't bear the hurt coming to consciousness in my body and mind. My various addictions helped me run, and stay numb, and for me, sex became the one that worked the best. But I gradually learned that buried truths, when compassionately understood, become treasures.

Preface

I wrote this book to reach people who are dying from sex addiction, or whose sexual innocence is dying a slow, needless death. I want to tell them there is a way out, available *right now*. I believe there are as many paths to healing as there are individuals on the planet, and this book describes just one: mine. If you're addicted to sex, I urge you, find your way out! Healing is your responsibility, and no one else can do it for you. Get started now, you deserve it. Don't waste a minute of the incredible life that awaits you!

I also wrote my story to offer the families and loved ones of sex addicts an idea about what they might be dealing with, with the hope that they could navigate the journey more easily than we did in my family. Appendix E, "What to Do If Your Boyfriend or Girlfriend Tells You They're a Sex Addict," provides ideas and resources I wish I'd had for handling the situation I faced in Chapter 11, "So I'm Dating a Sex Addict." In my experience, being close to a sex addict can be the best relationship of your life, or the worst, depending on how they answer the questions in Appendix E.

Even if you are not sexually addicted and you don't think you've ever known anyone who is, I invite you to think again. What about that girl your whole school, or maybe even your whole town, called a slew of horrible names to describe her promiscuity? Or the kid in your neighborhood who had the world's largest porn collection? Or the person from work who couldn't stop talking or joking about sex, beyond curiosity or fascination; they seemed obsessed with it. Perhaps they were addicted to sex and no one knew what to call it, or that help was even needed, let alone desperately.

When I was fourteen I used to get rides to school from an older neighbor girl who had covered the entire inside of her compact car with glossy pictures of nearly naked young men torn from teen heartthrob magazines. I used to stare transfixed at the chiseled bodies she'd enshrined. Later, I heard that she went on to dance naked

3

full-time at a strip club, and that she'd died in her forties from a drug overdose. Today that sounds suspiciously like sex (and drug) addiction, but back then I had no words for what I saw. She was just my neighbor. As you will see in this story, I was somebody's neighbor, daughter, sister, and friend too, and I worked hard to seem normal to everyone. But I still had a major, hidden problem with sex, and I needed help long before I found it at age thirty-one.

To me, sexual recovery has meant using a variety of resources to heal from the pain of sex addiction, including 12-Step program support, psychotherapy, bodywork, and many other forms of personal and spiritual growth. As the popular 12-Step slogan highlights, it means doing "whatever it takes" to get and stay sober from compulsive sex. People of all genders can become addicted to sex, and for thoughts about whether it's safe for female sex addicts to attend 12-Step sexual recovery meetings, see Appendix C, "Are Women Safe in 12-Step Sexual Recovery Meetings?"

I believe almost everyone has been negatively impacted by untreated sex addiction in some way. I think that in order to bring resolution to the problem, almost everyone will need to be educated and become part of the solution. And to do this, I believe we will all have to join in the conversation, and, in safe settings, risk revealing more about our painful inner truths. Nudity is everywhere in modern society. Individuals expose their bodies in public media, but few expose themselves emotionally. I want to see that trend reversed. I'd like to see more emotional nakedness in the public sphere, especially when it comes to sex. I'd like to see us all get "naked in public" through *vulnerable conversations* about what sex really means, and what happens when we use it, or see it used, in deceptive and harmful ways.

One quote from addictions expert and author Gabor Maté resonates deeply with me: "If you leave a young child in a dark room long enough, she will go blind." My childhood neglect and abuse left me blind to the true beauty of sex and love in myself and others, but sexual recovery taught me to see.

Most of all, I wrote this book to share a message of hope: neglect and abuse hurts, but *healing is possible*. If it happened to you, it was not your fault. You are beautiful. Your sexuality is precious and sacred. It always has been. You are not to blame. Even if your body enjoyed sexual abuse, you are *still* not to blame! Our bodies are designed to respond to sexual stimulation, even if our minds are not developed enough to make sense of whether or not something is ultimately good for us.

Because of the transformative effect of sexual recovery, I was able to create a new vision about sex, different from the one offered to me, my parents, and my grandparents before them. I believe that paved the way for me to eventually meet and marry my husband, the love of my life, who (spoiler alert) makes a brief appearance in Chapter 36, "What All the Fuss Was About." My story is intense, but it has a happy ending that was really a new beginning to a beautiful life—an experience that is so radically different from where I started, sometimes I can hardly believe it. But don't take my word for it: read on and see for yourself!

Introduction

THE JULY SEATTLE EVENING was balmy as I made my way to the sexual recovery 12-Step meeting for newcomers. It was 2001, and I was thirty-one years old. Descending the steps to the church basement, the shadowy stairwell gave way to fluorescent lighting and a pale gray-cream linoleum tile floor. Wearing a bright pink tank top and short white shorts, I had on the least clothes of anyone in the room. And it was a big room, full of men, not another woman in sight. At least thirty were already seated, with more arriving. There were men of all ages, though mostly older. And all were sex addicts, like me.

I don't remember what I was thinking—outside of saying hi to the one man who said hi to me—but my inner dialogue probably went something like this:

Oh my God, I'm dressed wrong.

Oh look, he's looking at me. Look how quickly he looked away. What IS that? Is that sexual sobriety?

There's another man looking at me. I look hot. I'm thin and tan. Another. I'm powerful here. I like it. Oh, I am in heaven.

It's cold in here. I should've brought a sweatshirt. Where should I sit?

I said hi, politely, to a man who greeted me.

He's creepy. I feel like shit. What's wrong with me? Why am I here? I don't belong here. I'm the only woman. God, the meeting is about to start. Where do I sit? No one wants to sit by me.

I don't care, sit down!

Introduction

This chair is cold. I hate these freezing folding metal chairs. I want out of here!

As I sat in the circle with my eyes down, I placed all my mental focus on my intuitive feelers, as I always did back then in groups.

Who's looking at me? Who's tuned in to me being here? Who's lusting after me?

In the center of my energetic web, I cast invisible tendrils all around the circle. I imagined that I could feel every vibration around me, and that I could control them all. I was the spider in the middle of its lair, the black widow in the pink tank top, ready to spring on my prey and devour it.

The meeting started with the customary introductions, but I tuned out the words. Wrapped in the familiarity of my web, I was getting high off the vibrations I was starting to feel from men in the room.

Then another sensation intruded, a wave of shame that made me feel like a teenager whose mom had just dropped her off at detention. I ignored it, forcing my thoughts back to the men. Per my energy read, I estimated that approximately twelve of the men were reacting to me. My goal was to get 100 percent of them to react, but I didn't know then that some of the members were gay and not sexually attracted to women. I also didn't know that some of the straight men were "sexually sober," and protected from my energetic intrusion by a deep awareness about sexual energy. They knew exactly what I was up to, and ignored it.

And then the sharing started. That was a little more interesting. Like a Quaker meeting, there was silence, then randomly someone spoke up, typical of 12-Step meetings: the first name intro, but with a twist. In here, they said they were sex addicts. Out loud. In front of everyone.

I vaguely recall that several men talked about their lives, but I don't remember anything that was said. Until I heard six words that have never left me, spoken by an executive type in a tailored suit. He had finely cut, short silver hair and shiny, manicured nails, and I can hear his words like it was yesterday.

He was telling the group about how he couldn't stop masturbating to porn, even though his wife had caught him multiple times and had given him an ultimatum: quit or else. He said he loved her, but he kept choosing the porn, and then lying about it. My half-hearted attention was suddenly riveted on something he said about the way he wanted to live his life instead, a motto his spiritual teacher had given him.

"My life is an open book." When I heard them, the six words seared through me, lighting up something deep and real inside, a longing that was so strong it bordered on excruciating, an ache I felt to my core. Whatever that place in me was, it had been dark, dull, and mostly forgotten for as long as I could remember.

"My life is an open book."

My web vanished, and I began to listen intently.

⋄ ⋄ ⋄

Looking back, I know that hearing those words rebooted me, fundamentally reorganized me around their power, and bonded me to them in a way that I'd only been bonded to sex before. They held up a mirror to my own shadowy secrets and ignited a bright light, and the reflection was ugly, but true. This man said his teacher had told him that the key to happiness was the concept of congruency, where what you think, feel, and do are in alignment. He couldn't do it, couldn't get his act together, and he was about to lose his marriage over it. He called that powerlessness, but he longed for something different, something better, and though he hadn't achieved it yet, he wanted to believe it was possible. Suddenly, I did too.

The echoes from that man's words have whispered to me faithfully ever since that night, despite life's ups and downs. They've prodded me, terrified me, guided me, and haunted me in my recovery. Although I hadn't formally started working the Twelve Steps, I'd had my first spiritual awakening—promised to those in 12-Step recovery—just by sitting begrudgingly in the room, forcing myself to listen.

Alcoholics talk about hitting bottom, and I knew on some level that I was almost there in my life. But having to go to a support group for sex addicts seemed like the worst thing that had ever happened to me. All my life I'd tried to be the perfect "good Catholic girl": I was an A student, homecoming princess, the cheerleading captain of my high school squad, and awarded Best Smile by my high school classmates. But the smile hid a slew of secrets. When my clandestine sugar binges and fast driving in high school devolved into more extreme food, alcohol, and sex binges in college, my behavior began to reveal that my polished life wouldn't stay shiny—like a mirror that begins to show its brown-veined underside instead of reflecting a bright face.

Even though I earned a master's degree in social work, I never learned that something was terribly wrong with my sexuality. Sex was a toxic landmine, quietly waiting to go off. I didn't understand that despite how normal my family seemed from the outside, I had been neglected and sexually abused as a child, in a variety of ways, and hadn't begun to make sense of it. The aftershocks of these chronic, hidden violations made me hyperreactive to certain kinds of sex, at least until after orgasm. Then, feelings of regret would hit me like a flash flood of slimy mud, my thoughts choking me: *What have I done? Why have I done this again?* This was followed by a hateful onslaught of self-criticism at my weakness for doing things I didn't want to do. I hastily buried my pain with busy activity, a new outfit, food, or fantasies of another exploit. By age thirty-one, I hadn't consciously remembered my childhood neglect and abuse, but my lifelong distractions were no longer working. So here I was, joining a fellowship of recovering sex addicts, people I thought must be the dregs of society.

It turns out, I was wrong.

There is a saying in recovery I've come to rely on: Tell the truth and tell it faster. Here's my truth: This 12-Step fellowship was the best society I had ever known, the club to which no one would want to belong. It would introduce me to the finest men I'd ever meet and, eventually, the finest women. In their company I would learn that admitting you're addicted to sex is proof of bravery, and showing up to become part of a solution is an act of courage. They would help teach me that my sexuality was damaged but not broken; it could be repaired. I would grow to understand why I'd become so barbed and bitter sexually, and learn how to soften into love.

I wish I could tell you I got it that evening, but I didn't. I didn't get sexually sober, I didn't get God, and I certainly didn't get being honest about sex. But that executive in the fancy suit gave me the one thing I needed to survive what would emerge from the Pandora's box that is inevitably opened by sexual recovery: he gave me hope.

Part One:
Looking Good, Feeling Bad
(Before Sexual Recovery)

"That which we do not bring to consciousness
appears in our lives as fate."
~ Carl Jung

Inset picture top right: Age 6, Kindergarten. Top left: Age 9, Christmas. Bottom left: Age 11, Playing dress up with my sister. Bottom right: Age 16, Dress up has become a way of life.

ONE

A Dark Family Legacy

You'd never guess from looking at the tidy, two-story Victorian home on Grand Avenue that it once sheltered a pedophile. It looked upper-middle-class, befitting its former owners' roles as a manager in the town's biggest factory and his society wife. One time, driving by it years after his crimes were revealed, my mom made a somber comment, almost in passing, "I don't think we'll ever know how many children he molested." Such was the legacy of Grandpa Westby, my mom's father.

As a child, I never liked going there. He and his wife were alcoholics, their personalities mostly blank in my mind or creepily gleeful, the way heavy drinkers can get. After years of concentrated work in therapy, memories of most of my past clarified, but recalling these grandparents was always more burden than blessing: lush raspberry bushes in their backyard where plump, red berries promised much, yet delivered only a pale, sour sweetness; the steep stairs to their attic room, dusty and pregnant with secrets, where my sister and I would play for hours with an electric card shuffler, entranced by its crisp whirring.

When I was nine, my eleven-year-old sister, Christi, bravely revealed the molestations she'd suffered at Grandpa Westby's house, telling our father, who then told my mother. After three days of confusion and deliberation, dad called Child Protective Services, and then the police. Grandpa was arrested, convicted, and mandated to sex offender treatment with "community custody." That meant he could live at home as long as he went to intensive therapy and kept all the other conditions of his parole, but if he violated them, he'd go right to jail. I didn't understand any of that back then, nor that I would grow up and work as a forensic psych evaluator for people accused of sex crimes. I just noticed they stopped coming over for Thanksgiving dinner and Christmas, for which I was glad. I was never left alone at their house again, and in my mind they became my "bad grandparents." To me, Grandpa Westby was a monster and Grandma Westby was a cold, wicked witch. I was relieved he never got to me, and our family didn't speak of it again.

My "good grandparents," on my father's side, lived an hour north of Seattle on the waterfront of a giant lake fittingly named Lake Goodwin. Their one-lane driveway was bordered on both sides by tall evergreens that stood like loyal sentinels watching over us. It seemed to take forever to drive to the lakefront and the white vinyl-sided, double-wide mobile they called home. In my mind, it was a palace.

Their land-kingdom was my version of heaven, and I stayed there often as a child. Grandma Sprout kept a big garden where even the white strawberries were sweet to my impatient pilfering. The shoreline was lined with cherry trees waving in the cool lake breeze, and I loved the friendly ducks that would constantly mill around, leaving feather treasures with their departure. I felt safe there and played happily by the lake for hours, making mud pies with my sister for tea parties. Once when I was alone, I sat on the mobile home porch with my eyes closed, quacking to the ducks. When I opened my eyes, I swear every duck on the lake had come to visit, dotting the green grass as far as my little eyes could see.

Grandpa Sprout was a chipper, six-foot-two, ex-professional hockey player. Born in Canada, he was part Irish and always moving, working out at the gym almost daily until he died. Growing up,

Grandpa Sprout was the one adult who showered my sister and me with cheerful attention. His jokes usually made no sense, but they were told with a silly sweetness that endeared him to me forever. Coming from a family of big drinkers, especially my mom, grandpa was the one adult who was happy and not drunk at the same time.

Grandma Sprout lived with chronic pain due to severe rheumatoid arthritis. Her gnarled joints made her wrists and fingers look more like tree limbs with twigs protruding at stiff angles than human hands. She could get up to cook for Grandpa or us, but as her disease progressed she wasn't able to clean the mobile home well or do much else. She gave up gardening and spent her days lying on her favorite davenport, watching her soaps on a tiny, red plastic, black-and-white TV or reading *Star Magazine* and eating a box of Russell Stover chocolates.

Grandma complained bitterly and often about her pain and its limitations, and about grandpa's many flaws. I never found out what started their fighting, but I heard the remnants of it in their constant bickering and muttered-under-the-breath criticisms about each other until death did them part, and for grandma, even after. The only person she showed real affection for was her doctor—more like reverence, since he prescribed her regular morphine shots.

When I was in college I told Grandma Sprout that I'd changed my major to psychology, and she surprised me by telling me she'd been to a counselor once.

"I went after grandpa died, because everyone told me I had to. They told me I should talk about it, and about Danny's death," she said.

Danny was my dad's younger brother, who'd died at age twenty-three from a gunshot wound inflicted by a friend at the family apartment when both were drunk. It happened before I was born; I heard the story from my mom because dad and grandma barely spoke of it. Danny was immortalized after his tragic death as the perfect son, and I always had the impression that, according to grandma, my dad could never quite measure up.

Grandma's face scowled as she went on. "The counselor was a young woman—too young! What could she know about me? I didn't want to talk with her. I went once and never went back. Phooey on counseling!" A feisty, second-generation Pole turned Canadian-American, once grandma said "phooey" on something, there was no turning back.

Grandpa Sprout hadn't been to counseling during his lifetime, according to my dad, but he'd been a big drinker with even bigger mood swings, with what dad called "a temper." Dad said grandpa went to a program for alcohol abusers before I was born and "hadn't had a drop since," but everybody knew he loved to eat. He would make any cook burst with pride the way he relished his food, mixing it together on one plate like a solid soup, shoveling it down so fast you'd swear it had never been there at all. And there was one food he loved more than all others: ice cream. When I was about six, he passed on this love to me.

Grandpa's blue eyes twinkled under his bushy brows as he ushered me into the kitchen, nodding that I should climb up on the barstool, which I happily did. He was a man of few words. He turned to the freezer and plunked a quart of ice cream on the counter (vanilla, his favorite), frozen in one of those rectangular boxes they used to have. He didn't open the box and scoop out ice cream into a bowl like a normal grandpa; he took a large serrated knife in his giant hands and sawed the box in half, plopping one half, ice cream up, on a plate for me, and the other half on a plate for himself. He handed me a big soup spoon, sat down next to me, and we went to work. The cool ice cream proved no match for the warm glow of joy that always filled my stomach. We never left a drop behind in those flimsy boxes.

Like grandma said, who needed counseling? Grandpa taught me that ice cream makes everything better. At least for a while.

TWO

Nancy Drew and Other Role Models

WHEN I WAS EIGHT YEARS OLD, Nancy Drew was my hero. After reading my first Nancy Drew mystery, I decided I wanted to be a detective just like her when I grew up. I loved to sit cross-legged on the orange carpet in front of our monster floor TV to watch her escape from danger and solve devious crimes that stumped even the grownups.

One day, while no one was around, I embarked on a sleuthing adventure in my parents' bedroom. I routinely searched the house when the opportunity struck, looking for hidden clues, change left in coat pockets, and other treats. This time I found one, but I didn't yet know it was a trick in disguise. In my dad's top dresser drawer, under his folded white-and-navy socks, I uncovered a Playboy magazine with my heroine, Nancy Drew, on the cover. Wearing a partially open khaki trench coat, her bare thigh poked out of the opening, hinting of nothing underneath. Her face was heavily made up and she held a magnifying glass. My small fingers trembled as I opened the cover to search the glossy pages within.

At eight years old, I believed it was really Nancy Drew in the pictures that greeted me, and that she was posing naked, looking even more glamorous than on TV. I didn't understand the difference between the fictional character and Pamela Sue Martin, the actress who played her. I was fooled into thinking that Nancy Drew, whose cleverness and bravery I loved, also liked to model without any clothes for everyone to see. I was shocked that her nude body was so compelling, even my dad kept pictures of her—and not mom—hidden in his dresser drawer. I knew I shouldn't tell anyone; dad's secret was safe with me. But as I carefully replaced the magazine under his socks, I felt a heavy sensation crawl over me and take root inside, mingling with the excited tingling that seeing the pictures had evoked. Years later I would learn words to describe that shadowy feeling: shame. Unable to understand the significance of what had happened, I came to associate sexual arousal with a subtle but persistent sense of dread.

One night, not long after that incident, I woke up to sounds of hilarity and sex play in the living room. I slowly crept down the hall to investigate. I found my dad sitting in his favorite recliner in his blue bathrobe. He was by himself, watching a late-night cable channel called Escapade.

"Go back to bed, this is for adults," he said thickly, hearing me sneaking up behind him. He lowered the volume, and I headed back to my room, but I could still hear it all in my mind. After that, when I was sure everyone was asleep, I would sometimes steal out to the living room to watch for myself. I kept the sound low, thrilled even as I felt terrified of getting caught. During the day I replayed the scenarios in my mind: a man surprising a woman naked in a department store changing room, and her responding by having enthusiastic sex with him; a pretty homeowner watching her shirtless pool cleaner work while her husband was away, and then stripping for splashy sex with him in the pool; some kind of sporting contest between thin, blonde women in string bikinis, where they mud-wrestled and had swimming races. The scenes made me feel good when I saw or imagined them, as if life and sex were always fun, glamorous, mischievous, and carefree. Like the time I saw Nancy in the magazine, these stealthy, late-night excursions and the fantasies they created were added to my stash of secrets. They became my happy place.

Around that time I discovered women's magazines at a friend's house, and like the *Playboy* cover, I became enthralled with images of Cosmo supermodels posed in sexy clothes. I was enamored by their beauty, but even more so by their direct gazes. They seemed bold and powerful, and no one else ever looked at me like that. I wanted more.

⬦ ⬦ ⬦

When I was nine and Grandpa Westby's molestation of my sister was revealed, things radically changed around our house. My mom had what she later referred to as a "spiritual experience." She said the voice of God, in the form of Jesus, came to her and told her that she needed to get her life together, and so she did. She gave her life to Jesus Christ that day, swore off smoking and drinking, joined AA, and enrolled our family in a nearby Catholic church. She made dad get rid of his porn, but I could still find the cable channels and, even with the new black squiggly line marring the picture, see and hear enough to excite me.

Although mom's bedtime drunken stupors ended, it seemed like she was never home. She was always gone at "meetings." When mom was around, she practiced a new hobby: eating. She filled the house with cardboard flats of gooey cinnamon rolls, gallons of ice cream, bags of chips, and tubs of frozen chocolate chip cookie dough. Mom designated a special drawer for candy bars that my sister and I started affectionately calling "the third drawer down." I loved helping mom make chocolate chip cookies, and considered our new lifestyle a big improvement. Before she quit drinking, I was often hungry, but mom would get mad if I asked for food. Dad was usually away as a traveling RV salesman, and when mom drank wine or vodka instead of eating, she wasn't so focused on cooking for my sister and me.

Mom's new bounty of sweets didn't last. Eventually, she gained so much weight she couldn't stand it, and then all the good food dis-appeared and I was left to scrounge unsuccessfully for some hidden item she'd missed in the back of the freezer. When my sister and I were enrolled in Catholic Sunday School and I learned to pray for the first time, my first prayers were for mom to go off her diet.

My second prayers were for Jesus, whom I learned about from my pert new Sunday school teacher. After class one day, the teacher took me aside for a private lesson. She leaned down, her face close to mine, and spoke with an unusually low, serious tone. "Jesus is the lord of all lords, Staci. Since your family is just starting to come to church, you are meeting him for the first time. But in order to really know Jesus, you must ask him to come into your heart. Then you will be saved, because he will know you are a *true* believer."

Seeking solitude for my special moment later that day, I wandered out the front door and into an unlocked motor home in our drive-way, a loaner from dad's lot. It had a dark, artificial wood-paneled bedroom in the back with a full-length mirror on the adjacent bath-room door. I sat on the thin bedspread and looked at myself, with my short blondish curls lying limp where my perm was half grown out, bleached by chlorine. Taking a breath, I asked for Jesus to come into my heart. At first, I asked him with my thoughts, which I was sure he could hear because he seemed to have magic powers like that. I tried to really, really mean it, but nothing happened. My heart didn't feel Jesus come into it, full of love or light or anything else. So I tried again, this time out loud. "Jesus, I believe in you. Please come into my heart and save me."

Then I waited in the musty silence, and again, nothing. The girl just stared back at me, shoulders hunched over, green eyes flat. I'm not sure what I expected to happen, but it was definitely more than nothing. Locking the narrow motor home door, I wandered back in the house and started hunting for cookies. Later that day I told my mom I gave my heart to Jesus, and she got a tender look on her face and gave me a rare hug. I hated it when she touched me, though I was a long way from figuring out why.

Back then neither my family nor I had the strength or support to make sense of the terrible impact of mom's alcoholism, dad's reactive rages and depressions, or the generations of sexual neglect and abuse so prevalent on both sides of the family. When dad quit drinking not long after mom, our family just moved on, "focused on the positive," as dad liked to say, and tried not to look back.

- THREE -

Spacey Staci

ALL THE GIRLS AT SUMMER CAMP were pissed at me, and I didn't care.

I was twelve and not a real Girl Scout, but Camp Killoqua opened its doors nonetheless to teach me archery, canoeing, and how to cook chicken in foil over a campfire. The camp's slogan was "Light the fire within," and my fire was lit during that week all right, but not from the outdoor activities, catchy dinnertime songs, or inspirational talks from counselors named Bunny, Bam Bam, or Minnow. My spark came from a dog-eared book the girls were passing around—its title long forgotten—filled with wildly graphic stories of men deceptively prevailing over the virginities of a myriad of female conquests. Once I got my hands on it, I forgot to play nice.

It started out as such episodes do, with girls whispering and giggling. I didn't know any of them, but they looked over at me watching them curiously from my lower bunk and decided to let me in on their special secret.

"Brittany brought a sexy book from home, do you want to see it?"

I nodded, and she ceremoniously handed it over. I flipped through a few pages and smirked, letting out a mirthless laugh like I'd seen such things a million times. I hadn't though; unlike at home this form of pornography had no pictures, just words. Then my eyes caught a naughty phrase—I felt my face flush, and time suddenly slowed down. Without taking off my grubby Keds, I crawled into my

24

sleeping bag, grabbed my flashlight, and burrowed under the covers to read.

"Hey! Give it back!" the girl said, surprised. The others joined in the chorus, calling me out of my cocoon to return the book to its rightful owner. I ignored them, already lost in the first story. If they'd gotten closer I would have growled; there was no way I was letting go of that book. I read it over and over that night, begrudgingly leaving it on Brittany's bunk the next morning after all the girls had left for breakfast. It didn't help; the girls barely spoke a word to me the rest of the camp. But at least I had new stories in my mind to keep me company.

When puberty hit at age thirteen, it was like somebody waved a magic wand and transformed me almost overnight from an invisible tomboy to something far closer to what I saw on magazine covers at the supermarket. My body grew taller, curves appeared, and my face shifted to reveal the chiseled Norwegian cheekbones of my mom's side of the family and Grandma Sprout's almond-shaped, upturned green eyes. This brought a radical change in the way people treated me, especially boys and men. At first I felt shy and confused by all the attention, but I soon followed in my older sister's footsteps and made the junior high cheerleading squad. This gave me practice being in front of people and being looked at. A dreamy boy asked me to "go with him," and after we broke up I soon had another boyfriend, starting a steady string of relationships that offered happiness for as long as their romance and affection lasted. Determined to be true to the teachings of the Catholic church, however, kissing was as far as I let things go. Except in my mind.

By the time I bleached my hair light blonde at sixteen, I'd grown enthusiastic about being admired. In fact, I was quite dependent on it to get me through the day. Boyfriend or not, I reveled in the appraising looks, whistles, and comments I received from boys and men in public. Their special treatment made me feel good, like I mattered, for the first time in my life. I began to vigilantly search for glances and heads turning wherever I went, but soon I noticed that this kind of attention was coming from my dad and a few of my friends' dads. That felt different. Their lingering glances and suggestive comments and jokes made my skin crawl, but I didn't know what to do about it, so I tried to ignore it.

I focused instead on becoming as irresistible as possible. I read fashion magazine articles about how to apply makeup and dress enticingly. I borrowed my older sister's trendy clothes and copied how she styled her hair. Comedies like *Porky's* and *Fast Times at Ridgemont High* became my clandestine guides about how to grow up, but they perplexed me even as they excited. Like dad's cable porn, the images in the racy teen movies competed mightily with the stern messages I heard in Sunday Mass about celibacy being holy and sex outside the bounds of marriage being bad.

I decided on a compromise: I wouldn't act like the sexy bad girls I read about in *Cosmo* ("Confessions of a High-Class Call Girl"), but I'd at least try to look as pretty as I thought they did. Afraid I might turn out to be an alcoholic like my mom, I avoided school parties and drinking with the fast crowd. I hoped being a cheerleader would give me the popularity I craved.

One day as I walked by my dad wearing my cheer uniform, he made a passing comment that had a major impact. "Staci, your thighs are just like your mother's, a little too thick. Your face is gorgeous, but you need to lose a little weight if you really want to look like a movie star. Your sister's thighs are about perfect."

My sister was tall and willowy, with voluminous chestnut hair and a dazzling smile, and I already wanted to be like her, though I'd never compared my legs to my mother's before. I accepted dad's appraisal as fact, instantly determined to fix my thighs. I cut out pictures of models' legs and pasted them in a blank photo album, filling the pages with images of the thin thighs I now coveted. I became obsessed with having a perfect face and body, and worked out so often to Jane Fonda exercise videos that I memorized her every word. Watching *National Lampoon's Vacation*, I was awestruck by Christie Brinkley's character and her red Ferrari. I decided I needed only one more thing to complete my sexy look: a hot car. Thanks to my dad's recent job change, I knew right where to get one.

◊　◊　◊

After getting out of traveling motor home sales, my dad became the proud co-owner of what my sister and I called "the lot." It was a small used-car dealership with a hodgepodge of cheap cars lined up for sale under the awning of a converted gas station; tantalizing come-ons scrawled in white shoe polish across their windshields read "Superfast" or "HOT!"

For my sixteenth birthday, dad indulged me with the gift of an eight-cylinder Ford Mustang Fastback, and let me pick out any color I wanted for a custom paint job. I chose a pearly robin's-egg blue, and decided my teen persona was finally flawless, except for one problem: I kept crashing the car. I never seriously injured myself or anyone else, but with each fender bender, my car lost some of its sparkle and shine.

In my post-crash interludes, I borrowed even more excellent replacements, thanks to the impulsive car-buying habits of teenage boys. My dad would sell them pricey muscle cars with polished paint jobs, and the boys would pour every last penny into turbocharging the engines. When they went broke and were unable to keep up the car payments, dad would snatch the cars back via one of his repo men. He'd promptly resell them at higher prices, and sometimes, if they didn't sell right away, he'd lend them to me.

I took full advantage of dad's little racket. I felt like a princess whenever I visited the lot, cruising rows of cars for a replacement for my dented Mustang. Once I borrowed a banana yellow kit car with only slightly cracked, smoky, faux DeLorean wing window-doors that lifted up, instead of out. A few times I drove cars that were so fast they were obscene, and I'm sure illegal; I loved them all. I once transported Grandma Sprout to the doctor in a Datsun 280ZX that was so low to the ground poor grandma could barely get in or out of it; she was mortified by the sans-muffler roar of the engine.

I loved to drive; it got me out of the house. Even though mom had been sober for years by then, the tension between my parents was constant; between that and dad's frequent looks and lectures, home was the last place I wanted to be. At night I'd take off and fly on the back roads near the Boeing plant in Everett, where mom worked. Police were scarce and the roads were wide and deserted, especially after dark. As I shifted and gunned the engine, I reveled in the powerful vibrations of the large motor, pretending to be a star in an MTV video as I blasted Don Henley's *The Boys of Summer* with the windows down and the wind whipping through my hair. One time a boyfriend and I decided to meet for a drag race, and not only did I beat him, but his car—a blue Chevy Nova—actually caught on fire and I had to drive him to the main road to flag down help.

It was all exciting and hilarious, but it would be years before I realized that there was more to the story than youthful vanity and thrill-seeking. The real reason I crashed the car three times during my first two years of driving? I was suffering from a post-traumatic stress symptom called dissociation, which affected my ability to drive.

Dissociation is the mind's ingenious way of protecting itself from overwhelm by dividing painful thoughts, feelings, and body sensations into manageable chunks, and storing them subconsciously. It's

28

like a circuit breaker, but it's only designed to be temporary until safety can be restored and the mind can make sense of, or "associate," the horror of whatever happened. In my traumatized family, safety never quite arrived, and by the time I was sixteen dissociation had become a chronic reflex to cope with pain. I call it "freezing and floating," and though it definitely helped me survive, dissociation can have some downsides.

My mind's adaptation kept the pain frozen inside, but the protective anesthesia meant that I couldn't feel much sensation at all. As a result, I felt deadened, like I didn't really exist. I would constantly glance at my rearview mirror while I drove as if to make sure I was really there. I'd often add mascara or lipstick to try to improve my reflection, never a good idea while operating heavy machinery. Driving fast helped me feel, and under such conditions the car crashes weren't surprising. Everyone blamed my youth and carelessness, and friends nicknamed me "Spacey Staci."

- FOUR -

My First Psychiatrist

I WAS IN MY BEDROOM, standing in front of the full-length mirror in a bikini. A stern eighteen-year-old with long, straight bottle-blonde hair stared intently back at me. The swimsuit was made from white crochet, with rainbows stitched across the cups and bottoms, and was a prize inheritance from my older sister, Christi. I wore it whenever I could, but now it didn't fit. It had become too small, and not the sexy kind. It was the too small bulging-out-in-the-wrong-places, the too small this-would-never-make-a-*Sports-Illustrated-Swimsuit*-issue-cover kind. I was furious, and felt victimized, not stopping to consider who to blame; certainly not me for binge-eating the last six months, since Grandpa Sprout died of a sudden stroke; the binges blocked all feelings about the loss. I didn't make the connection back then, but eating sweets not only tasted good, it made me feel closer to him, temporarily. Especially ice cream.

Gaining weight was a major calamity. By eighteen, I'd internalized my father's regular judgments about my body and weight, and the critic inside my mind had grown far more cutting than anything dad ever said. Looking at my slightly rounded tummy in the mirror, my mind launched into a vicious attack of all my physical failings. Again. When I couldn't stand it anymore, my fury coalesced into determination. I threw on a beach cover-up and flip-flopped out to my mother. She was sitting at our dining room table in front of a magnifying mirror, applying her "face," as she called it.

My mother never left the house without her "face" on. She would

30

line up her tubes and bottles, pencils and brushes in perfect order, like a sorceress preparing ingredients for a magic potion, carefully applying each layer. I used to watch her, enthralled, eager to get my own tubes and powders someday. By age eighteen I'd collected plenty, and had my own daily makeup ritual down pat. I even had my own makeup motto: *Don't leave home without it.*

"Mom, I want to go see Barney."

Her eyes widened, amplified by her lighted make-up mirror. Barney was her psychiatrist-therapist, and since I'd never shown any interest in psychiatry before, she asked why I wanted to see him.

"I want to get on Prozac."

My mom took Prozac. My dad took Prozac. Back then dad talked constantly about the virtues of the amazing new antidepressant medication and how it had changed his life. He'd rev up for another one of his lectures as my sister would catch my eye and roll hers, muttering, "Here comes lecture number three-hundred and fifty-seven." As a career salesman, when dad wanted you to buy something, he was convincing.

"Depression is a problem with the brain, Staci. Some people are just born with not enough good chemicals in there, and they don't feel right. I'm like that, and so is your mother. You'll probably need antidepressants too, because mental illness runs in families, and with your mom and I having it, chances are high you do too. That's why mom always drank, because she was trying to feel right."

Dad never mentioned his own past drinking or his rage episodes, but at this point in the lecture, if mom was there and in a talkative mood, she'd chime in.

"That's right. The first time I took a drink of alcohol, I felt normal. The problem is, until AA I could never stop!" And then she'd laugh with that tough-old-bird cackle. I'd dismissed dad's praises of the virtues of Prozac until now, but something I'd heard at school changed my mind. Someone had mentioned that Prozac could help me lose weight.

◊ ◊ ◊

I'd been exposed to a possible downside of Prozac a few months earlier, on a sunny spring afternoon after coming home from cheerleading practice. Pulling my recently repaired Mustang into the driveway, I scattered loose gravel onto the hedges that bordered the lawn. I entered our brown, split-level ranch house, slammed the front door behind me, and raced up the stairs to the kitchen. My mom appeared as I was scanning the fridge. She had a dour look on her face.

"I need to tell you something, honey. Our neighbor Bobby killed himself today. He hung himself in the Clark's living room."

I hadn't known Bobby except in passing because he was several years older and in a different class. One time, my family went over to his house for a barbeque, but for some reason we never reciprocated the invitation or socialized with them again. Hearing mom's news, I suddenly imagined Bobby's hanging body, backlit by the bright vista of the Puget Sound waterway outside their floor-to-ceiling living room window. I shuddered.

"Why?" I asked. I popped two slices of Wonder Bread in the toaster to make buttered cinnamon toast, suddenly craving some comfort food.

"We don't know really, but he was depressed. He'd just started taking Prozac." I was shaken by the news about Bobby, but despite his tragic suicide, a few months later, when my bikini wouldn't fit, he didn't come to mind. I considered Prozac a diet pill and had forgotten all about the possible risks.

Dad wasn't home the day I decided to see mom's psychiatrist, so I was spared his knowing nod at being right about me. I'd never tell him that I wasn't depressed. At eighteen I didn't even know what depression was, and mental illness was the furthest thing from my mind.

◇ ◇ ◇

The first thing I noticed when walking into the doctor's office was that he was overweight. His eyes appeared unnaturally large behind thick glasses, and were a watery, gentle kind of blue, constantly blinking. He told me to call him Barney, like mom did, and asked right away why I came to see him. I gave him an answer I'd heard from one of dad's pop psychology talks. Like his dad before him, my dad liked reading self-help books.

"I don't feel good about myself."

"What don't you feel good about?"

"My weight. And I'm depressed. I want to get on Prozac."

Barney looked at my five-foot-seven-and-a-half, 140-pound frame, and then surprised me with his concerned, slightly exasperated reply.

"Why do you worry about your weight? All the young women worry about their weight, and it makes no sense. You are beautiful!"

I was even more startled by what happened next—I burst into tears. I hadn't cried for at least a decade, not even when my beloved grandpa died six months earlier, and certainly not in front of a strange man, doctor or not. But his words were said with genuine bewilderment and sadness, real feeling, and they touched me with their simplicity and kindness. Somehow I knew Barney wasn't speaking about my appearance alone, he was speaking about my inner essence, and suddenly I could feel it, and it hurt. I didn't experience my essence as beautiful. Not for a long time. Maybe not ever.

That was the end of the dialogue. Barney went on to talk the entire rest of the session, mostly about himself. I recall only two other things that happened toward the end of the hour: 1) He showed me the book *Codependent No More* by Melody Beattie, and talked enthusiastically about how great it was, how it changed his life, and how he couldn't recommend it more highly, since my mom was a recovering alcoholic; and 2) he wrote out a prescription for Prozac on a small square of paper and handed it to me.

Leaving his office, I decided the visit was a success. I told him the minimum and got what I wanted, as I usually did; I had no intention of going back. When I picked up my own little green-and-cream capsules later that day, I didn't hesitate a beat. Just as Barney ordered, I popped them in my mouth. I was excited for Prozac to start suppressing my appetite so I could quit binging and reclaim the power tool I was sure I'd lost and desperately wanted back: my svelte body.

After only three days of taking Prozac, however, I could tell that something inside was terribly wrong. I felt as if I was starting to mentally implode, as if my life force, which had been running forward sluggishly, reversed internally, and then clogged. It was like Prozac coated my mind with a swampy sludge that started to choke me, and I feared that continuing to take it would somehow be lethal. I remembered Bobby then, and pictured his lifeless form, slowly swinging as if in a macabre warning. Disappointed to be heading to college feeling fat, but choosing survival instead, I tossed the bottle of pills. I'd have to find another way to lose weight.

FIVE

Guys Only Want One Thing

I TWIRLED A LOCK OF BLONDE HAIR around my finger to keep from biting my nails, determined to grow them long for once. I'd survived the bubbly rigor of sorority rush, and was now one month into my college experience. I sat cross-legged on the floor in a posh living room surrounded by thirty-two new "sisters" at a pajama party, no boys allowed. We were getting to know each other.

Membership in the sorority house was highly coveted, and hopes were high I'd bring glory to the house by following in my older sister's footsteps. When she joined as a freshman two years earlier, she'd wowed the Greek system by becoming a Husky football cheerleader and being featured as Miss December in the highly popular *Women of the University of Washington Sororities* calendar. My goal was to do the same, and hopefully more.

During the final rush party before pledging, I was surrounded by co-eds in silky, jewel-tone dresses sipping lemon water in champagne flutes. The conversation was a low murmur, a piano tinkling in the background. A statuesque redhead leaned close to me and whispered conspiratorially.

"Did you know the Omegas are the girls the guys take out, the Zetas are the girls they take to bed, but *we're* the girls they want to marry?" Secretly wishing I could join the Zetas, the fact that I had a sister in this house meant rejection by the other popular sororities. It was assumed that younger sisters, called legacies, would automatically pledge the same house as their older ones. Lacking another acceptable option, I did exactly that, so here I was at the newbie retreat, wishing I could have afforded designer pajamas.

Rising above the excited chatter of our new pledge class, a bold girl with mischievous eyes called out, "So! Who here has had sex?" I looked around the room at the lovely faces framed by long hair like mine, a few daring short styles among the circle. One by one, the hands rose confidently. Mine didn't, nor did two others, and the rest of the group erupted with laughter.

"Our three little virgins!" my new sisters teased, as if we were quaint, a throwback to innocent days of yore.

"We'll have to get you laid!" someone called out, sparking more laughter and fervent conversation about who should be fixed up with which frat guy to deflower us. Suddenly I felt embarrassed that all the sexual experiences I recalled to that point were pretty tame, and always stopped short of real sex. My mind flashed through a series of memories, starting with my very first kiss, which took place at another girls' sleepover in the sixth grade.

◊ ◊ ◊

We were at Kat's house, eight other twelve-year-olds camped out in sleeping bags in her downstairs den. We watched a movie, ate popcorn and candy, and then settled down to supposedly sleep, but the real evening's event was yet to come.

We'd arranged for a group of twelve-year-old boys also having an overnight at a nearby house to sneak out after dark to visit us. The girls had been furtively whispering about this for weeks, and I was filled with excitement about seeing Christopher again, my first boyfriend ever, after almost a month of no contact during the summer.

Minutes after midnight we heard the tap, tap, tap on the sliding glass door, and Kat ran over to open it a crack. "You can't come in, and we can't come out!" she said breathlessly, keeping it down so her parents wouldn't wake up.

They talked for a while in hushed tones, some girls running over to the door briefly and then darting away, while I stayed safely huddled in my sleeping bag, terrified. Finally a girl came over to me and whispered, "Chris is here, he wants to talk to you!" The moment had finally arrived. I stood up, smoothed down my long blue nightgown and walked slowly over to the sliding glass door, my heart pounding.

"Hi," he said, softly.

"Hi," I whispered back, shyly. We stood together silently, and looking back I'd say he was gathering his courage. I was content to wait; I loved staring at his face in the moonlight. A baseball cap covered his short brown hair, and his brown eyes were bright and shiny as they gazed into mine. His lips were dark and red.

Suddenly I heard Kat's frantic hiss from behind me. "Hey, you guys gotta go, my dad's waking up!" I felt a jolt of panic, but just then Chris leaned in and pressed his lips gently to mine. He paused to catch my eye one last time, and then was gone, disappearing into the night with his little pack. I heard Kat's parents stirring upstairs, but I was in dreamland and couldn't care less.

Oh my God. He kissed me! He KISSED me! I've been kissed! I've been KISSED!

I was content just kissing with a steady stream of boyfriends in junior high and high school, until I met my first serious one—Tyler the basketball star—during my junior year. After a romantic summer of dating, I fell in love with him and our physical explorations occurred slowly, with care. He was always gentlemanly with my religion-inspired "wait until marriage" rule. For me, keeping the rule was easy because, even though I adored him, I never felt erotic pleasure being touched anywhere below the neck.

I didn't know then that I'd been touch-starved from birth, or that such neglect, along with my buried childhood sexual abuse, had left my body numb. To this day, I can't recall a single instance of either parent touching me in a way I experienced as nurturing during childhood. I usually hated touching other people too. Whenever I tried it, I felt an odd prickly sensation, and an urgent impulse to jerk my hand away. It was a little better with boyfriends, but for everything Tyler and I tried, all I really wanted to do was lie in his arms and have him stroke my hair.

My parents must have suspected that I'd gone further with Tyler than any other boy I'd dated, because right before prom they sat me down for a talk about sex. I could tell they were nervous; this was something they felt they had to do, but didn't want to. I sat on the living room couch, with my mom on my left and my dad across from us in his well-worn recliner.

"We want to talk about sex!" Dad boomed, trying to sound light-hearted, and failing. Dad was a big man with a big voice, six-foot-two and heavyset, and nothing he did came across lightly. "We don't want you to do it," he added, again as if he were joking. I wanted to be anywhere else in the world but on that plaid couch, staring down at the floor.

"I know," I said, and I did. I'd picked up via jokes and passing comments that the family value, aligned with the church, was that I shouldn't have sex until I was married. But this was the first time my parents had ever sat down together to tell me directly.

"Your mom and I know from experience that having sex before marriage is a bad way to go," Dad said. "Tell her Lani."

Mom frowned, but reluctantly began her story.

"The first time I had sex, I was your age. It was in the back of a car with my boyfriend at the time, and we were both drunk." My face was a mask, revealing nothing, but inside I was stunned by her revelation. "He didn't love me," she added quietly. "In fact, he was

38

cheating on me with my best friend at the time. I really loved him, and I when I found out later, I was devastated."

Dad continued, "So you see, guys your age are jerks. They only want one thing—sex—and they don't care about you, even if you love them. It's important to wait until you get married to have sex."

I meekly said, "Okay," and our conversation was over. They looked relieved; mom went to the kitchen to start dinner, and dad made one last lame joke, probably thinking he was breaking the tension, before opening his newspaper and disappearing behind it.

I went to my bedroom and shut the door, my world suddenly changed. I'd always thought, since I'd thought about such things, that my parents had waited until marriage to have sex, like the church required, and that's why they wanted me to. Now that I knew mom hadn't—I was still clueless about dad—I felt confused, and betrayed. *Why should I wait if she didn't? What did they know? Is sex all Tyler wants? Why should I care what they say?*

Despite my disillusionment, I still wanted to be virtuous, and held off from going "all the way." The night before Tyler left for college mid-summer I found the courage to tell him I loved him, and promised to write every day until we met again. But after he was gone, missing him grew intolerable, and my hurt clenched into a fist of anger whenever I thought of him. I had a fun first try with alcohol at a frat party, but as the weeks without Tyler stacked up I started distracting myself with more alcohol, dances, and the unrelenting flirtations now available to me every night in the Greek system. I broke up with Tyler abruptly and, in hindsight, cruelly, just before my sorority sleepover, and tried not to think about him.

◊ ◊ ◊

"Lighten up on them," a sorority girl said, breaking me out of my reverie, "I think it's cute they're virgins!" Everyone joined in with more laughter, and then the stories started about everyone's incredible first sex: where, with whom, and exactly how. I was riveted, my embarrassment at being sexually inexperienced abruptly shifting to determination. I decided I needed to have *real* sex as soon as possible, my parents and the Catholic church be damned. As soon as I returned to the sorority mansion, I placed an out-of-state call to Tyler, who would soon be returning home for Thanksgiving break.

After arguing over our breakup, I declared the real purpose of my call: I was established in college now and more mature, and I wanted to have all-the-way sex. Tyler consented, and we hurriedly made arrangements to meet at my parent's home, where I would be staying over the holidays. He was to sneak into our basement to meet me while my parents were asleep upstairs, a lot like my sixth grade sleepover at Kat's. Only this time, things didn't turn out so blissfully.

I heard his knock on the basement window, though it was too dark to see anyone in the cold November night. Sitting up on the bed, I reached over and slowly slid open the glass panel, scooting over so he could climb in. His big tennis shoes landed on the round waterbed, a relic from the 70s, sending it sloshing.

"Shhhhh, my parents are upstairs!"

"I know, I know," he said, sounding nervous and excited. I felt jittery too, but more resolute than anything else. My mind was set on changing my status from virgin to woman, so in my case, it was the girl who just wanted one thing.

Tyler was considerate and patient, but no matter what he did, I couldn't relax. Everything I still felt for him—love, anger, hurt, sadness, longing, disappointment, and bitterness—jumbled together inside and scrambled my thoughts. When we finally fumbled into the promised ecstasy of merging our bodies, I mimicked sounds I'd heard from the only role models I had for what women were supposed to act like during sex—the porn stars I'd seen on cable TV. But

40

in reality my body was contracted with anxiety and pain. Instead of sex being mind-blowing like my sorority sisters had promised, when it was over and Tyler left, I sat alone on the warm waterbed feeling disoriented and hurt. I decided sex was awful and that I would have to be drunk before I ever did it again. Just like mom.

Tyler called me a few times after that night, but I avoided him. Back at the sorority hall, one call I did take was from my parents, in the claustrophobic phone closet upstairs. They were both on the line, and mom began the confrontation.

"Honey, we need to talk to you," she said, but she was quickly interrupted by dad.

"Your mom found a used condom in the basement!" he said, his voice slightly raised. "Does it belong to you? Have you had sex?"

"Barrie, that's really her business," Mom said, trying as usual to pacify him.

"It's my house, and my business what happens in it!"

They went on arguing, and I hoped they'd burn themselves out, but at some point there was silence and I knew I had to say something.

"It wasn't me," I tried.

"Of course it was you!" Dad countered. "No one else was down there!"

"I don't know what you're talking about," I said, trying to muster righteous hurt, but landing closer to a whine. "I didn't do it!"

"Okay, okay honey," Mom said.

"It's not okay! She has no right to use my house as a brothel!"

"Barrie, that's out of line. Staci, we're going now. I'm sorry."

I hung up the phone. I needed to find something to eat.

- SIX -

Drinking, Eating, and Cheating

MY SECOND QUARTER IN THE GREEK SYSTEM meant more fraternity parties flowing with vodka-fruit cocktails, called spodies, mixed in and liberally poured from huge plastic barrels. After my first experience with alcohol, there was rarely an in-between for me; I either drank nothing or I found myself on the cold tile of a bathroom floor, wrapped around the toilet bowl. I developed crushes at several different frat houses that I visited for sloppy, post-party hookups that sorority girls called mashes, but I quickly found a new boyfriend, a gregarious drummer named Matt.

After drunken almost-sex in his room the night we met, I started spending most of my free days, and many nights, in Matt's fraternity house. We declared ourselves exclusive, but fidelity was the last thing on my mind, especially after even a sip of alcohol. In deference to Matt, I cut back on my rounds to other fraternities, but couldn't quite give up the last two: the aloof guy with the out-of-state girlfriend, and the guy I kept stringing along who said he loved me. I liked the security of a steady boyfriend, but the novelty and risk of flings on the side felt far more exciting: dad's porn channel *Escapade* brought to life. But the mornings after, I felt guilty.

Junk food became my get-through-the-day drug. Whenever the inconsistencies of my life became more than I could bear, I'd let off steam by jumping into my high school graduation present, a cranberry red Alfa Romeo convertible, and embark on a secret comfort food scavenger hunt. Anticipatory adrenaline coursing through my body, I would drive around, zipping through whatever fast food drive-through caught my eye and inhale a junk food dinner. As my body became numb and heavy, I'd stir up more thrill by speeding across town toward a mini-mart, the kind that sold junk food so laden with preservatives and sugar it could barely be called food.

Flush with the freedom of living away from home, where no one knew what I was up to, I told myself I could have anything I wanted. I was kidding myself, because the nearby convenience store clerk, eyeing my bounty with a mocking smirk, knew all too well what was going on. I tried to avoid his eyes as he loaded my score into a bag: Reese's Peanut Butter Cups, Snickers, a Big Hunk, and a pint of Cherry Garcia ice cream. In an attempt to balance out all the sugar, I'd also grab a slice of zesty pizza and a huge Diet Coke chaser; regular Coke was too sweet.

Putting up the convertible top so no one could see me at work on my feast, I'd often take only a bite or two before moving on to the next item. My worries drained away as my mind floated upward, lost in another delectable self-assault.

Ahhh, the relief, I thought, as the chemical rush obliterated any painful anxieties that might dare intrude. When I drove back to the sorority after wiping my face of grease and cream, I'd scour the streets for a free parking space for what seemed like hours, usually parking illegally and hoping to avoid another ticket. Soon it would be dinnertime, when I would enter the fancy sorority dining room and sit among my new sisters for the evening meal, returning again to the sedate numbness I both ran from and chased. In health terms, my behavior was crazy, but emotionally, my various binges kept me feeling sane. Food overloads were similar to my nighttime sexual transgressions: they blotted out pain and replaced it with pleasure, power, and control. Any lingering "bad" feelings were quickly banished, replaced by anticipation about the next feast.

Despite attending parties and formal dances that seemed glamorous and full of adventure, I didn't let myself get close to my sorority sisters, except for brief alcohol-fueled merriments that, like the other binges, always wore off by morning. Mostly, I turned inward and kept eating in secret, gaining ten, fifteen, twenty-five pounds. I had no name for my repetitive cycle of food fantasy, binging, sleeping it off, waking up feeling sick, going to class, and then starting all over; it was just something I did. A similar pattern played out with my stealth fraternity visits at night, although I tried to cut back on those by ordering medium pizzas instead from a hole-in-the-wall delivery called Pizza Answer. After polishing off the whole pie, I always felt too bloated to leave the sorority. As the months went by, my escapades grew less thrilling but not less compelling; I couldn't seem to stop.

One day, during a visit home to see my parents, I noticed a book my mom had left out titled *Feeding the Hungry Heart*, by Geneen Roth. I grabbed it without knowing why, and took it with me to read on an upcoming Greyhound bus trip to Eastern Washington. I'd planned to meet a high school friend for the Apple Cup, the annual rivalry football game between her school and mine.

Sitting on the bus, I watched the western evergreens give way to sandy-colored fields and hills, sagebrush scrubbing the horizon. My sorority bag was once again stocked with sugary indulgences, like a child who brings her blankie everywhere she goes. Lulled by the repetitive rumble of the diesel engine, my thoughts drifted back to another moment on another bus, when I was ten years old on the way to elementary school.

I sat alone, as I did every day, and stared out the window. This day, there was a bee attached to the glass. I didn't know why it was stuck there, and I watched it buzz frantically, trying to get free. As the bus accelerated, the bee became pressed against the clear pane.

As the bus entered a ramp onto the freeway, the pressure of acceleration pushed the bee against the glass so hard that a drop of fluid left its body and slowly trailed down the window. Then another drop started, the buzzing faded to stillness, and the memory faded too.

I hated that memory; I'd always identified with the little bee, though I didn't know why. Now I have words to describe how I felt as I watched it die: trapped, sad, powerless, confused, and utterly insignificant. And so, so angry. But as a child and young adult all I could feel was a dull ache in my stomach that I tried to eradicate with food or video games at the local mini-mart.

Back on the Apple Cup Greyhound, I started reading mom's book about food. I ate nothing, despite the stash of goodies next to me on the worn seat. Soon I was engrossed; I'd never read a book that talked so openly about eating, feelings, and a new word: compulsions. People in the book had compulsions to do things they didn't want to, but couldn't help themselves. Like me, they ate in crazy ways, and they hid it. Some of the people in the stories were able to stop, and feel better. I still believed "getting better" was synonymous with losing weight, and I had no idea that sex could be a compulsion. But I began to consider that emotions might have something to do with how and why I ate so much. Reading those stories made me first feel less alone.

I didn't change instantly, but reading the book and its promise of something better contributed to an idea I did act on: to travel to France as an exchange student my sophomore year. Somewhere deep down I knew I needed to get away from the Greek system, so I set about exploring how to make such a journey.

Loans, applications, a passport, and a visa later, at the age of nineteen, I flew to Paris and caught a fast train to Avignon in Southern France. I moved in with an exchange family for the winter and told myself I would use my new lifestyle to lose weight and straighten up:

45

no more cheating. On a deeper level, it was my first real initiative to strike out for something different than what I grew up with. Unlike the little bee stuck to the school bus window, my feet were starting to kick free of the glass.

Although I still often drank to excess with my fellow exchange students, I avoided men and focused all my energy on a new fantasy: to become thin and stylish like the French women I admired. My weight loss routine involved following a strict food plan and exercising almost every day in a women's gym near my school in the city. I ate a chunk of plain baguette for breakfast, chewing as many times as I could to make it last longer. Lunch meant carrot slices and thin soup at a French diner called Flunch, and dinner consisted of miniscule bites of whatever my exchange mother, Claudine, prepared while I avoided her pointed glares at my insulting lack of consumption. By mid-quarter, I'd lost fifteen pounds and felt physically lighter, but my mind remained as heavy as ever.

This became obvious to me during my regular workout. Sweating on the treadmill at high speed, I'd stare out the window at a tall street vendor on the busy sidewalk below. I no longer felt my body or the burn of running, my mind spellbound as I watched him craft perfect round crepes, one after the other. His ritual was as exacting as a priest preparing communion at Sunday Mass. He poured and sculpted creamy batter onto a round black griddle, and as it heated, he painted the flat pastry with Nutella or fluffy whipped cream covered with sliced red strawberries. Each day I imagined that he would roll and hand one of his finished delicacies to me, and I would eat it slowly, savoring every delectable bite. But as the days stretched to months, I never let myself have one.

The fact that I wasn't fixed despite my successful weight loss became even more noticeable when I received a care package from Matt for Valentine's Day. Beneath the thick brown paper, the bright red wrapping revealed a two-pound box of See's chocolates, Nuts and Chews. I told myself I would only have one piece and throw the rest away, but down they went, nutty chew after nutty chew, until the box was almost empty and I started to feel sick. Panicked that I might gain back any weight, I decided to purge them, something I hadn't tried since junior high school. I debated only briefly whether to use the sink, toilet, or bidet in the little French bathroom I shared with the others.

Deed done and all traces carefully cleared, I remembered my other try at vomiting in junior high. I'd learned about it at my first cheer squad movie night, in a hushed story about another girls' sleepover where the most popular girl in school had come out of the bathroom with vomit on her fingers and a smile on her face, advising the others that it was a great way to stay skinny. I'd gone home and tried it myself when no one was around, hating the acidic burn in my throat, but hoping for the best. Later that night, my sister cornered me in my bedroom and confronted me.

"I know what you did," she said, her green eyes narrowing dangerously. Her normally chipper voice was a deep growl. "You left your puke all down the side of the toilet bowl." My eyes widened, but I didn't dare deny it.

"Don't you EVER let me catch you throwing up your food again! It's a horrible thing to do, and I won't let you get away with it next time." I complied, never daring it again, until six years later and five thousand miles away from her wrath. But even though I wasn't caught in France, the bitter sore throat hangover left me feeling worse than before. I promised myself I'd never eat sugar again and that I would continue my "healthy" eating even after I returned home.

When I returned to Seattle twenty-seven pounds lighter, Matt was thrilled. He led me straight to his room at the frat house, where he had scattered red rose petals on every surface. Yet despite our seemingly joyful reunion and the fact that I'd stayed faithful while I was away, I knew something was still wrong with me. My efforts hadn't cured the thing that I wanted it to cure; the thing I still didn't have a name for. I was always worried about something, and now that I'd stopped cheating and reached what I thought was an acceptable weight, I suspected it might go deeper than that. Once home in Seattle, all I could think of was how to make the constant worry-static in my mind go away. I didn't know there was a name for it: anxiety.

For a while I replaced food binges with shopping. With a big chunk of loan money left over from my trip abroad, I sought to complete my fantasy makeover with a new wardrobe befitting my now-slender body. I drove to the mall and roamed from store to store trying on clothes and buying everything I liked. Soon I acquired a critical mass of purchases so bulky I couldn't carry them to my car. Frustrated there were no shopping carts in malls, I left some bags behind a store counter while I struggled with two trips. The fashionable blonde clerk gave me a look similar to the convenience store clerk who sold me piles of junk food, though mercifully, her expression was more pitying than mocking.

◇ ◇ ◇

Once again, broke and exhausted from obsessing about food, I fell back into visiting one of the two frat guys I'd vowed to never see again. Distressed, I confided in my sister about my fear of gaining back the weight I'd lost, and she surprised me by admitting she'd had trouble with eating too—for her it was eating too little and letting herself get too thin. She said while I was away in France she'd started working with a counselor, who recommended she join a therapy group for co-eds with food problems, and she suggested we join together. All I remember from the six weeks in the group was that my beautiful, skinnier-than-me sister seemed to get special treatment from one of the male facilitators, and I felt jealous. I was always jealous of any attention Christi got that I wanted.

Drinking helped me avoid food binges, but it escalated past the point of finding myself wrapped around toilet bowls to not finding myself at all. Waking up in bed without remembering how I got there scared me, and I tried to cut back on drinking again. Unaware of my infidelities, around that time Matt decided to pin me, the fraternity equivalent of a pre-engagement promise of marriage.

True to his romantic nature, Matt orchestrated a dramatic surprise in the sorority dining room. One spring evening, forty frat guys in sharp navy blazers and ties entered the hall, surrounding me at the table right after we'd sat down for dinner. I smiled as my fellow sisters giggled and cheered. Matt broke through their ranks and bent down on one knee before me. He and his chorus started singing a sweet three-part serenade about true love that clenched my stomach even as I beamed with apparent delight. As he lovingly fastened the gold and pearl fraternity pin to my blouse, I felt wretched inside, wondering if anyone there had seen me recently passed out on another fraternity's front lawn. Terrified my double life might start to publicly unravel, I decided again to find some help.

My sister seemed to like her new counselor, so I asked if I could see her too. I didn't want to try medication again but hoped talk therapy might help. I was told that it would be better if I saw a different person, so Christi and I could have our own counselors. My sister gave me the name of a psychologist her therapist recommended named Dr. James.

⋄ ⋄ ⋄

I sat nervously in the waiting room on the third floor of a waterfront building near the university filling out forms on a clipboard. A tall blonde woman in a gray suit greeted me, offering a pinched grin as she led me into her delicately decorated office overlooking the lake. Dr. James asked why I'd come, and I told her I'd started eating too much junk food again and was afraid of gaining more weight.

Her eyes appraised my body, and I thought I caught a look of revulsion pass behind her wire-rimmed glasses as she said, "Well Staci, it's really quite simple. To keep your weight down, you need to stop eating junk food and exercise. Do you even know how to eat in a healthy way? Do you exercise regularly?"

I stared at her, thin as a bird and looking far more fragile, and felt a sudden impulse to crush her arm and twist it, to see if her bones were hollow and birdlike. I was certain by now there was more to it than eating and exercise; that whatever was wrong with me went deeper than that. I knew the book *Feeding the Hungry Heart* had told me the truth, that it was my heart that was hungry, not a problem with my bad habits. I instantly neither liked nor trusted Dr. James, and had no desire to tell her anything more. I politely finished the appointment, and told her I'd talk with my mom about rescheduling, but didn't. I returned to comfort food binges, but now I started to hate myself for my weakness.

At twenty-one years old, I didn't grasp the possibility that my food binges, alcohol abuse, compulsive shopping, and deceptive promiscuity might qualify as my very own addictive cocktail: my chemical-behavioral version of Prozac. I didn't know that I was using this combination to medicate and distract myself from the inner turmoil that was endlessly trying to get my attention. The pain that was buried did not want to stay there; like a tiny green shoot cracking through concrete, it wanted to emerge into my conscious awareness to be grieved and released. I didn't know how to let this happen, but I was starting to realize that my life was too chaotic and that I couldn't figure out how to make it better on my own.

I told my sister I didn't like Dr. James and I had to see her counselor.

I said I didn't care if we saw the same person; I needed to see someone now. It was a relief when Christi finally said that Margaret, her psychotherapist, had said yes.

SEVEN

My First Psycho-Therapist

MARGARET WAS A SHORT, PEAR-SHAPED WOMAN with wavy gray hair and round glasses. She'd gone back to school at age fifty to get her Ph.D., and operated a private practice out of a small, stuffed-animal-filled office built onto her home. Blunt and sharp as a tack, Margaret's words often stung as she pointed out my many dysfunctional defenses. She was quick to laugh at me and everyone else, and at first I liked her, even as I was secretly afraid of her.

Margaret said she had to provide a code to prove to the insurance company that I had something worth paying her to treat. She showed me the insurance form and talked about my diagnosis, or the label that described my "mental illness."

"I've looked at all the possibilities, and what I think fits you the best is called dysthymia," she said.

"What's that?"

"It's a chronic, low-grade depression. You can function in school, but you never quite feel happy or well. Your relationships aren't very deep. You don't have all the symptoms of a major depression, where you can't function at all, but you have enough of them to warrant this diagnosis," she explained.

"Okay," I said, and we dropped it. That was that, my first known psychiatric label. My first actual diagnosis must have come from Barney, the psychiatrist I saw for Prozac when I was eighteen, but he never mentioned the specifics. Since I was covered under my mom's health insurance, I was glad I didn't have to pay.

I didn't know what the symptoms of my depression were, but Margaret thought I'd become dysthymic because I'd had a bad childhood. I thought she was way off; I told her I'd had a wonderful childhood, even though at twenty-one I remembered little of it before age sixteen. The fact that I was not conscious of much of my past was something I figured out in high school when my friends used to tease me about it. I'd laugh, unworried; it was just my normal. I had never heard of the concepts of dissociation or protective amnesia.

Margaret thought my spotty memory was alarming, but I minimized her concerns.

Therapists always think their clients had bad childhoods, I told myself. Really, mine was perfect! My parents loved me. My mom threw birthday parties. I'd seen the pictures, which filled in for happy memories.

"What about your mom's drinking?" she challenged.

"Oh, she quit all that when I was nine," I said. "She found the Catholic church and started AA, and things got much better. It really was fine!"

Margaret did not agree that my family was perfect, and there was no convincing her otherwise. She insisted that my lack of clear recall was caused by trauma, which she described as emotional injuries, kind of like scars, that can stack up over time. She thought that's why I was always somewhat depressed, because emotional scar tissue didn't have as much feeling.

I didn't understand, but I started to feel better from talking with her every week, so I kept going. I stopped stuffing myself to the point of stabbing pain, dull aching, and sour breath. I also quit drinking so much, which was a big relief. But I didn't stop cheating, or keeping secrets.

◊ ◊ ◊

At Margaret's insistence, my parents dutifully came to therapy sessions with my sister and I to process the bad experiences from our past by talking through them. Margaret said I should start getting to know my parents as adults and encouraged me to set up one-on-one time with them. She advised me to stand up to my dad's belittling humor ("How dare he treat you that way"), my mom's tardiness and disorganization ("She is demonstrating that she doesn't value you by making you wait; it's disrespectful"), and to limit my contact with them while I determined if they could earn back the right to be close to me.

Meanwhile, Margaret was getting closer with us, especially my sister. She talked about bringing my sister to a psychology conference with her, explaining that the best way to help my sister was to use a therapy technique called reparenting, in which she offered herself to my sister as a healthy "attachment figure" outside the family and outside the boundaries of typical therapy in an office. My parents agreed, knowing little about therapy and eager, like the rest of us, to please the imperious Margaret.

And so the lines that typically defined ethical therapy started to blur. Margaret gave my sister extra sessions. She invited her to stay afterward to have dinner with her family—her husband and two grown sons, who were both single and still lived with her.

Margaret explained that since I didn't have the same diagnosis as my sister, I didn't need the same kind of approach. But she did ask me to travel with them to another psychology conference out of state. I agreed to go, feeling special yet uncomfortable at the same time. I insisted that I get my own room, while Margaret and my sister stayed together.

After we returned from the conference, I decided I didn't want to go on any more trips with them. I felt left out, like a third wheel. They would laugh and share special inside jokes that they would have to explain to me. When I told Margaret I didn't want to go on further trips, she seemed glad. She told me that her therapeutic approach was unorthodox yet successful, but that many people would not understand, so I shouldn't tell anyone about it.

"Your sister has a right to confidentiality," she said. "It is not your place to talk about her therapy." I agreed, and for a long time told no one about our trip, or the other trips my sister began to take with Margaret and her family.

A year later, my parents began to get frustrated with the course of our therapy, grumbling about how Margaret seemed to have too much control over us. Indignant, I denied it, insisting that I was twenty-two now and old enough to make my own decisions.

Today I believe that my parents were right. Margaret was using us, especially my sister, to meet her own emotional needs. She used her command of psychological language to deceive us into thinking her intentions were principled, when actually they were selfish. I liked her attention and what I thought was protectiveness, but ultimately she would become my role model for the kind of therapist I never wanted to be.

One intense session proved to be the last for my dad. My parents arrived together and sat on the love seat in the small office, while Margaret reigned in her overstuffed chair in the corner, my sister and I flanking her on both sides. Usually Margaret started the sessions, set the agenda, and then deferred to my sister at her right, or rarely me, the left gun, to raise our issues. But this time my dad arrived with something on his mind.

"I need to say something; it's been really bothering me," he began, and I could tell he'd been ruminating over this for a while. His voice was shaking slightly, his big hands balled into fists at his sides. My mom appeared rigid, scared, and small next to him. Dad mostly followed Margaret's lead in sessions, so starting things out was new for him.

"Now we've been coming here, paying money, and "processing," as you call it, for a long time. But I have to tell you, I don't think it's helping. I mean, no matter what we talk about, there never seems to be any resolution. We make progress in one session I think, and Lani and I go home feeling like we're getting somewhere, but then the next week we come back and it starts all over, all the problems, all the complaints about the past. You seem to be turning our daughters against us. There's never any forgiveness!" He paused and I looked, wide-eyed, at Margaret, who was swelling up like a puffer fish, about to reply.

"And another thing," Dad said, gaining momentum. "Lani and I don't think it's right that you keep taking Christi on trips. I mean, that's way out of line for a therapist. We've gone along with this therapy because you said it would help our daughter, but the fact that we can't tell anyone about it seems all wrong."

Margaret was now in the end stages of swelling, becoming energetically huge in the room, though when she spoke her voice was quiet and chillingly confident.

"You are continuing to show resistance to helping your daughters heal. You demand forgiveness, though you haven't changed at all. You are a bully and you need to be held accountable, but when you are, you don't like it and you blame me and this process. I have explained to you that this therapy technique is the best for your daughter, that it saved her life, but that it is new and still not fully understood. You act like you accept it, but now because you aren't getting your way, you complain. If it weren't for your past emotional abuse and neglect, and your wife's father's sexual abuse, your daughters wouldn't even need therapy. You are disrespectful and out of line."

I'd never seen anyone stand up to my dad that way when he

was angry, let alone a five-foot woman, and I was impressed. Dad reacted by standing up to his full six-feet-two-inches, towering over Margaret, saying, "I don't need this shit," and walking out the door. For a second I thought he might spit.

Margaret's expression was smug, like she'd won something. My sister looked mad and mom looked frozen. Margaret went on to explain that dad was demonstrating emotional immaturity, and that my mom would have to make a decision: abandon us too and "enable his quitting," or stay to support her daughters. Mom said she'd be back, and the session ended. Margaret debriefed my sister and I about what to do if dad wouldn't apologize and come back to therapy. She encouraged us not to have any contact with him outside her sessions and to tell him through our mom that we did not feel safe doing so without Margaret there. Her complete minions, we agreed.

Mom made her escape a few sessions later.

Margaret had recently taken my sister on a trip with her to China, and while there Christi became gravely ill. She was twenty-four-years-old, so Margaret had no legal obligation to tell my parents, and didn't. When our mom found out that my sister has been sick abroad and Margaret hadn't called, she was furious. Margaret informed her that it was the kindest thing to do, to protect her from unnecessary worry. Mom, normally compliant with authority, did not agree.

In this same family session, my mom found out that I'd also gone on a trip with my sister and Margaret to a psychology conference, and that was the last straw. She tried to protest, saying it seemed wrong, but Margaret cut her off, confronting her as she had my dad, and accusing her of not supporting our needs. We were only halfway through the session, but mom stood up to leave. I followed her to the doorway, bursting into tears.

I felt five years old, suddenly reliving a memory from the apartment in Yakima, Washington, where we were living back then. My

parents were fighting, and I saw my mom rushing out the door, saying she was going to the store to buy a pack of cigarettes. I wanted to
go with her, but she left without me, the big wooden door slamming
in my face. My sobs bubbled up, unwanted and uncontrollable, until
dad stomped out of the kitchen toward me. I turned to see his huge
frame coming fast, and I was terrified. He picked me up, swung me
over his knee, and spanked me, hard. Then he sent me to my room
with a singular assignment: "Quit crying!" This happened regularly
when I was upset as a child, and at some point I figured out how
to avoid the spanking; whenever I felt like crying I would go to my
room and quietly stay there until the threat of tears safely passed.

Back in the therapy session, the door to Margaret's office was still
open, and my mom was rushing up the driveway toward her car.
I called out, "Mom, please don't abandon me!" but she didn't turn
around. I collapsed on Margaret's couch, bawling as if I were that
five-year-old instead of twenty-two. Margaret somehow cued my
sister, who moved next to me on the couch and stroked my heaving
back. Margaret told us that our mother was unable to be there for us,
but that it was important that we take control and inform her that we
would not talk with her until she would reengage with the process
and come back to therapy. We followed her advice, which kicked off
a six-year estrangement from my parents.

- EIGHT -

Shamanism and Nightmares

DESPITE OUR FAMILY BLOWOUT, I remained enamored with therapy. I was amazed that just talking with Margaret seemed to solve my out-of-control eating problem, and my drinking was manageable for the most part. Having been the quiet one in the family, I loved getting to talk about my life and problems for a whole hour every week, and how Margaret actually listened instead of lecturing me like dad always did. It was a first.

After finding a few psych classes absorbing, I decided to give up my dream of becoming a broadcast journalist and change my major to psychology. I wanted to become a therapist like Margaret, so I signed up to volunteer for the late shift at the Seattle Crisis Clinic to get experience helping others.

I hit it off right away with a fellow volunteer named Kenneth, a soulful sailor and would-be therapist. Kenneth had a bushy beard and eyes so dark they were almost black. He said he was in training to become a shaman, and when he learned that I was raised Catholic and had no idea what shamanism was, he took it upon himself to offer me a full tutorial. This started with a long list of books with interesting titles like *The Reluctant Shaman* and *The Way of Wyrd*. I read them all with relish, taking in perspectives on reality I'd never imagined. Unlike my experiences in Sunday Mass, which I attended less and less often, I felt like someone was finally starting to tell me something practical and powerful about spirituality.

I loved Kenneth's attention, and as our acquaintance grew, I started flirting with him, even though I was still promised to Matt and Kenneth was married with three kids. We went out to dinner, he took me on his boat, and I visited his house for lunch. I met his wife, Samantha, and their young daughter and sons. Hiding behind the pretense of a mentoring friendship, Kenneth and I had a secret, romantic, hands-off affair. I told Margaret nothing about this relationship, convinced she'd make me end it. I justified to myself that beyond hugs, Kenneth and I had never touched, so I wasn't doing anything wrong.

After our volunteer year ended, Kenneth wanted to stay in touch. He encouraged me to come with him to a local shamanic workshop, and I happily agreed. While driving us to the training, his voice grew somber, a departure from his usual cheerful charm.

"Staci, I need to tell you something. I'm attracted to you—you must know that. But I'm also confused, because I'm fifty, and you're twenty-three. Is this real for you, or are you stringing me along?"

Overwhelmed by his directness, my eyes lost focus and I stared off into space as if I hadn't heard him. I was dissociating again.

"Will you look at me?" he demanded, raising his voice. "I just said something to you that's important to me, and I want you to look at me!"

I would not look. Despite my blatant flirtations, Kenneth's directness terrified me. I believed then that talking openly about our attraction *would* make it an infidelity, whereas flirting in secret really wasn't. In my mind, admitting the emotions would be far worse than cheating on Matt with guys from school, because even though Matt was my boyfriend, we weren't legally married. I refused to talk with Kenneth further, and we entered the large classroom in awkward silence. My discomfort was quickly replaced by curiosity about the class, and I focused all my attention on the instructor, Leslie, a slender brunette holding a huge round animal-skin drum in one hand

and a wooden beater in the other. She tapped the drum five times to call the class to order.

After a short summary of shamanism, Leslie explained that she would drum rhythmically to lull us into a trance, from which we would travel spiritually to one of three different realms, called the upper, middle, and lower worlds. In this altered state, we would visualize going down a hole or chasm and emerge in another landscape, where we might encounter spirit guides or animal helpers. We could then ask them for information to help us better navigate our daily lives. Even though it might seem like we were making the whole thing up, Leslie assured us that we would be tapping into a realm of truth with our minds that was quite real and powerful, and that we could practice and improve this ability over time.

We were instructed to partner up, lie down on the floor slightly touching our partners, and close our eyes. I turned to an orange-haired woman seated next to me, who introduced herself and agreed to travel to the spirit world on my behalf. I didn't notice anything special during the drumming other than feeling uncomfortable lying so close to her, but after it was over she told me she'd seen my power animal, a raven, four different times.

When it was my turn to let myself go into trance to look for her power animal, I began to shudder and shake as if I were having a seizure. I heard the drum, but I couldn't see or imagine any of the suggested visualizations, only a confusing rush of gray and black, while my body twitched as if flooded with electricity. It wasn't painful, just frustrating. Afraid my partner would be disappointed, I told her that I saw a big gray bobcat with white around its eyes. Feeling guilty at her excited response, I decided I wasn't cut out to be a shaman.

After the workshop, Kenneth and I kept our dinner plans, arriving at a funky teahouse in my neighborhood. He was energized by the training and impressed when I told him about the raven power animal the orange-haired woman had found for me. Our upsetting earlier conversation was gone from my thoughts; it had automatically been stuffed in a mental hidey-hole where all such scary things went.

I broached another topic, spontaneously telling Kenneth about how Margaret had developed a special relationship with my sister, and that recently, Christi had moved into Margaret's home. I described how left out I felt, especially when she traveled the globe and went on cruises with Margaret's family. Kenneth reacted strongly to my revelation.

"I have a personal rule not to question people's therapists, but for this one I'll make an exception," he said. "Margaret groomed her from the beginning, don't you see?"

"What do you mean?" I asked, forgetting I'd first heard the word *grooming* when I was nine years old—the social worker had used it when investigating Grandpa Westby for abusing my sister.

"Child molesters do this," Kenneth explained. "They manipulate their victims to do things they wouldn't normally do by testing them first. They try out harmless things, like a friendly hug, and then build up the kid's tolerance to more outrageous stuff. Like stroking their hair and then their arms, and then more and more private places. A lot of times they flatter the kids to reassure them that what they're doing is really okay. Later, if the child protests, the offender can point to all the earlier touching, and tell the kid they clearly wanted it, or led them on, because they never said no. Are you sure Margaret's not being sexual with your sister?"

"No way. Margaret's asexual. It's like they're best friends, but she orders Christi around."

"Even if it's not sexual, it can still be harmful. There's such a thing as emotional grooming too, especially by people in positions of power, like therapists. Grooming can foster dependency, so you never leave.

Margaret started grooming your sister by crossing small boundaries with her, like having her stay late after sessions, then escalated to taking her on trips, and now they live together! What she is doing is really wrong, Staci, and harmful to your sister. You're being harmed too; it's a triangle, and a fucked up dynamic."

I stared at his sympathetic yet troubled dark eyes, suddenly not hungry for the food in front of me. I felt confused, but also somehow better, as if the fact that I got less attention from Margaret than my sister wasn't so bad after all. Yet despite Kenneth's protective outrage, I couldn't imagine life without therapy. I didn't want to start over with a new therapist, and I feared if I left Margaret, I'd lose my sister too. I was also afraid I'd go back to overeating and gain weight again, so I didn't confront my dependency on Margaret. But I did make one change after that night: I started avoiding Kenneth.

◇ ◇ ◇

A week later I decided to surprise Matt with a spontaneous visit, and stopped by the house he rented with a few fraternity brothers. As I stepped onto the porch, I noticed a stack of mail poking out of the mailbox. I gathered it up and sifted through it, noticing a brown paper-wrapped magazine with Matt's name on the label. I tore off the paper and stared at the woman on the cover, her tan, smooth skin, flowing dark hair, and impossibly proportioned body draped in sheer blue, hiding nothing. I imagined Matt looking at her and decided I couldn't measure up, which triggered a mental cascade of self-loathing. As soon as I walked in the door, I turned my anger toward him.

He was alone, sitting on the couch in the cluttered living room, and I held the magazine up as my greeting, demanding an explanation.

He stumbled to answer, but the gist of it was that we hardly ever had sex anymore, and he had needs that porn was taking care of.

He was right about our diminishing sex life. Since I'd been getting closer with Kenneth the last year, I'd been spending less and less time with Matt. Seeing him reminded me of my secrets, a feeling I didn't like.

"I'm sorry," he said. "I'll cancel the subscription. I didn't want to hurt you. Come here." He gestured for me to sit next to him on the couch and put his arm around me, taking my hand in his. "I'll get rid of it. It's no big deal. I really want *you*, but when you say you're tired or busy or whatever, I don't want to pressure you. I love you." His tenderness relaxed me, but rising dread soon replaced the relief I felt. His secret was out, but I was still very much in hiding.

"Um, I have something to tell you too," I started in a small voice. He let go of my hand and leaned away from me, crossing his arms.

"What?"

I followed with a tearful confession of some of my infidelities, leaving out about half, including how close and flirtatious I'd really been with Kenneth. I told myself I didn't want to overwhelm him, but my omissions were all about self-deception and damage control.

Yet even with what little I shared, the injury to our relationship was beyond repair. We began couple's therapy with Margaret to try to work it out. I stopped cheating and started trying to be as adventurous with Matt sexually as I had been with the frat guys on the side, but I was never quite up for it unless I was drunk, and then I couldn't remember much of what we did. After a dismal attempt at homemade porn, I finally quit trying, and our fights escalated to a frantic pitch, at least on my side. Matt broke up with me a few months later. He was kind, telling me it was because we'd grown apart and asking if we could still be friends.

I immediately returned to binge drinking with friends, and

distracted myself by having sex with a guy I met in a downtown Seattle sports bar who told me he was separated from his wife. I pretended our tryst in a nearby park was adventurous and exciting, but most of it was a hazy blur. Only one moment registered: as I looked at his face inches below mine, it suddenly became distorted, as if I were seeing him through the wrong end of binoculars. Instead of pressed against mine, his body seemed worlds away. I declined his invitation to spend the night at his place so he could cook me breakfast in the morning, shuddering inwardly at his neediness.

My hangover the next day was no surprise, but it came with a rush of tears that wouldn't stop. Distraught, I called Margaret to confess, still leaving out a lot. In our next session, she said I was wise to have used a condom, but advised me in her wry monotone that, clearly, I was not ready to date anyone.

"You need to bring down the drama first," she said. "No more drinking at all. If you keep drinking, you will grow apart from your sister, and then you'll be left with no one."

Frightened, I agreed to stop drinking and hooking up with men. I spurned my party friends and settled instead on a pattern of movie-and-ice cream nights alone in my studio, curled up in an old pink recliner I had found for free on the side of the road. I stayed single and avoided all men, and for a while things quieted down. I graduated and started a master's program in social work, but along with my discoveries about social work and mental health, I started my own tutorial: pornography.

Impulsively, I began renting X-rated videos from a trendy sex shop and watching them before bed instead of regular movies. I told myself it was okay because I was a liberated feminist like some of the outspoken, hairy women I'd watched from a distance at school. Social work studies of oppression and social justice revealed that I was far more than "Caucasian"; I was a "race-ignorant, white-privileged, thin, middle-class, heterosexual, able-bodied, fat-phobic female with Americanized beauty superiority." Keeping to myself, I didn't make close friends those two years, but I did fall hard for porn.

The fantasy images I consumed made me feel so high, I no longer needed ice cream. I discovered the Internet at the university library, where I furtively tried to connect with anonymous men by typing provocative words in sex chat rooms, meanwhile hoping no one could see my screen from behind. I found myself overwhelmingly aroused from these episodes, but I quickly dissolved my guilt within my new identity as a sexually progressive woman.

I wanted more than what I saw on the screen, so I went to a fetish night held in the dark bowels of a downtown club I heard about in a chat room. Unsure what to expect, I was startled by the techno-punk cacophony and people in various stages of undress skulking and slithering around, proudly hating each other. Alarm overcame my thrill, and I went back to cybersex, alone.

◇ ◇ ◇

After graduation I found a steady first job in my field and finally had a little extra money at the end of each month. I adopted a sweet orange kitten I named PK, and began to pay off my student loans. Under Margaret's direction, I started saving money for the first time in my life. I tried to stop the porn and chat room visits, which were leaving a nasty streak of discomfort in the wake of their gratification. I was a professional now, not a college student, and I wanted to make more wholesome decisions.

But as my external life reached a new level of stability and I gave up the world of cybersex, something changed internally. My sleep became overrun with nightmares—night terrors in which I'd wake up in a sweat and it would take hours to get back to sleep. My mornings became marred by headaches from clenching my jaw all night, so I made an appointment with a dentist and was fit with a biteplate that I soon couldn't sleep without.

Margaret told me to write about my bad dreams and how I felt about them, so I could read them to her in therapy. The themes repeated, similar and horrifying: me, a trapped little girl trying to fight off unrecognizable but familiar men, and enduring unwanted sex acts. Sometimes I would wake myself up trying to kick off phantom attackers. During one such dream, I saw a cube with colored squares on each side, spinning and twisting. I read my journal entry aloud to Margaret in a session:

> I dreamed of a Rubik's Cube—three sides were matching, knowing it was so close—when all sides were matched I would remember everything. The Rubik's Cube sank down deep into the ocean.

I became anxious about going to sleep and stayed up later and later, distracting myself again with junk food and TV, once more gaining weight. My energy level plummeted as sleep deprivation set in.

One day, while sitting in my sunny third-floor studio apartment eating an apple with a knife, I looked out the open patio door and admired a line of tall poplar trees swaying in the wind. I carved off a slice of the bright red peel and noticed a brownish mark on the white flesh. Curious, I sliced into it and a black earwig exploded from the apple—crammed into too small a space, it burst out three times the size of the hole it was confined in. I leaped up, ran out onto the patio, and threw the apple as far as I could, wriggling earwig clinging to its surface.

I went back inside, shaking and tearful. I felt as if the earwig was somehow me, reflecting ugly, black insides confined beneath a waxy, red surface. It reminded me of my life, and my mind ran through disjointed images of the degrading sex I used to consume and had found myself craving again. Even though I'd quit renting the videos for a while, the images hadn't stopped playing in my mind. I turned on the TV to change my mental channel, and despite myself, soon headed to the video store to pick out another porn movie. It was the only thing that really worked to force the apple, earwig, and everything else out of my awareness.

I continued to see Margaret, though we made little progress, and our sessions grew increasingly strained and tedious. Margaret decided to refer me to a specialist in hypnosis. She thought my chronic nightmares might be a form of lost early memories trying to return to my consciousness, and that a hypnotist might help me clarify things. So I made an appointment with Dr. Dunn, a certified hypnotherapist, who apparently worked part-time for the Seattle Police Department. Margaret would remain my primary therapist, and I'd see Dr. Dunn for two consulting sessions.

NINE

Hypnotherapy

DR. DUNN'S OFFICE BUILDING INTIMIDATED ME. He worked in the heart of downtown Seattle, on an upper floor of a shiny glass skyscraper with furniture in his waiting room worth more than my car. When his office door opened, I was surprised by his tousled salt-and-pepper hair and casual tone. He struck me as a surfer type, but with a Ph.D.

Dr. Dunn explained how hypnosis worked, but said we wouldn't be trying it in our first session. Instead I told him about my new job at a nursing home and answered his questions about my nightmares, my spotty childhood memories, and Margaret's concern that our work together wasn't going anywhere. I revealed nothing about Margaret's unethical relationship with my sister. Embarrassed to be there, I wrote a check at the end of the session and agreed to come back again to try hypnosis.

A week later I was leaning back in his comfortable chair, eyes closed, as he coached me to relax and then counted down from ten to one in a gravelly "hey dude" voice, which I found soothing. He instructed me to imagine myself walking down a hallway with doors on all sides, and turn to a door with a sign on it labeled Happy Memories. I could see the hallway, see the door opening and me walking in, but what happened next astounded me.

Once I walked through the door, the room gave way to the outside, and I saw a clear image of Lake Goodwin and the long wooden dock jutting out from the shoreline. I saw the morning mist steaming from the water's glassy surface, and sensed the hush of the early hour just past sunrise. I watched, mute, as my nine-year-old sister, Grandpa Sprout, and seven-year-old me tossed our water skis and towrope into the motorboat. We were quiet like the lake, as if we were all sharing a special mystery with the dawn. As the low motor puttered us away from the dock, my sister's eyes crinkled with glee because she was going to be the first to ski. I felt the pride of my younger self, puffed up as my orange lifejacket, as Grandpa informed me that my job was to be the First Mate Safety Flag Officer, so I should watch her carefully from the back of the boat.

My view suddenly shifted to my favorite Christmas ever, when I was nine. It was the first one without Grandpa and Grandma Westby at our house, and the first one with mom—and all the adults—sober from alcohol. I loved all the new toys I unwrapped, because for once I was given things I really wanted, like a black light, instead of random kids' stuff. My sister and I ran to our shared room to try it out, fascinated with the purple-orange glow of our skin in the dark. We listened over and over to her new Kenny Rogers album, *The Gambler*, memorizing the words to all the songs and singing along, giggling wildly at our strange neon-white teeth.

Then a third memory came in a rush—a thunder-and-lightning storm overhead at our duplex in Yakima. I was four years old sitting with my family at our dinner table, which had been moved out to the deck of the small apartment. It was a warm summer night, and an electric breeze tickled my skin as I looked up in utter awe, without fear. My sense of being a little girl in a little body left me and I felt my mind expand out, out, somehow merging with that storm and dancing along the jags of light, flashing and clapping in joy for all of life.

Dr. Dunn's voice coaxed me back to his therapy office, and I heard his counting again, up from one to ten, as he cued me to see myself walking up a staircase and to feel my body in the chair. I opened my eyes, and he asked what I'd seen. I felt exhilarated, still full of awe from the lightning storm, and something else, something new. For the first time in my life I had more solid recollections of my past from the inside, not just jarring flashes or what I heard from family stories or saw in pictures. The sharp memories of happy times felt transforming, as if I was no longer floating through life like a lost duckling in deep water, frantically paddling my feet but never really moving. For the first time in my life, I felt on firm ground. I felt real. I wanted desperately to continue hypnotherapy, but Margaret said no.

"You need to let your brain integrate the memories you've already found," she said when we were together again. "Dr. Dunn agrees with me. This was about opening a door, not changing therapists."

Furious, my secret porn video rentals turned toward themes of rage and violence. My relief at reclaiming happy memories of my past disappeared, and soon I felt worse than ever. The nightmares returned, and something in me started to snap, broken and hopeless. I abruptly became suicidal, and started to imagine getting a gun and shooting myself in the head.

The idea of a gun became so real I could see its shiny, black metal surface and hear the clunking sound of my teeth clamping around it. Exhausted by running from sleep, I began to contemplate how to get one. In my fantasies I was frustrated by the waiting period between the time I could buy a gun and when I could pick it up; I wanted one now. I started driving by Butch's Gun Shop, the name spelled out in huge white letters on a brown slatted wooden roof. These thoughts became strangely comforting to me, a new death-lullaby, but I also hated them, and felt powerless when they came. The moods would steal over me, dark and deadly, so horrid that I named them "the mean, dark brown-black hollows." I wrote it all down in my journal and, for the first time ever, Margaret showed fear while working with me. She made me promise not to get a gun, and to call her if I took any real action toward getting one.

I quit driving by the gun shop, but I didn't tell her about my new diversion, which was to poke my face and legs with a safety pin. Little pricks brought little round red drops of blood, which calmed me down and made the gun obsession less compelling. The pokes didn't hurt, not really. Bright red dots on white tissues hidden in the trash, another little secret.

Back then, I thought it was bizarre that making myself bleed could make me feel better, but now I know that self-injury can bring pleasure from the body's natural opiates and symbolically express pain while covering up what can't yet be spoken or felt. Compulsive cycles often involve self-destruction in various forms, and to combat my general sense of helplessness, I added one more pattern to my arsenal to restore my sense of control.

◊ ◊ ◊

"Dad called out of the blue, after all this time," my sister said over dinner one night at my studio apartment. It had been six years since we'd had meaningful contact with my parents. "He said he had a weird feeling. He asked about you, without me even telling him about your depression!" Margaret had an open release of information to tell my sister everything about my therapy, so she knew about my sessions, my dark moods, and my suicidal thoughts.

"I told him you weren't doing well and I was scared, and Margaret and I talked about it. We decided that he should come back to therapy with you, to support you through this." I was not given the option, but went along with Margaret and my sister's plans, as I always did.

Margaret, my dad, and I met a few weeks later in Margaret's Seattle office, a more neutral territory than her home office where our family last met. Margaret explained that my depression was getting much worse, but I didn't want to take medication, so we were trying to use therapy and journaling to find the source of my pain. She believed there could be clues in my dreams, and wanted me to read some journal entries to him to see if he had any idea what they might mean. The first dream I read was obviously about child sexual abuse, and was way too graphic to read to my father, but I didn't realize it and Margaret didn't prevent it. The second dream was this:

> I dreamed I was over at the neighbor's house and I found an old secret place and an old book. The pages were blank, but I pulled them off one by one, and hidden below I found some pages with much writing on them. It seemed I knew it was about sex, sex memories. Then I found more information stapled to a hardcore porn magazine...I can't remember much more.

My dad listened, nodding, then said he had no idea what the dreams meant. Instead of trying to interpret them, we talked about the past I had remembered in therapy so far: how afraid I'd felt of him as a child; terrified of his rage and spankings, I was convinced he could kill me. He was shocked to hear this and agreed to work with me to help me feel safer. My suicidal urges abated as we connected, week-by-week over two months; him apologetic and asking to hear more, and me feeling braver each session. I told him things I'd never said, and under Margaret's watchful eye, he actually listened.

Encouraged by the progress my dad and I seemed to be making, my mom gave him a gift to give to me, a necklace. He handed me the small white box in the parking lot after a session, and I opened it to see a shiny, silver half-heart.

"Your mother is wearing the other half," dad said. "She's really hoping you'll call her." I put it on, later incurring Margaret's ire when

I showed her and told her the story. In a blistering critique, she said I was giving my mom the wrong message by wearing it, and that I wasn't honoring the therapy process.

My dad later explained his sudden return by saying he'd had a strong gut feeling I was in danger, and broke the six-year estrangement to call my sister and ask about me. Though he still hated Margaret, he pretended to go along with her control to see if I was okay. I remain grateful that he listened to his intuition, because his presence back in my life helped me feel better in a way that therapy with Margaret hadn't. It was the most intimacy I had ever experienced with my father, and it probably saved my life. But it didn't shed light on why my dreams were overrun with images of sexual abuse and exploitation. Awareness about how broken sex was in our family remained a decade away.

TEN

Near-Death Inspires "Termination"

I PAUSED OUTSIDE MARGARET'S OFFICE DOOR, my eyes lingering, tracing etches of grain in the painted wood.

This isn't going to go well, I thought, turning the knob.

I began the session cautiously, with a typical update about my week before finally getting to my big news: this was going to be my last session, because I was discontinuing therapy. The therapeutic term is *termination*, and Margaret's reaction was instant, her eyes narrowing like a terminator herself.

"You have regressed," she said. "You are acting like a child, and this is a big step backward in your work. You still do not honor the process of therapy, after all I have done for you!"

"I know it seems sudden, but I think this is right for me," I said haltingly. "I don't know why, but I trust this."

I was as surprised as Margaret by my decision. For all the years I'd been coming to see her, I never thought about how long we might work together or ending therapy.

Until my car accident.

It had happened three weeks earlier after leaving a new friend's thirtieth birthday party. We'd played eighties music and silly games and danced, and while driving home I marveled at how much fun I had. This especially amazed me because no one was drunk or high.

High on life, I thought happily.

I sang along with the radio, watching the wipers getting ahead of the beat. It was pouring Seattle rain in sheets of hazy gray outside the windshield. I slowed to a stop at a deserted intersection and was waiting for the light to turn green when SMASH! A car plowed into me from behind at full speed. I would later learn that four high school guys were out for a cruise in a parent's Cadillac Escalade and their brakes went out. I was looking forward when it happened and hadn't seen them coming.

Then things got really strange. When the SUV hit, my head was thrown back and I saw the ceiling of my car, by then a blue Toyota Tercel, its pale gray fabric overlaid by something else…something shadowy, but not malevolent. A blurry shape hovered there, like a thin, concave cloud. Though it had no face, I sensed the shape was aware, intensely alert, and beckoning to me. Although I had no memory of seeing it before, the dark presence seemed intimately familiar, and timelessly patient. Somehow, I knew it was both an entity and a passageway, a portal, and it was inviting me to pass through. Without hesitation, I said yes in my mind.

Instantly, my mind shifted, and I began to experience everything with far more vividness. My awareness shrank to the size of a pinpoint, and I shot like a rocket out of my body and up through that shadow, rising above the rain and clouds.

I am flying! I can fly, I know how to fly! I've always known, but must have forgotten until now, this glorious moment! I watched the pale half-moon go by, and then saw flashes of stars getting brighter, glowing and shining, bursting, like fireworks. I continued flying up, faster and faster, past even the molten sun. It felt ecstatic to be free, finally free, knowing, without knowing, that I was going home.

Then the sky changed and I saw streaks of darkness, smudges and layers of a blackness so bleak I shuddered, glad to fly by without slowing. All at once the light returned, a wall of golden light, creamy soft and sparkly, and I dove into it and through it, and was embraced in feelings of joyful welcome and celebration.

Consciousness here was utterly different than before, rendering my everyday experience isolated and barren. I could feel the presence of other beings, because they somehow joined me in my mind. Thought was communal and connected; this realm was more vibrational than verbal or visual. We shared thoughts telepathically, unique voices with different rhythms and inflections, each more tender than the last. I felt love pouring in from the beings around me, infinite yet personal—it was warm love for me as I existed on every level, every space and depth, pooling deep into my awareness like liquid light, melting my own shadows away until they became love too, until everything I knew softened into love.

One of the vibrations became more prominent, a masculine thought-voice that I recognized with a burst of happiness: *Grandpa Sprout!* Yet his presence was more than just the giant of a man who provided the only safe harbor I'd known as a child. Here he was, vast in his kindness, unfettered by the occasional impatience and burdens of his life I'd not understood back then. Here, he was expansive and completely free.

He explained without words that I had a choice before me, and that only I could make it: would I stay in this place, or choose to return to my life as I knew it on earth? He added that there was someone I might consult to help me decide, if I wished. Would I like to meet an aspect of my own soul who was always here, watching over me, while I moved on earth?

I sensed her there, waiting for me, though not like she was standing still across the room. What I really felt was the gentle nearness of a most cherished sameness of mind, yet grander beyond my comprehension—as if she were a part of me who was magical and divine, better than I could have ever hoped to be, and her affection for the smaller "me" was boundless and eternal. We merged easily, effortlessly, and traveled together without moving, across galaxies, taking a grand tour of the cosmos that she explained with thoughts was for play and perspective, in that order.

We moved back in time to visit another aspect of me, this one from before I was born on earth. This "self" revealed that she had a mission, one that at age twenty-nine I'd apparently barely begun. Would I release my task, or return to earth to see it through? I felt the eagerness of the not-yet-born me, pulsing with love and anticipation, relishing the honor of an incarnation that was sought by countless other souls. Then I saw this me again from a distance, but my mind couldn't quite comprehend the setting. I translated it into seeing this version of myself walking through a grove of flowering fruit trees, accompanied by a being with light brighter than any I'd felt so far, bright as the sun, but a sun of pure love instead of fiery heat. It felt masculine, and a poignant tenderness flowed from him, washing over the me in the vision.

You do not know, I heard him think to that aspect of me—and there was protectiveness in his vibration. *You do not know what it is you will face.*

Let me go, the preborn me implored. *I have something to give, let me give it. I care not the consequence. It cannot be worse than standing by to watch yet another utter end.*

The bright being paused, as if for a deep sigh, and then answered. *Yes, my dear one. You may go. Go now, in peace and love.*

Then I saw the pre-incarnation me as a spark, a fast firefly soaring eagerly away from the grove of trees, out of the light, past the layers of darkness, past the stars, sun, and moon, entering through my mother's body into the core of her ovum, joined by my father's sperm. The spark burst with life, and the view faded.

My soul-guide and I were then joined by another vibration, the brightest one; the one the preborn me was walking with in the trees. All at once I knew everything that happened after my birth; every moment, event, and feeling; every act and reaction; every exchange of love, betrayal, and abuse up to the point of the car accident that had brought me here.

Now you know, he said softly. Now you know some of what you will face, and we can show you as much as you wish before you decide.

I've seen enough, I heard my mind say, unwavering. *I want to go back.*

In the snap of a second I was alone again in the totaled Tercel, my steering wheel slowly coming into focus. Then I heard a car door open and shut, followed by muffled voices. I felt deeply calm as a young man appeared at my window.

He cupped his hand around his mouth and pressed it against the glass and yelled, "Are you okay?"

"Call an ambulance," I replied. I heard him agree, mumble an apology for hitting me, and then the scream of sirens from a distance, growing louder. Two firemen removed me from the car and strapped me to a gurney, and I noticed in a detached way that they were both strong and pleasantly handsome in their dark uniforms. Then, lying in the back of an ambulance, I heard more sirens, and began to feel wet tears streaming down my face. The euphoria I'd experienced while in the place of light was fading, replaced by a sharpening pain in my neck and shoulder. My body felt unbearably dense and heavy.

A female paramedic bent over me and said gently, "You'll be okay, you made it. You're going to be okay."

I know. That's why I'm crying.

In the rush of hospitalization and rehabilitation therapy that followed, the beauty and promise of my near-death experience faded into a shroud of sadness. Within a week I could remember almost nothing of it, but something inside me had shifted nonetheless. I became fueled by a new determination to find love in my life, real love, and I realized that therapy with Margaret was a pale imitation. I needed much, much more.

Back in her therapy office, Margaret peered at me through her owl-like glasses, her dark eyes as shrewd as ever. She could tell that for the first time in eight years, I'd come to a decision that was truly beyond her reach.

"Well then," she said, "you may never mention my name again, nor write about me, nor contact me. Ever. Do you understand?" I nodded.

"You have abused me many times. You have always been diffi-cult to work with. I didn't even want to take you on as a client. I only agreed because I was seeing your sister, but you have fought me every step of the way."

As Margaret concluded her itemization of my failings as her cli-ent, I did what I almost always did when she told me I'd done some-thing wrong in a session—I apologized. But then, I did something new: I stood up and walked out the door, closing it behind me.

I also did not keep silent. After a tearful reunion with my parents, I called the American Psychological Association ethics helpline to file a complaint. I was told my situation did not represent a serious ethical issue, but I was certain they were wrong. I sent a letter to the Washington State Department of Health, accusing Margaret of unprofessional conduct. She was ultimately found guilty of a minor charge and released to practice again, which I didn't think was severe enough though better than nothing. Her consequences might have been more serious if I'd been willing to testify, but I was too exhausted by the car accident rehabilitation, an intrusive investigative process, and the fact that I wanted nothing more to do with Margaret. As I feared, my sister stayed by Margaret's side and cut off all contact with me for several years.

Only later, finally free from Margaret's influence, would I realize how jealous and possessive she was, and that healthy therapists do not act like she did. I was sad to lose the connection with my sister, but the relief I felt being out from under Margaret's controlling influence was exhilarating. I decided I was cured of my depression, and that Margaret was the main cause of all the problems in my family. My parents were happy to agree; we moved on without much discussion, and my parents took me on a cruise to the Caribbean with the proceeds from some land they sold. I was twenty-nine-years old, through with therapy, and from now on, I promised myself, I was going to do exactly what I wanted. And what I wanted most, after six years of being single, was to find a boyfriend.

- ELEVEN -

So I'm Dating a Sex Addict

"IT'S MY FUNK FACE. Everybody has one, you just have to find yours," said Jason, a fact that slightly concerned me. On one hand, the music he was introducing me to as we danced in his living room was whole-body scrumptious, the beats of P-Funk causing my hips to gyrate sinuously of their own accord. On the other hand, Jason's face as he moved was a cross between ecstasy and constipation, and I wasn't sure I wanted to find my funk face if it was going to look like that.

I'd actually met Jason for the first time several years earlier, when a friend's boyfriend had unexpectedly brought him along to the Seattle Folklife Festival, and the four of us spent the day together listening to music and, later, dancing. The caller directed us in a folksy square dance to the rowdy cadence of fiddles and banjos. We twirled around and around along with fifty other couples in the exhibition hall, and I laughed like a child on a merry-go-round.

Back then I'd gushed about Jason to Margaret, describing the lanky, unemployed jazz musician with brown eyes and the most endearing haunted look, probably because he was a creative type, up late writing music. Later I'd learn he was up all night watching porn.

Margaret's response was the same whenever I brought up any man I was attracted to, like my boss, my professors at school, colleagues at work, and now Jason: I still wasn't ready to date. I accepted her wisdom, without question, as a sad-but-true fact. But now, only days free of her, I called my friend and asked her to find out if Jason was available. He was! Our first two dates were a wonderful mix of

Thai food, talking, walking, and seeing a production of *The Velveteen Rabbit* at Seattle Children's Theatre. I felt elated as we held hands all the way back to his rusty pickup.

On our third date, as Jason dropped me off outside my apartment, I told him I loved him. He'd just kissed me for the first time, and the swell of whole-body pleasure it kindled was entirely new, contrasted to the numbness I'd mostly felt before. I was sure it must be the real thing—I didn't yet know the difference between infatuation and the deeper nuances of love. At my proclamation, Jason's eyes widened, but not in elation.

"Oh, um, that freaks me out."

"Why? You make me so happy!"

"Yeah, but…well, you don't really know me. I mean, it's only our third date."

My nascent affection started to curdle in the acid of his rejection.

"So what?" I protested. "Love is like that, it just hits. God, don't you have a romantic bone in your body?"

Jason took a step backward, seeking a safer distance from my abrupt shift from glee to anger.

"Let's not dwell on it," I snapped. "Forget it."

"I won't forget it, but…" Jason stumbled, trying to recapture some kind of connection. We agreed to meet the next day, no plans this time. Maybe just hang out at his house, take a nap together. Of course this was code for sex.

The next day, my rapid tour of the small suburban home Jason rented with his best friend ended at the open door to his bedroom. With a ripped futon stretched out on the floor and dirty clothes strewn around it, the room looked more like a pit. What saved it from total serial killer décor was the absence of duct-taped foil covering the small window, although the tacked up maroon sheet was pretty close. The tacks didn't even match. Jason stopped at the doorway, turning to face me. I looked up at him, admiring his smooth pale skin, wavy brown hair, and slightly mournful hazel eyes.

"There's something I have to tell you, before we go any further."

I waited, unconcerned. Despite my disappointment with the room, I was happy, reveling in my new infatuation and ignoring everything else. Tingling with anticipation, I smiled and said, "Okay, what is it?"

"I'm a sex addict."

Looking back now, I find Jason's honesty admirable. I would later come to learn, once I figured out I was also a sex addict, how hard that particular self-reveal would be. But back then, the impact of hearing his awful disclosure was instant.

I left. That is, I physically stayed in the doorway to his room, but mentally I dissociated again. I tuned Jason out, because the second I heard the words "sex addict," I started getting overriding input from normally dark corridors inside my own mind. His revelation triggered memories of Grandpa Westby and the horror of finding out he'd molested my sister when I was nine. After grandpa was safely in jail, I'd told a social worker who was interviewing me about his lingering glances and creepy pats on my knees. She'd called this "grooming behavior," and said that he might have been preparing me to be his next victim.

In my swirling confusion after Jason's admission, I concluded that all sex addicts were child molesters, I was dating a man exactly like Grandpa Westby, and I'd stupidly let him groom me into it like a nine-year-old girl. I felt trapped and helpless again, like the bee stuck to the glass.

Jason was still talking, but I barely heard him. He explained how he learned about sex addiction from his dad when he was eighteen, and the father-son pair started going to support groups for sex addicts. I was no longer tingling with anticipation; I couldn't feel my body. My brain was at DEFCON 1, a clanging alarm reverberating throughout all levels. I couldn't figure out how to get out of there without upsetting him, fearful he might become violent in some way. I didn't yet know that although Jason had exploited himself and used other women during his sexual acting out, he'd never been violent or abused a child. I didn't know back then that "sex addict" did not mean the same thing as "sex offender," or that although some sex addicts commit illegal acts as part of their addiction, most never hurt children. I would go on to spend the next fourteen years exploring this distinction in my personal and my professional life.

What I actually said was, "Oh, no big deal. I was in therapy, but I finished all that and don't need it anymore. And I've done lots of crazy stuff too. My high school boyfriend and I broke up, and I was really mean to him. I treated him like shit, wouldn't call him back. I've had lots of sex problems, getting drunk and then wanting sex, and then avoiding guys after, you know. And I've made porn before!"

I couldn't stop myself, I went on and on about my sordid past, describing how I cheated on Matt and our many fights, like the time I jumped out of his moving car and crumbled into the ditch, sobbing. Jason didn't break up with me, like I hoped he would after hearing all my nightmare girlfriend stories. We were just getting started. It turned out we had similar terrible pasts, and I was caught in yet another dramatization. I'd enrolled in another form of sex addiction school, a course on love addiction, and this one would have a five-year term.

A healthier person would have paused after such an intense revelation, or asked for more information to sort out what it meant to date someone addicted to sex, but in the weeks after Jason's disclosure, I didn't ask a single question. I didn't want to know more about sex addiction. With my sister cut off from me, Jason was my only steady relationship. No matter what he called himself, I already wanted to be with him all the time. His attention was a balm to my emptiness, and from the moment he picked me up for our first date, I felt I couldn't live without him. After my initial panic at his reveal, I promptly banished any thoughts of his addiction. I didn't want to lose him, and I focused on the positive for all it was worth.

And there were positives. Jason charmed me because he was beautiful and soft-spoken and talked about his feelings; I'd never heard a guy my age do that before. He said he didn't look at online porn anymore; he went to 12-Step sex addict meetings and read self-help books instead. He also attended weekend personal-growth workshops, along with all his therapy group friends, which impressed me. I loved going to his jazz gigs, and found his original songs stirringly woeful. And Jason's touch was nourishment after a lifetime of touch starvation. I couldn't get enough, and I decided my new post-therapy life was perfect. Until we started fighting.

At first we only argued once in a while, but soon the arguments became more frequent, until the lingering effects of the previous one didn't quite dissipate before the next one occurred. As the first blush of dating paled, antagonism became the white noise of our relationship, like static from an off-channel radio that we couldn't figure out how to switch off.

It started when he got mad at me for flirting with his male friends, which I denied completely. Things escalated when I felt angry after learning about a relationship he had with a woman—Alicia—in his therapy group. I thought it was way too close, but Jason insisted it was no big deal. I hated the long, late-night conversations in which he confided in her all the details of his life. He even told her specifics about our sex life, which really infuriated me, but he said it was all part of his therapy. I complained that he wasn't making enough money; we also fought because I wanted him to see that he was too dependent on his therapist, but he wouldn't. And after five months of sensual delight, we began to fight about sex, so even that refuge from the rest of our conflicts grew tainted and terse. Frantic efforts to spice things up with novelty, public risk, and new lingerie were bandages on a broken leg fast turning green: they didn't fix anything.

By our one-year anniversary it dawned on me that my relationship with Jason had escalated from early, exciting ups and downs to a kind of relational bipolar disorder, with agitated manic highs and long, silent-treatment lows. He planned a fabulous weekend getaway to celebrate our year of dating, romantic and secluded, but we fought bitterly most of the trip. Our dwindling ecstatic times were eclipsed by a rising baseline of hostility and depression.

One day, Jason offered a new perspective about our chronic conflict.

"You know, I was talking to my friend Ed about how we always fight, and he said you might be a codependent."

"What's that?" I asked, annoyed.

Jason explained that it was someone who kept trying to fix addicts, but ended up feeling worse instead of better. I shook off Ed's label, convinced he was trying to blame me for my boyfriend's problems.

Sure I'm mad that Jason never works, has no money, no direction, never plays his music anymore, is dependent on his therapist, is too close with Alicia, only owns three shirts, and is generally depressed all the time. But anyone would be, so how is that my fault? My life is fine…other than not having enough money.

I was working a temp social work job at a hospital, having quit my full-time job not long after starting to date Jason. At first I'd considered his musician/odd-job lifestyle free-spirited and cool and I wanted to be more like him.

Temp work gives me so much more flexibility, and I can spend more time with Jason! I'd told myself. *Besides, everybody's using credit cards to make ends meet these days.*

But my reality was far less romantic: since ending therapy with Margaret and diving head first into my new romance, I no longer had the energy, focus, or emotional strength to work full-time. Always exhausted, I could barely finish a two-week social work assignment before needing a week off to rest. My fatigue was becoming debilitating, and pretty soon only an orgasm could lift my mood enough to get me out of bed.

To find out why I was so tired all the time, I went to see a prominent specialist in natural medicine and energy healing for a full workup, charging it to my credit card. After an extensive battery of tests, she said she could find only one thing wrong with me, which she summarized as "the presence of energetic scar tissue." I had no idea what that meant, and no money for whatever treatment it might require, so I didn't go back.

One day during a break in my hospital shift, I wandered into a resource center with free pamphlets and booklets stacked in a display case. My eyes settled on a red one with a white stick figure on the front titled *What Is Codependency?* I took it home and read it, underlining the parts I related to—almost every word.

I flipped to the end of the booklet for solutions, finding recommendations for therapy and self-help groups, aka 12-Step meetings for people with the same problems. Still glad to be free of Margaret, I wanted nothing to do with therapy, but in what would prove to be one of the best decisions of my life, I went to a 12-Step meeting. Twelve years after Barney the psychiatrist recommended it, I started recovery for codependency.

TWELVE

Codependency 101:
This Is Bigger Than I Thought

TWENTY PEOPLE SAT IN A CIRCLE in the tidy church parlor, chatting in muted tones. *Hmm, this group is way quieter than mom's AA gatherings ever were.* After mom had joined AA when I was nine, she took us to her "birthday chip meetings" a few times. No one sang to her, but she'd be given a round coin called a chip for one more year of not drinking, and everyone would clap, drink coffee, and celebrate with generously frosted sheet cake. Even without alcohol, it was always a boisterous crowd.

This meeting was more subdued. A heavyset woman with long, straight hair and wine-red lipstick started things off with an introduction. After a few readings, new people were invited to introduce themselves, by first name only. I received the slightly singsong greeting by everyone in unison common to 12-Step meetings.

"Hi Staci. Welcome!"

"I'm passing around a newcomer's packet for Staci," the leader announced. "Sign your name and number if you're available to take calls." When the packet made its way around the circle to me, I noticed there were two names and numbers scrawled on it, from the only two men in the room.

I told myself it was because I was so gorgeous, though for once gloating didn't make me feel superior. After the meeting I didn't call either man, but I did go back the following week. *Nothing else has helped, so why not?*

After a few weeks of listening to other people talk, I became antsy to do something more. I decided to follow the recommendation for all new people, which was to find someone to sponsor me. I learned that a sponsor was a person who took you under their wing and mentored you, who helped you get settled and do the work necessary to get better. I zeroed in on a tall, sarcastically funny woman in her 60s named Janine. She talked about healing from something I'd never heard of, a "toxic relationship." I decided that must be what Jason and I had, and that she could probably help me. After the meeting I shyly approached her to ask if she would be my sponsor, and to my relief she said yes. We started talking on the phone regularly—Janine said I could call her every night at nine if I wanted. I usually did.

I started feeling a little less lonely, finally finding a word for the lifelong ache in my stomach. Janine listened to my complaints about Jason and his therapy group "girlfriend" Alicia for a while, but finally said we needed to do some specific work together if I wanted anything to improve. She explained that this was what everyone meant when they talked about "working the steps."

I don't recall how we worked the first three steps, but I do remember her advising me to write in my journal about Step Four, which she described as a thorough analysis of my character defects. I started writing about my failings, using the questions in the program's book for guidance. The words flowed easily onto the page, because years of therapy with Margaret meant years of listening to her critical comments about me. Even though our therapy didn't really change them, I'd at least learned what my faults were.

4th Step Character Defects in Codependency Recovery: My "searching and fearless moral inventory."

› I believe I am above the law—I don't pay a parking meter and I believe I won't get caught.

› I am overconfident; I don't take in new information because I don't believe I need it. I'm not humble. When I feel strongly about something, I don't listen.

› I am impatient with sacrifice that takes a long time in coming/paying off.

› I set expectations without discussing them with others and then get mad when they don't meet them. I don't believe I have the right to talk about my expectations, or that I should have to.

› I pretend everything is fine when it isn't and then get mad at others for not seeing my distress or not caring; I minimize what's true so others don't feel uncomfortable, then get mad at them for not understanding or support- ing me. I hide myself, then am disappointed when I feel distant and disconnected from others.

› I make nonsupportive, mean jokes at others' expense because I'm jealous of them. I try to peer-pressure oth- ers when it's me that feels afraid. I feel scared but don't know this; instead I get mad at others for not being helpful/loving enough.

› I am bossy, I believe I am smarter than everyone else and am intolerant of their slowness or lack of compre- hension. I tell them what to do and how to do it, and judge and criticize them when they won't. I want to con- trol others; I believe others are incompetent and I seek to direct situations and actions so I'll get the actions I most want. I fear the unknown and use control to avoid it.

› I want what I want when I want it. I'm greedy, without having to work for it or sacrifice for it. I'm not willing to try hard or suffer pain in order to get what I want. I believe the world owes me since I've been neglected and mistreated, and I feel angry at the world for this.

› I am possessive: the things I think are mine I want as mine; I don't want to share or give them up. I don't consider that what I have has been given to me. I am possessive of people, and try to control them to keep them near me. I feel threatened if they want space or pursue outside friendships/interests. I am jealous. I feel jealous when someone I am attached to shows genuine interest/love in something/someone besides me. I get mad or withdraw in petty protest or tease others, or I judge and criticize others who have qualities I want for myself.

› I am terrified of loneliness and abandonment, and cling to others (Jason) to keep from feeling these feelings. I avoid intimacy by joking.

› Resentment: I don't tell others if I feel hurt or mad, but instead hold in resentments toward them. I get distant, cold, intellectual; I tease in a critical way. I blame others for my decisions and bad outcomes.

› Impulsive/compulsive/obsessive: I get fixated on things and act without thinking to avoid feelings, like with food, sex, spending, etc.

I called Janine and told her I'd finished the Fourth Step. She told me that since the Fifth Step read, "Admitting to God, ourselves, and another human being the exact nature of our wrongs," I needed to read my Fourth Step list to her aloud, in person. My enthusiasm for the whole process was seriously dampened at that point, but we arranged to meet at her apartment in a nearby neighborhood.

We sat in her modest living room, and she led us in saying "The

Serenity Prayer" together. This was a mindless custom to me at the time, but I would eventually come to love the simple petition, and repeat it countless times. Originally written by Reinhold Niebuhr, the prayer spread and quickly became a cornerstone for AA and many other 12-Step programs worldwide:

> God grant me the serenity to accept the things I cannot
> change,
> Courage to change the things I can,
> And wisdom to know the difference.

"Okay," Janine said, "let's hear it." I read through my writing without interruption, feeling my face become flushed and hot. It was one thing to write it all down on paper, but much harder to admit these awful things about myself out loud, to someone I hardly knew! When I finally finished, I looked up to see her face alight with a big smile.

"Good work Staci, and thank you for sharing! Most people don't ever get honest with themselves, but you did. A self-inventory is the key to a new life, and you've taken a major step forward in your recovery." She stood up, beckoned me to join her, and wrapped me in a tight, heart-to-heart embrace. I felt stiff and awkward in her arms at first, but she kept holding on, patting my back gently. I let out my breath, and gradually became aware of the warmth of her sturdy body, melting my resistance. She was so close; I could smell the bright citrus scent of her freshly washed hair.

After she let go, I looked around the room as if I'd just arrived. My eyes were drawn to the sliding glass doors, cracked open to reveal a bountiful garden outside. Her living room was comfortable, with a rainbow-colored afghan draping her couch that she told me one of her friends knitted for her. Janine had lots of friends from the codependency recovery program—female friends. I wanted that too, real female friends, not superficial acquaintances. Someone to be close to, besides Jason. I'd had some in the past, but they always seemed to fade away.

Janine's feedback to me wasn't finished.

"You're not quite done, though. You need to write more about your problems with sex."

How little I knew about what that would mean! To this day I'm not sure what I said that inspired her assignment, maybe it was how I dressed or acted at the meetings. But whatever it was she saw, she was spot on. I had a lot more going on with my sexuality than I was admitting—even to myself—and Janine's invitation to explore more in this area was the finest, most challenging gift she gave me.

Exhausted, but eager to please my new sponsor, home I went, and soon sat back down to write. Closing the journal much later, my typical state of protective numbness gave way to a new feeling, and it wasn't good. Thorny and painful, I instantly hated it. Thinking about what I wrote felt like getting bitten by big red ants—quick, sharp pains I tried to crush. I didn't yet know I was lying on a swarming, crimson anthill, or how many more bites were yet to come. What the rest of my introspection would reveal was going to hurt for a long, long time.

At the next Friday meeting, Janine greeted me with a smile and enfolded me in another hug, which surprised me again. Touch, especially spontaneous, affectionate touch, wasn't something I was used to.

People didn't really do "good touch" in my family. I recalled a picture of me taken when I was five, wan grin on my face, my arms wrapped around my mother's legs. Her expression seemed to reveal a desire to kick out and shake me off, as if she were restraining herself for the camera.

Yet even as they scared me, I found myself liking Janine's hugs, and I liked listening to people in the meeting share about the imperfections of their lives. I remember one man talking about a Kafka quote he'd heard, saying that for him, 12-Step recovery was "the axe for the frozen sea within us." I was sure I had a frozen sea inside me, too, and hearing him talk about his made me feel a little warmer.

After the meeting, Janine gave me another hug and asked if I'd finished my additional Fourth Step writing assignment. I nodded, and she invited me back to her apartment the next day to read it, adding, "When you're writing an inventory, it's best to get it done sooner, rather than later."

As I walked up to her front door, I noticed that her building looked different than I remembered, more exotic. The dusky brown siding was topped by a rose-colored roof, with palm trees in front that stirred in a gentle breeze, as if they were welcoming me. Janine answered the doorbell wearing sweats and a faded blue T-shirt, her bobbed gray hair pulled back in a low ponytail.

"Hi!" she smiled, ushering me again into the living room. There was a sweet, spicy cinnamon scent in the air, and as I sat down she brought me tea and asked how I was feeling.

"Okay, I guess. I'm still fighting a lot with Jason, but I'm trying to be less, well, mean."

"Good for you!" She explained that she always had terrible relationships with men until she'd found the program and realized she needed to get to know herself instead of always focusing on her alcoholic husband's problems. Things improved for her, though the first few years had been rough.

"After I started my step writing," she said, "I cried for one full year."

Uh oh. A full year? I hated to cry, or to feel any pain. Suddenly I wanted to bolt, but I was distracted by Janine's encouragement to get started. I hesitated. Reading what I'd written specifically about sex made me seem awful, and it dredged up things from my past I'd never reflected on before, let alone told another person.

When Margaret had asked about childhood sexual experiences in our early therapy, my brief answer then was that I'd "played doctor" with a few other neighbor kids, like everyone did, and she'd never pressed me for more. But writing it all out for the Fourth Step inventory had jogged my memory, and I recalled three episodes with other kids I wasn't sure were so playful after all. The first happened when I was eight, then nine or ten, then eleven. We were all about the same age, and everybody went along with what happened without protesting. But as I thought more about it, the memories brought an awful mix of feelings, deep in my stomach: nausea, revulsion, and growing alarm. As those memories crystalized, I also realized that around the same time, an adult man had done sexual things to me. I didn't think it was Grandpa Westby, but I couldn't quite remember. I saw a blurry image of a man with dark hair, but his face was in shadow. I remembered he had a menacing presence.

I looked at Janine and thought, *Oh god what does all this mean? Am I going to have to cry for a whole year?* After one more prompt, I gritted my teeth and started reading aloud:

Sexual Inventory:

> › **Self Image:** I believe I am incredibly beautiful and thus better than others—more powerful. I believe I can make others do what I want because of how I look and my desirability.

> › **Vanity:** I escape by focusing on my appearance.

> › **Sexual Control:** I believe I can have sex with anyone I want. I can make anyone attracted to me. I can put a spell on others—especially men. I can hypnotize them and they will do my bidding. No one can say no to me.

I have used sex appeal to influence/manipulate Jason into being with me even when he didn't want to.

› **Intolerance for refusal:** I believe if Jason says no when I want to be sexual I HATE HIM, and he is saying I'm bad, shameful, worthless, and dirty.

› **Powerlessness:** I believe my sexual energy is uncontrollable. I want to hurt myself sexually; I hate my own fear of my sexuality. I hate all churches for their fear, degradation, criticism, and belittlement of women and sexuality—for blaming women's sexual natures and bodies as bad, fearful, and dirty. I have acted out this hatred by hurting myself, punishing my own sexuality, shaming and criticizing my body, hiding my body and sexual feelings, and teasing. I believe if I hide my body, men won't desire it, women won't be jealous of it, and people won't be mean to me anymore.

› I also feed on men's fear of me, of my appearance, <u>of</u> their fear of their attraction to me—I'm like a vampire, growing powerful on their weakness.

› I believe Jason can talk me into being sexual with him by words/energy/sexual actions to arouse me—he can manipulate me into being sexual. Even if I don't want to—I go along with him because I'm afraid if I don't he will leave me. I'm afraid he will hurt me/hate me.

› I hate my body, especially certain parts. They keep me from being perfect.

› As a child between the ages of eight and eleven I played doctor with neighbor kids around my age while our parents were busy and not paying attention. Was I being hurt, or hurting them? When I think of this, I have vague memories of times I was touched by an older man with dark hair. I don't know who it was, and I never told anyone.

Janine listened quietly until I finished the whole thing. Her eyes closed, she didn't say anything for a few moments, which seemed to stretch on forever. When she opened them, her face was serious. Not harsh, but no longer kind either.

"Staci, this is bigger than I thought. You need more help than I can give you. I know what you're talking about because I was sexually abused as a girl too, but all these beliefs…you need to go to another program for this."

She told me about a special 12-Step program for people with sexual problems, with local meetings like ours. I agreed to go, but rebelled inside. *Why should I have to go to that kind of meeting? Jason's the sex addict, not me!*

Janine seemed relieved, as if she'd been holding her breath. I didn't finish my tea, leaving a third of the clear brown liquid in the bottom of my flowered mug as she showed me out. We didn't pray, but she gave me a brief hug in her shadowy foyer and said I did well. I felt confused, and she must have noticed my expression because she added one more reassurance: "Don't worry, you'll find what you need. And congratulations, you've finished your Fifth Step!"

I walked alone to my car, not feeling proud or relieved that I'd finished the dreaded Fourth and Fifth Step "moral inventory." The first round was bad enough, admitting I was a terrible, selfish, petty person. But in the second layer, I'd searched the depths of my character and discovered something I never expected, memories of sexual experiences I had buried as incomprehensible.

Oh my God. Was I sexually abused, like Christi? Who was the dark-haired man? Was my playing doctor with other kids actually hurtful to them? To me?

Years later, my forensic sex offender training and experience would teach me what I never learned in school about childhood sexuality: that it exists, that it's normal, and that kids are endlessly curious about sex and various kinds of touch. Exploring their bodies with other kids is how they naturally learn, and this can be an innocent, fun, special part of growing up.

My training would also teach me the sad fact that children who have been sexualized too soon, physically molested, or exposed to pornography sometimes reenact what they experienced with themselves and others. Experts refer to this kind of behavior as childhood sexual reactivity*, and it is different from the natural sex play of nonexposed children. I call it "behavioral storytelling," and it can be confusing, scary, and shameful for everyone involved.

But back then I understood nothing but revulsion about what I recalled. I was overwhelmed and blamed myself for everything, with no ability to consider the larger context of what happened, what was normal, and what wasn't. I thought I was horrible, everything was my fault, and now that I'd told Janine, it was all unforgettably, irrevocably real.

---

*According to child psychology experts Eliana Gil, Ph.D., and Jennifer A. Shaw, "Many children who have been overstimulated sexually cannot integrate these experiences in a meaningful way. This can result in children acting out the confusion in the form of more advanced or frequent sexual behaviors, heightened interest and/or knowledge beyond what would be expected of that age." E. Gil and J.A. Shaw, *Working with Children with Sexual Behavior Problems* (New York: Guilford Press, 2013), 21.

Part Two:
Light In the Shadows (Getting into 12-Step Sexual Recovery)

*"For a seed to achieve its greatest expression,
it must come completely undone.
The shell cracks, its insides come out and
everything changes. To someone who
doesn't understand growth,
it would look like complete destruction."*
~ Cynthia Occelli

Top right: Age 16, Attempting to look like a Cosmo girl. Top left: Age 21, Getting ready to go out clubbing. Bottom left: Age 31, Early recovery: buzz cut and baggy clothes. Bottom right: Age 33, Two years into sexual recovery.

THIRTEEN

Sex Addiction Recovery 101: Welcome!

THE MEAN BLACK-BROWN HOLLOWS of depression were back—sludgy, dark feelings that weighed me down and clawed at me like the shadowy specters in the movie *Ghost*. Rarely working, I gave up my apartment and moved into a college friend's spare bedroom in a strip mall part of town. Most mornings, I stayed in bed waiting to hear the front door close letting me know my roommate had left for work, and only then getting up to scavenge for food. For weeks, my main daily activity involved lying on the living room floor under a blanket and listening over and over to Coldplay's *Yellow*, hoping the haunting lyrics would replace thoughts I couldn't bear to hear myself think. Instead of overeating, I ate little, dropping weight and, for the first time in my life, didn't care. But I kept going to the Friday night codependency meetings.

I stopped calling Janine, and she stopped approaching me at the end of meetings, neither of us able to bridge the awkward chasm my disclosures had cleaved. But one night I heard a program slogan with a twist that caught my attention: "Easy does it, but DO IT." I wasn't doing much of anything and, for lack of a better plan, I remembered Janine's last piece of advice: go to the program for sex addicts.

I was surprised when an Internet search revealed not one, but three different sexual 12-Step programs in the area, called fellowships, with meetings all around town. *How many sex addicts are there in Seattle?*

After procrastinating for a few more weeks, I finally got myself out the door one Sunday evening and followed the directions to a worn converted house on a busy city street I'd driven by hundreds of times and never noticed. It was called an Alano Club, and its rooms held 12-Step meetings of all kinds.

As I approached the building, the pungent odor of cigarette smoke drifted from a group of heavily tattooed men chatting on the front steps. My mind flashed to when I was four, hiding my mom's cigarettes under her black fake leather recliner, hoping this would stop her from puffing out that dark, acerbic smell. I awkwardly wove my way through the small gathering and began to search for Room One.

Where the perverts go, I thought darkly. Room One, with its yellowed walls, was devoid of art or furniture, except for a table in the corner and a circle of folding chairs around the perimeter. Sitting in the room were fifteen men ranging from their thirties to upper seventies, maybe a few were younger, but not many. These men looked different from the men on the steps. They were clean-cut, mostly white, a few Latino and black, and not a tattoo or trench coat in sight. I felt numb again, crossing the threshold and trying to act as if I belonged.

An attractive white man in his mid-thirties with bright blue eyes approached immediately. He was shorter than me, and wiry.

"Welcome!" he said enthusiastically. "Is this your first meeting?"

"Yes. I mean, I've been to other meetings, but this is my first one like…this." My mind started racing.

Oh my god, why is he so cheerful? Is this really a room full of sex addicts? He looks so normal! Everyone here looks normal. Wait, that guy over there is staring.

"Okay, great! This is for you." He handed me a pamphlet and explained that it was written especially to welcome new women. "We're gonna get started, but if you have any questions after the meeting, let me know." I would later learn that the brochure was written by one of the first female members of the fellowship, from another state, and that they were waiting to be handed out in meetings all across the world. Back then they collected dust, because women almost never showed up.

I sat down and flipped through the pamphlet as I waited for things to start. My eyes were drawn to a heading about how new women might handle being attracted to others at meetings, but my reading was interrupted by the meeting leader.

"Hi, I'm Fred, and I'm a sex addict." I cringed, wondering if I'd have to introduce myself that way too, but I soon noted with relief that introductions were voluntary.

During the first fifteen minutes, the group doubled in size, all men, and I felt like they were closing in. My gaze found my feet, focusing with tunnel vision on the fine creases in my soft black leather loafers. I heard only muffled words from the opening readings until the man on my right suddenly passed a book to me, and I realized that it was my turn to read aloud. Suddenly, I was back in junior high hearing my teacher saying, "Staci, slow down." Not thinking about the words, I read slowly and with inflection, trying to impress the sex addicts with how articulate I was. As soon as the meeting was over I fled the room, women's pamphlet still clutched in my hand. Safely locked in my car, I chewed my cuticles, tasting blood and trying to focus.

What the hell was that? What's wrong with me? Why was I the only woman there?

I could not make sense of what had happened, though today I have more understanding and tenderness for my disorientation. Growing up with almost no mention of sex in my family, except for dad's unwanted lectures and junior high jokes ("How do you make a hormone? Don't pay her!") and mom's complete avoidance of the topic, left me believing that it was not okay to talk directly about sex.

Other people might comment about it (though they *shouldn't*), but no one ever asked me to say anything, except for the time my parents confronted me after finding the condom.

The Catholic church taught that I shouldn't even want sex, let alone talk about it, and certainly not in a big group, let alone a big group of strange men. Sure I'd *had* sex and looked at porn, but I still never *talked* about it, not even with my friends. I vaguely remembered some kind of sex education in school, but just dry, boring, meaningless facts.

I'd had some exposure to 12-Step meetings from going to mom's AA birthday chip meetings as a child. I learned from those gatherings that people in AA were different than other people—they hugged each other, they cried in front of the whole room when they were sad, and they said things about themselves aloud that no one in church ever dared admit. Like bad things they'd done and were sorry for. But still, the focus there wasn't sex.

Attending codependency support meetings for a few months, I was now used to people sitting in circles, talking to everyone and no one in particular, and getting painful things off their chests. The no cross-talk rule in these groups meant that no one interrupted or commented on what was said. That helped me feel safe talking there too, knowing that, unlike therapy with Margaret, no one would criticize or laugh at me. I was comforted by hearing that other people hurt like I did, that I wasn't the only one. They'd felt awful too, but many of them talked of getting better and feeling happy again. I could tell it wasn't fake by their expressions and genuine laughter; I never laughed anymore. Those circles had gradually become havens in my life, until my Fifth Step revelations revealed that codependency was not the only compulsive process going on, and probably not even the main one. Sex, too, turned out to be a massive hidden problem, and

Janine's advice was correct. I needed a place where people knew what sexual addiction was, and were willing to talk about it.

But to walk into a sexual recovery meeting, where every single person was openly admitting, by being there, that they had a major problem with some kind of sex, was alarming. The bold truths I heard spoken were like a blowtorch to my frozen sea of sexual feelings and memories, melting my protective denial. I was terrified I would drown in the flood of salty water. I decided that I hated that meeting, hated the idea of sexual addiction, and that I would never go back. *Ever.*

Two days later, Jason dropped a bombshell.

"I've decided I need to take a break from sex for a while," he announced. "My therapist said it's the best way to calm our relationship down. I need to get clear, and she said that will help me."

I was livid. "What? You're going to inform me, without even asking what *I* think? Your therapist tells you to do something and you do it, just like that? Who are you with, me or *her*?" It was a familiar fight theme, but this no-sex rule was new. I felt my eyes narrow, calculating how I might change his mind, switching tactics. As he revved up to defend his choice as healthy and reassure me we could still cuddle and spend the night, and that this was only temporary, I tuned out his words. I felt like a child who covers her ears and chants "I can't hear you" over and over.

"Fine," I said frostily when he finished. I decided that any more talking was a waste of time.

Later that week, Jason went back to his therapy group carrying an "accountability sheet" confession about how he broke his commitment not to have sex with me. I was pleased to prove that no matter what he said, if I touched him, he'd change his mind. I considered it a personal triumph over Jason's therapist and her ridiculous boundaries. *She might control his life, but she can't control mine!* I'd forgotten everything I'd written about problems with sexual control from my Fourth Step inventory.

But Jason returned from his next group determined—no sex for ninety days. He didn't want me to even try, calling my seduction disrespectful. And the next attempt I made, he stopped me, saying if I didn't quit, he'd go home. Stung by his rejection, I decided to punish him by refusing to cuddle or spend the night with him, and life went from tolerably bad to completely vile.

Without the comfort or distraction of sex or even snuggling with Jason, the bleakness of my life became obvious. I impulsively quit my temporary social work job and started a temp clerical job, which was less demanding but paid less. Money grew even tighter, and I began to charge more of my regular expenses, such as groceries, on credit cards. I resented when I spent time with Jason, but was lost otherwise, my head crowded with secrets that isolated me even when I was not alone. Although I didn't realize it, my depression was worsening again. I'd begun to experience withdrawal from the compulsive sex that was a staple of our relationship, compounded exponentially by the loss of all nurturing touch.

I tried going back to the Friday night meeting for codependents, but since no one there talked about sex, I was too afraid to bring it up. I continued to have little contact with Janine, but one night I approached her after the meeting and told her I tried the other meeting to get help with "the sexual stuff." She smiled, said "Great!" and turned to talk to someone else. No hug.

Desperate to find something to ease my increasing anxiety, I pushed through a pile of papers on my bed stand to find the pamphlet about women sex addicts I'd been given at the meeting the previous month. Hunched into my pink recliner with my knees tucked up to my chest, I read every word. I felt both dread and relief as I saw myself described in detail by a perfect stranger—*how did she know?*

Because, came the answer, *she had the same problem as you. But unlike you, she did something about it.* The anonymous author's advice was to go to six meetings, but I couldn't go back to that room full of men. I decided I'd try a different fellowship for sexual recovery, one that looked like it might have more women.

FOURTEEN

Love Addiction Recovery 101: What's an Intrigue?

WHEN I FIRST HEARD A WOMAN introduce herself as addicted to sex and love, I felt an unwelcome flicker of recognition inside. Later I'd learn that the term *sex addiction* was often more focused on compulsive sex acts, and *love addiction* on compulsive relationships, but that the terms were often used interchangeably.

At that meeting there were three women there and six men—a much smaller group than my first meeting. I tried to listen, but my sense of time had strangely sped up, and the next thing I knew everyone was holding hands and saying "The Serenity Prayer," signaling that the meeting had ended. After that it was fellowship time, where people stood around chatting. I was standing there awkwardly, unsure what to do, when one of the women turned to me.

"Glad you're here," she said, her dreadlocks pinned fashionably behind her ears. She was pretty, without makeup, a loose white T-shirt and green capris revealing a dancer's physique.

She looks cool, like Halle Berry gone grunge. Maybe it's not just losers who come here.

"Do you need a phone number?" she asked, surprising me. She wrote hers down on a slip of paper and handed it to me before I could answer. "You can call me for support." I shyly took the paper, feeling like the invisible girl in junior high suddenly getting attention from a popular senior. As she turned to talk with others, I walked over to a table and started flipping through a book, my eyes surreptitiously returning to her.

How did she get here? She seemed to know all the men, but wasn't flirting with them. I noticed another woman, white, younger and slightly overweight, who seemed eager and distracted, and a third, who sat rail straight in her chair and didn't look at me or anyone else. I never called that pretty woman, but I liked her attention, and decided to go back.

For the next month I went to meetings three to four times a week whenever I wasn't working, listening to readings and people sharing about the trouble in their sex lives and relationships. People talked of using porn and the problems it was causing, and how some people had multiple liaisons going on at once, secrets galore, and wanted to stop, but didn't, or couldn't. Some men spoke of buying sex, and a few women talked about selling it. I heard about affairs, which I could especially relate to, but most of all I liked hearing other women talk, although I remained too scared to say a word. I was startled to hear a woman say she'd had a lifetime problem with something she described as "compulsive masturbation."

So that's what it's called.

It was usually all I could do to show up and listen, but one day, I don't know why, I introduced myself and shared a little about my difficult relationship, my boyfriend who thought I flirted with other guys, and my nonexistent sex life. When I finished, everyone said the same thing they said to everyone else who shared, "Thanks, Staci." Two simple words, yet the impact of the group's attentive listening and acknowledgement was intense. My racing heart didn't slow down until long after I finished talking.

After meetings ended I'd immediately leave, never calling anyone from the group, though newcomers like me were encouraged to. I didn't know what I'd say if I did call, and was afraid of what the person

I called would say back. Trying to see women, especially women my age, as sources of support instead of competition was hard for me; I was suspicious of them. I was used to sizing up every woman I saw and rating her attractiveness: who had the thinner thighs, the better body, the prettier face or hair, the more stylish or expensive clothes? I would rank the winner in a nanosecond: me or her, with a reactive burst of triumph or jealousy. The idea of making myself vulnerable to a woman felt overwhelming. With men I felt in control, but in my experience women were often mean, or envious, or both. In this new culture, the goal was to get sober and *not* hit on each other or steal someone's boyfriend. I was enticed and repelled at the same time.

One day after a meeting a man approached me. He was about thirty and attractive in a rugged, Seattle-flannel way.

"Um, hi Staci, I'm Dillon. Can I talk to you?" I was taken aback that he called me by my name even though we hadn't formally met. The 12-Step custom of stating one's name when sharing created an odd kind of familiarity. Dillon then explained that he'd been having sexual fantasies about me ever since I first showed up at the meetings and he had wanted to start an "intrigue." He came to understand it would be wrong for him, acting out his addiction, so he stopped. After an awkward pause, I realized he was apologizing.

"Um, thanks," I said. He said thanks back, wished me well, and left the room. I sat down, alone now in the circle of chairs, and tried to make sense of what he'd said.

He was fantasizing about me and wanted to start an intrigue, but didn't. What's an intrigue? You mean a man can make a choice about whether he fantasizes about me or not? No way! I thought they all did, because they were men. What the hell is going on?

◇ ◇ ◇

I couldn't have articulated it back then, but I now define attraction as one-way, while an intrigue involves two people acknowledging and fostering a secret attraction, primarily through innuendo and an exchange of nonverbal sexual energy. In the house I grew up in, especially once I started developing sexually, the buzz of one-way sexual attraction was often present. As a child I was too young to understand the source of my discomfort, but later I realized that some of the adults in my family were reactive to the kids they were entrusted to protect. Through sexual jokes, appraising comments about our developing bodies, comparisons to movie stars and each other, and worse, we got the message that certain adults were focused on us in a way we didn't understand, but that didn't feel good. And the ones who weren't fixated didn't seem to notice, or do anything to stop the ones who were.

It was an invisible energy web in which, as a child, I was helplessly entangled. My sister and I intuited this sexually toxic grid back then, regularly speaking the unspeakable in our little girl play, when I was eight and she was ten.

While riding in the backseat of mom's white AMC Pacer, our ritual was always the same. Whoever wanted to start the game would call out, hissing, "The SPI-I-I-I-I-DER (pause) and the FLY-Y-Y-Y-Y-Y!" She was two years older, so she always made me start as the fly, and she always started as the spider. Whenever I heard her menacing voice, I'd thrill inside with the spookiness of it. I'd lie with my head on her lap, facing up, as she traced a spiral web on my face, repeating, "The SPI-I-I-I-I-I-DER (pause) and the FLY-Y-Y-Y-Y-Y," each time in a louder raspy whisper, until her finger reached the tip of my nose. Then she would pinch it hard. That was the spider's bite, the crescendo of the game, after which we'd switch places so she'd be the fly and I'd get to be the spider.

It was always better to be the spider. Perhaps that sentence sums up my gravitation toward the role of temptress, and eventually becoming addicted to sex. I no longer wanted to be the victim, the fly. Though I still didn't recall the details of my own sexual abuse, at some point I decided I'd had enough of being the victim. I wanted to be the one in control, the dominant one. Playing neither role in the drama was not an option for me—no matter how much I tried to pretend otherwise, my unconscious past dominated my sexuality, and I couldn't yet understand a way to stop acting it out. I wanted to be powerful, but I'd actually become powerless.

◊ ◊ ◊

Dillon's admission after the meeting about his fantasies, and his decision to stop them because he was in sexual recovery, was enlightening and baffling at the same time. I now know that such confessions are not recommended as part of a healthy recovery, because telling a fellow sex addict about an attraction often inflames their own obsessions. But for me, his disclosure also sparked a competing awareness: that the amorphous force I felt growing up, the spider web I first felt in my family and then unconsciously re-created wherever I went, might have a name and the possibility of an end, or at least a transmutation, in recovery.

It was a heady concept. Could the force of attraction I'd structured my life around be brought to consciousness, discussed, and controlled? What was that force? Sex? Sexual attraction? Sex gravity? It had seemed to me a fundamental law, as immutable as gravity— you dropped an apple, it fell. You put me in a room with a man, any man, and I'd sexualize him. I'd want him to want me, and my thoughts would reflect this with fantasy and gratifying body sensations. If he reacted, I'd feel even better, and that would become a source of pleasure whenever I saw him. My only problem was Jason, who didn't like it when he saw me perform this subtle dance with other men. Knowing he disapproved didn't stop me; I simply tried harder to hide it.

I puzzled over this incessantly—was it truly possible to *decide* who I fantasized about? Which man I focused on? To choose *not* to focus on someone, even if I was attracted to them? I knew there were various levels of intensity in my attractions, from mild to mad. I thought I might be able to make choices around the mild attractions, but the medium to mad ones? A shadowy corner of my mind had a definitive reply: *No fucking way!*

I knew Dillon was trying to be helpful with his truth-telling, but I was afraid to see him again because now *I* was intrigued. As with Jason, I took his sober, respectful new approach to me as simply one more challenge to overcome, even though I was beginning to grasp that, in sexual recovery, this kind of behavior was off-limits.

Watching my journal entries narrow from rants about Jason to fantasies about Dillon, I began to suspect that my codependency sponsor had been right: this compulsive sex thing might be bigger than I thought. I recalled my journals from junior high and high school, filled with name after name of the boys I was crushing on, little hearts drawn around each one, always two or three at a time. At that age it was mostly fantasies from a distance about boys besides my boyfriend, or stringing boys along with flirtatious attention, but by college it had grown to more. Through the entire five-year relationship with Matt, I'd almost always had one or more secret flirtations or physical affairs going on. And when I'd stopped seeing men altogether after my therapist had forbidden it, porn and sex chat became my substitute. Until I met Jason.

I didn't want to go back to cheating, so I decided I'd better not get within a hundred feet of Dillon. But if I left the noon meetings, where else could I go for help?

An image popped into my head from the first sexual recovery meeting, the one with all men at the Alano Club, and I shuddered. I recalled how scared I was afterward, and how I swore I'd never go back. Remembering advice that Janine had once given me about dealing with fear, I pulled out my journal.

"You have fears?" she'd said in her no-nonsense tone. "Write 'em down in a list, and then look at them! That's a big part of what taking an inventory means." As I read back over my list, I realized that being the only woman in that first meeting, and that sex was so bluntly talked about, were not the only things that frightened me. What alarmed me even more was something I remembered hearing that no one talked about at the smaller fellowship I'd switched to. In that first meeting, a few people talked about desires to take advantage of others sexually, urges to hurt them, and how they intervened.

Impulsively, I decided to return to that other fellowship, but to try to find one of its smaller meetings. I went back online and noticed one that was oriented toward new people. Even though I might once again be the only woman, the idea of getting help from people who were trying to overcome their own predatory urges brought some relief, along with anxiety.

Maybe they can help me understand my urges to dominate men.

But, like almost every step of forward progress I made in sexual recovery, this one was followed by another burst of internal rebellion. I was able to make myself try the newcomer's meeting of the first fellowship, but this time the sexually addicted part of my mind fought back, deciding that if I had to go, I would at least put on a "suit of armor" to help protect me. If I was going to be surrounded by all men again, I wanted to feel in control. My armor took the form of short white shorts and a hot pink tank top.

- FIFTEEN -

Sexual Sobriety Defined

As the months passed, I became a regular at the formerly all-male sex addicts' meeting. When one woman finally appeared, a self-identified lesbian, I was relieved and excited. I approached her after the meeting ended, offered an eager welcome, and handed her my phone number. She looked at me like I was insane and never called. In fact, she quit coming to that meeting entirely, though she did stay in sexual recovery.

I knew because I started going to other meetings on other days of the week, and began to see some of the same faces. I was generally ignored, politely greeted, or given sidelong looks, but was never openly ogled. I was amazed. Since the age of sixteen, I hadn't been in a room full of men and not magnetized attention if I wanted it. I hated being ignored, but I was also intensely curious.

Why aren't they reacting? What are they so focused on instead? As we sat, week after week, in our circles of folding chairs, and the warm summer days ebbed into cool mornings and early sunsets, I became a spider on their wall, studying them.

Who are these men, and how exactly does their society function, if not by sex? One time I arrived early and took a seat in the circle away from the men already there. Every chair in the circle filled up, but the chairs on either side of me remained empty until long after the meeting started. Then a latecomer walked in, and his eyes widened as he realized he had no other seat options. I pretended not to care, laughing inwardly at his discomfort as he sat to my left, careful not to touch me.

Cooties.

Now I know that to many of the men I represented danger, I was "the enemy." I looked like the object of their desire in an inner struggle that was wreaking havoc in their personal lives, the one they came to meetings to get away from. Like the lesbian woman who never called, they wanted to keep a safe distance.

The meeting structure was always the same: opening readings, then sharing, where people introduced themselves and talked while everyone else listened without interruption. People spoke about their lives, their sexual compulsions, and their successes and failures with getting sober. I never talked, but sat quietly, often simmering with resentment and wanting to leave and never come back. Yet I found the depth of honesty, which I'd never heard anywhere else, strangely comforting, and listening to people tell their truths kept me showing up week after week. The contrast to growing up in an alcoholic family was immense, and despite my anxiety being there, I couldn't get enough.

One night after the meeting ended, I noticed a stocky, raven-haired man about my age get up and approach another man, a tall redhead with a goatee. They stood near me, faces alight with something. *What is it?* I wondered.

"Hey, man, good to see you!" The raven-haired man opened his arms in welcome.

"Hey, Sam, you too!" the redhead replied. He also opened his arms, and they embraced. It wasn't sexual, and they weren't gay. The look on their faces was delight, their eyes glowing as they greeted each other. It was genuine affection. I was right there, available to flirt with, tease, or even hug after the meeting, like everyone else was doing. They ignored me as they hugged, happy and safe, laughing and catching up.

WTF. I felt small and invisible. But then, in addition to the bitterness, another feeling came, a heart-pang I struggled to make sense of. It was longing. Not for seduction or sex, though they were both good-looking and I was attracted to them. The longing was for what they had; I wanted that affection. I wanted a friend who looked at me like that, someone I could look at like that, and share a real hug with.

I didn't know how to get it, but I thought back to Janine, my codependency sponsor, and how she used to hug me. I especially remembered after I read my Fourth Step list to her—the inventory of all the awful things about myself—that, instead of condemning me, she congratulated me for my courage and gave me a hug. I was so surprised! It felt like the first real hug of my life. I'd revealed my worst, everything I'd tried so hard to hide, and still she pulled me close and held me. But I also remembered that after I read her the second part of my writing, about sex, her hugging stopped and she told me to try sexual recovery for help. *Maybe I should try harder,* I thought. *Maybe I should try to figure out what it means to get sober with sex.*

My eyes found the scarred wooden tables stacked with books and pamphlets I'd always ignored. Finally, with something to do at the end of the meeting besides sit frozen or flee, I approached a man standing near the table. He was in his mid-fifties with glasses and a brown goatee, and he greeted me politely, offering to help. I told him I wanted to read about sobriety. With a grin, he handed me a pamphlet.

"I recommend this one. It'll help you figure out what's right for you. But it helps to go over it with a sponsor." I snatched it like a hungry dog, wary and without thanks, and walked away. I didn't want another sponsor who might send me away again. I went home and read the pamphlet, suddenly becoming obsessed with defining sexual sobriety.

The pamphlet suggested I divide all of my behaviors related to sexuality into three categories: the good, the bad, and the really ugly. It sounded so simple, yet this practical tool to define my own sexual boundaries filled me with a sudden surge of hope.

Can I really stop this? Can I really make a sobriety plan and stick to it? I decided to work harder than I had, to really "work a program," like they said in the meetings.

I finally have a tool! My attitude quickly shifted from one of rebellion to superiority—I was going to have the best recovery of anyone. Then my mind shifted back to callous disdain for the entire process.

The idea of sexual sobriety is insane! I read on and learned that my worst acting-out behaviors were defined by what made me feel the most worthless, caused the most harm, and resulted in something called *unmanageability*. My mind went into battle-mode, turning on itself.

These 12-Step words are so stupid. What does unmanageability even mean?

Call it whatever you like, you've got it! You can't manage your life.

It's not that bad...lighten up! "Sex addiction" is such a melodramatic concept. Sex is fun!

Oh, really? Fun? Is it fun to get yourself into umpteen awful situations, like that guy's after-hours bachelor party, watching a woman get paid to grind on the groom, terrified out of his mind, while his so-called friends watched, and everyone knew about it except his bride-to-be? Was it fun to get wasted and piggyback on that raging guy you met at a bar, only saved from drunken sex, or worse, by Debbie grabbing you and shoving you in her car, while the guy screamed at her and tried to grab you back? The friendship didn't last long after that...was all that really fun?!

Sullen silence.

Face it. Sex rules you, and you think it's the other way around. If that's not powerlessness and unmanageability, I don't know what is. The only way you'll ever get sober is to be shut up in a convent forever.

I felt a surge of hostility, but had to admit that my life wasn't so rosy. I thought back to the two men and their happy greeting. Because I'd heard them talking in meetings for months, I knew that one was a successful software programmer and the other was happily married, running his own business. I, on the other hand, was working temp jobs, sinking further into credit card debt, and scrounging for a life. Jason was supportive now that I was going to sexual recovery meetings, though we avoided going to the same ones, but things remained strained between us. I really did need a new focus.

Arriving home that evening, I took out a piece of white notebook paper, turned it lengthwise, and divided it into three columns. I didn't know what to write in which column. I quit.

Back at the newcomer's meeting, I started listening more carefully to the men who'd already written their sobriety statements, and who actually read their lists out loud to the whole group, to stay accountable. I related to much of what I heard.

We may be different genders, but they're succeeding at not doing a lot of things I'm still doing.

Still at war inside, I abruptly found myself distracted by a man I'd never noticed before. With his brown, curly hair and dark brown eyes, I decided he was definitely my type: a polite veneer, but with the prospect of danger lurking beneath the surface. This man had the intoxicating combination of boyish charm and murderous intensity, and my thoughts of defining sobriety were overrun by an instant, intense attraction. Listening to him became the highlight of my meetings. I learned he was married with a newborn son, but that didn't stop me; I hung on every word he uttered. When he talked about his stress at work and his struggle to not look at other women and pornography, I nodded sympathetically, but inside I was thinking, *look at me, here I am!* Suddenly I felt a lot better. It became easier to show up at the meetings, hoping he'd be there. Outside the program gatherings, my mind was distracted by anticipation about when I might see him again.

Around this time, a sturdy Italian man who introduced himself as Anthony approached me after a meeting. Even though he was in his mid-forties, I had heard him referred to as a "recovery old-timer" because he claimed fourteen years of sexual sobriety.

He smiled disarmingly as he introduced himself, "How are you? Do you have any questions about how the program works? About the literature?"

I tried to copy his friendly tone. "No, I'm just learning a lot, thanks." After he left, I felt relieved; I wanted to be free to focus on my new favorite object, the brown-haired, brown-eyed man. I drank him in with my eyes, trying to be subtle about it in case Anthony or someone else noticed. I started obsessing about him, even as I tried not to fantasize, because I knew he was married and that couldn't be sober. I failed. I was getting comfortable again with another secret attraction, despite the oft-repeated recovery slogan, "You're only as sick as your secrets." When it came to sex, I was still far more comfortable with secrets than the truth.

One day after the meeting, I found myself edging toward the brown-haired man. When he turned and left the room, I followed.

I want to ask him about his recovery program, I told myself. I trotted up the steps to the outside of the church. The air was crisp but I felt warm, my heart beating faster. Turning a corner, I looked around, and saw him heading toward a pretty brunette who'd come out of the meeting for partners of sex addicts. He smiled and gave her a big hug—my heart sank.

That must be his wife, the mother of his baby boy, I thought, ashamed. I went home and started filling in the columns to "define my sobriety." In the left, the worst-of-the worst column, I wrote:

Intrigues with men

Compulsive masturbation, with or without pornography

Dressing provocatively to seek sexual attention from men

Hurting myself physically

Anonymous sex

Then I wrote my sobriety date: Today.

- SIXTEEN -

Haircut and Gay Allies

MY FIRST OFFICIAL ACT as a sexually sober person was to cut off
all my hair. Consistent with my fear of intimacy, I didn't like anyone touching my hair. I always felt anxious letting someone get that
close to me, and then too embarrassed afterward to see them again. I
remembered my older sister's efforts learning to weave French braids
when we were kids by practicing on me, and how she would painfully pull my hair and bark "Sit still!" when I squirmed. My mom
must have touched my hair often before I was able to fix it myself, but
I had only one memory of that from when I was about ten years old,
and it wasn't a happy one.

We were sitting on our red-and-green plaid couch, and as she was
saying something to me, she reached over and tucked a strand of my
long bangs behind my right ear. The gesture seemed absent-minded;
it could have even been a nurturing moment, but for me it wasn't.
My ear prickled, as if too warm, and I felt an urgent need to untuck
my hair, only stopping myself because I was afraid it would hurt her
feelings. As soon as we finished talking and her attention was elsewhere, I flicked my hair free.

For most of my life, I never went to the same hairstylist more than
once.

"You're a hair hopper!" one stylist in a fancy downtown salon
screeched, playfully chastising me when I told him I'd never seen
the same person twice. "Oh, we know all about people like YOU!" I

joined his loud laughter with a false chuckle, inwardly adding him to my list of one-haircut stands. Not long after that, I found Laura.

Laura wasn't simply a haircutter and stylist, she was a "hair balancer." I met her at a talk she gave at a local spiritual bookstore and liked her immediately. It helped that she was beautiful, with long, radiant auburn hair, but she was also warm and funny. Laura told us the story of how her hair had once been terribly damaged by a professional perm left in too long, after which she was only able to salvage three inches of frizz. Desperate, she contacted a man she'd heard about who used the esoteric principles of sacred geometry, intuition, and intense focus to bring a person's whole being into harmony by balancing their hair. After receiving a treatment, her hair grew out thick and naturally curly. She went on to get trained herself and later wrote an article titled "Hair Trauma" to describe the emotionally scarring experiences many people have involving their hair.

It would have been easy to laugh this off as bogus, but I was curious. I'd been to some of the most expensive salons in Seattle and still hadn't found what I was looking for—maybe this was it.

It was. The minute Laura placed her hands gently on my shoulders and took some deep breaths, I felt calm and safe. Her hands were precise and efficient, and I barely noticed the scissors near my head—a longtime unexplained fear of mine. Laura was the hummingbird of hair, flitting from clip to clip until I looked in the mirror and saw something special emerge. After she was done I always felt a deep release, as if someone had pulled out a long-forgotten sliver and my skin sighed in its absence, finally. From that moment on, I wouldn't let anyone else touch my hair.

◊ ◊ ◊

The day of the "big cut," I sat in Laura's comfy chair and watched as she gazed in the mirror at my long, sun-burnished locks. In the past, we'd chat happily about life during hair balancing sessions, or I'd sink into a relaxed silence as she worked. This time, I had only one thing to say.

"Cut it off."

At first she was enthusiastic about my going from long to short. "A pixie cut?" she asked, her chocolate-brown eyes dancing with the possibility.

"Shorter," I replied. Her brows furrowed slightly at my grim tone, but she went to work, and down the hair fell, catching on the folds of the purple cape draped over me. Snip, snip, snip, my hair dropped in large clumps, one after the other, as I stared intently in the mirror at my changing image, my expression flat. Laura breathed deeply as she worked, intuitively giving me the silence my solemnness demanded. This was more than a haircut, it was atonement for my sins, and a shearing of my sexual antennae.

"There, what do you think?" she asked, stopping at a spiky short cut that suggested sass and snap.

"Shorter," I replied tersely, and she returned to her flow. Around she went, making minute cuts, then pausing once more.

"What do you think? Here, look at the back." She held up a mirror. It was so short in the back that it looked almost shaved. The only place I had any real hair left was on top.

"Shorter," I repeated, but Laura didn't move.

"Staci, if I go any shorter, you're going to look like an Auschwitz survivor."

My eyes caught hers in the mirror, and my stomach released some of its bubbling tension as I replied, "That's exactly what I want."

Although I didn't make the connection until long after that day, I later recalled that when I was a child, my maternal grandmother had a slim booklet on her living room shelf that contained pictures of prisoners in the German concentration camps of Auschwitz. I used to look through it sometimes when no one was watching, mutely absorbing the appalling images of impossibly thin bodies discarded in piles, or of faces so gaunt they looked like living ghosts. I never asked grandma why she had it, nor suspected that because her parents emigrated from Poland to Canada before World War II, she might have had family or friends left behind who were subject to such atrocities. If so, she never spoke of it.

During the haircut, I'd forgotten about those horrible pictures; I just wanted to punish myself. Getting serious about sexual recovery had finally dissolved my lifetime of numbness, and I felt a bubbling mass of crusty lava melting away my apparently normal facade. Since defining my sobriety and trying to stick to it, shameful thoughts about my past constantly intruded on my mind. Self-recrimination competed with cravings to fantasize or look at porn, or do other sexual things I was simultaneously trying to avoid. I hated the struggle. I hated my sexual urges. And I hated what my new stand for sexual sobriety was starting to show me about myself. The impulse to cut returned, but in order to stay sober according to my new definition, I enlisted Laura's help to use sharp edges in a way that wouldn't draw blood.

Looking back on this extreme change in my appearance, I realize that I didn't know how to shut down my addictive sexual behaviors without shutting down *all* my sexual behaviors. This was a loss for my partner Jason, but I didn't care. For a long time, I felt only hatred for my sexuality, and afraid to open myself back up to sensuality at all. It would be a while before I could reclaim beauty and sexual delight without feeling like I was exploiting myself or anyone else.

⋄ ⋄ ⋄

I shoved all my sexy summer clothes in the back of my closet and pulled on baggy sweats and a sweatshirt before heading to my first post-haircut meeting. I did not put on makeup, nor try to style my barely-there hair. I arrived at the church and walked down the stairs to the basement with my eyes down, sitting in the first chair I saw. I didn't know then that it would be years before I would wear makeup again. I just felt awful and could no longer stomach the effort to pretty myself up.

As usual the meeting was full of men with more arriving: twenty, thirty, forty. After the daily reading, it was announced that, because there were so many new people, the group would be divided in half by an accordion wall, to give people more time to talk. Newcomers were encouraged to go to the smaller meeting on the other side of the wall, and experienced members would join them and answer questions after the sharing ended. I noticed that the brown-eyed, brown-haired man wasn't there, but this time, with a jangling pulse of self-recrimination at my weakness and corruption for seeking out a married man, I went to the newcomer's side.

The meeting was led by Anthony, the longtime member who'd recently introduced himself to me. I'd paid more attention to him since then, learning he was a fireman transplanted from New York. Whenever he talked, his contagious laughter seemed even to surprise himself as it burst forth in regular intervals, no matter what his life dished out. The meeting topic was the Alcoholics Anonymous basic text, known by insiders as the "Big Book."

I was confused. *Why are we reading about alcoholism here? What does that have to do with sex addiction?*

I'd seen the book before. When I was nine and mom first started AA, the book showed up at our house one day, and was lodged front and center on the dusty pressboard bookshelf at the top of our entryway stairs. The book became a big blue sentry in an obvious place, white script on its spine leaving nothing to the imagination: *Alcoholics Anonymous.* She carried it in her big purse when she left for AA meetings, like a new student heading off to school. I resented that she always went to meetings and was never around—I resented that blue book because it took her away from me.

Why is it here again, at the newcomer's meeting for sex addicts?

My angry ruminations inspired me to ask the question aloud to Anthony during the Q&A for newcomers.

"We don't have a book of our own yet, so AA has kindly given us permission to use theirs," he answered. "But believe me, it works! Underneath whatever substance or behavior you're addicted to, the basic problem is your thinking. I think the AA message works great for all addictions; just substitute the word *drinking* with *thinking*."

After the meeting ended, something unexpectedly wonderful happened. I was immediately approached by two men. We'd never formally met, but being in meetings alongside them for months had taught me intimate details about their lives, like the fact that they were both gay.

"Oh my *God*, I love your *hair*," fawned one, a striking Hawaiian named Hal with flashing dark eyes.

"I like it too," the other said softly, a musician who introduced himself as Oshin. He was Asian and slim, with expressive dark eyes, and hair almost as short as mine. His bangs were styled in a perfect flip, and he exuded an interesting blend of masculine and feminine. He reached out, not quite touching my short brown spikes, and added, "You look like Audrey Hepburn!" I was stunned to silence by their praise, blushing as they went on talking as if we'd known each other forever.

This was the beginning of my first program friendships, and my introduction to the wondrous world of gay men in sexual recovery.*

---

*For an excellent book on this topic, see Cruise Control: Understanding Sex Addiction in Gay Men, by Robert Weiss, a visionary leader in the field of sexual recovery.

In my obsessive hunger for male attention, I'd never really considered that some men were not attracted to women. My suburban upbringing had left me ignorant, and though I'd learned about minority social justice in college and had seen gay porn, I was about to directly experience the grace of gay men for the first time. Their love and support created the first real sense of safety in my adult life, taking sex off the table and replacing it with playfulness, and passionate discussions about jazz, porn, and recovery. I started calling them regularly for support, and they called me back. And soon I landed a longer-term temp job, so money started to flow again.

"Girl, you gotta get a sponsor," Hal said over the phone one day after listening to me complain about Jason, my obsession with the brown-eyed man, and my struggle to imagine giving up porn forever. I was afraid of what a sponsor might say, but I knew Hal was right. I finally had some support, but I needed more direction.

At the next meeting I heard, as if for the first time, the usual announcement about the list of names and phone numbers being passed around, with checkmarks by the names of those willing to be sponsors. When the clipboard came to me, I traced my finger down the column of checks until I saw the name of a longtime member: Diego A.

Hmm, I thought. *This guy's a possibility. He's gay, so like Hal and Oshin he's probably safe, even though he's gorgeous. His past is crazier than mine! And he's been sober a while, so when I eventually try to seduce him, he'll say no.*

Diego was a striking Latino with jet black hair who wore stylish gray suits and trendy sweaters. He was tall and thick, like a linebacker, but moved with a startling mixture of bulk and refinement. I'd heard his story, and it was intense: he'd compulsively combined unprotected sex at bathhouses with methamphetamine cocktails for years. He talked in the meetings about how that way of life had almost killed him, and how it had actually killed almost everyone he knew back in the day, through AIDS. After getting into recovery, he became sober and turned things around, and he was now a successful manager at a large local hospital's psychiatric ward.

A *psych ward, how perfect*, I thought. With my new friends' encouragement, I approached Diego after a meeting and asked if he'd be my sponsor. He looked at me discerningly, as if calculating how serious I was, and said we could meet for coffee to talk it over.

"Bring your sexual sobriety definition," he said. "In writing."

Later that week I sat nervously in a crowded coffee shop near the church, my list folded in my pocket, and watched him walk in with a blue book under his arm. I left that meeting an hour later with a new sponsor, a more detailed definition of my sexual sobriety, and that blue book under my own arm.

"You'll need it," he'd said as he handed it to me. "We'll use it to work the steps, starting with Step One: powerlessness over sex addiction."

Within a week, I decided to save money by moving out of my friend's house and into my parent's summer getaway, a double-wide mobile home an hour outside the city that they rarely used. It was parked on 700 acres of mature forestland north of Seattle not far from Lake Goodwin, where I'd spent the happiest times of my childhood. My parents agreed that I could live there rent-free if I paid my own utilities, and I figured I could live off my meager savings and look for work locally once I was settled.

The mobile home was nestled among the trees along with hundreds of other trailers, campers and double-wides, most of which were vacant in the cold months. I had peek-a-boo views of a few neighbors' places, but kept to myself. The tall firs provided a sense of privacy and beauty, especially when the winter sun angled through green branches, its light glowing in the dust of a passing pick-up truck. It was an ironic and perfect escape from the shards of my old propped-up-perfect life, a lonely trailer park where I might grow into someone more honest and real. And there was one feature about the place that would prove essential to my fragile sobriety: no Internet connection.

- SEVENTEEN -

9/11 Despair

I WAS STARTING TO GAIN TRACTION with sobriety, adding up the days when I didn't do the things on my "No" list, which I now frequently read aloud in meetings:

"No hurting myself physically; no affairs or intrigues with men; no sex outside a mutual, caring relationship; no compulsive masturbation, with or without pornography; no alcohol or drugs; no toxic (abuse) fantasy; no pregnancy or STD risk; no cybersex."

I'd recently updated my list, and added "no alcohol or drugs" and "no toxic (abuse) fantasy." Although I'd never tried hard drugs, conversations with Diego helped me to realize that ever since college, getting drunk or high was inevitably accompanied by secret intrigues or risky sex.

"Not everyone in sexual recovery gives up alcohol or drugs," he explained. "The focus is on sexual behavior, but for me, sex, drugs, and alcohol were all related. I couldn't give up one without the other two." I knew I could give up pot because I'd never really liked it, but I wasn't willing to quit drinking forever. We agreed on a compromise: I'd go dry for three months, and then see how I felt.

Fantasy was another matter altogether. I didn't think it was possible to give up all sexual fantasy, but through my work with Diego I learned that my recurrent infidelity fantasies were like mental practice for cheating on Jason, and could raise the risk that I might follow through. When I finally got up the courage to admit my abuse fantasies, Diego speculated that they might be a distortion of the

132

nebulous memories from my own sexual past. I wasn't sure about that, but acknowledged that even though exploitation fantasies were the most arousing to me, I always ended up feeling bad afterward. I started paying attention to when people in meetings described techniques for interrupting their own fantasies, like praying or mentally picturing a stop sign instead of the old scenarios, or imagining their thoughts were clouds slowly passing by, and I practiced them often.

But after only a few weeks without alcohol, and without the "drugs" produced in my mind during fantasies or consuming illicit sex of some kind, my old symptoms of anxiety and depression returned, amplified. Living alone out in the woods was isolating; I saw Jason far less often, and I wasn't driving to Seattle for as many support meetings.

On September 11, 2001, I was fragile enough that when the planes crashed into the World Trade Center buildings in New York, I crashed too.

I sat alone in front of the tube television in the double-wide trailer, transfixed by the images before me on the screen. Disoriented with shock, I imagined the confusion, terror, heat, choking dust, and desperation the victims must have felt, most succumbing to sudden or slower deaths. I felt overwhelmed. Watching the images over and over opened up a hidden well of despair within me I'd spent my life walling off, but I couldn't tear myself away. Floor by floor the towers dissolved, and brick-by-brick the edifice inside my mind that held back my own shadows also crumbled. Sitting yet again in front of the 9/11 horror show a week after the attack, I noticed an odd, detached thought pass through my mind, like a cloud: *I am giving up now.*

I felt a deep letting go inside, as if some part of me had been clinging to the side of an internal burning tower and was now tumbling down into a black void. After that, I quit searching for a job; I gave up fighting or performing or doing much of anything. As I watched those people fall to their deaths on the screen, the part of me that had always "kept on keeping on" fell too.

Though my debt had been steadily growing since I met Jason, I'd always been able to pay my bills on time and keep up appearances with a decent credit score. Now I had no income and began taking cash advances on three different credit cards to pay for basics. I didn't tell anyone. I stopped going to meetings or returning calls, instead watching TV accounts of the "terrorist attack" nonstop. I slept nine to twelve hours a night, and took long naps every day. Fears grew about where my life was headed, and I lost the capacity to make an "inventory" list of them, or even respond to my feelings. I compulsively watched Mister Rogers, the only thing that seemed to offer any comfort. Card by card, my credit limit began to run out.

I hid the truth from both my family and Jason, and returned to eating junk food nightly until I sank into a bloated sleep. Unable to process either the global or personally symbolic meaning of 9/11, I regressed further into a range of coping skills familiar to many traumatized people: freeze in place, hide, eat for comfort, and sleep. When Fred Rogers sang "It's a beautiful day in the neighborhood" to me, my mind sought respite by dissociating from the reality of what I saw on the news and pretending it really was a beautiful day.

Whenever I was awake and away from the TV, my painful struggle with sexual obsessions continued. Even though I no longer had access to Internet pornography, memories and the exploitative graphic images I'd once consumed grew more vivid in my mind. As I tried to block them, intrusive fantasies about sex were replaced by litanies of self-hate, and I felt as if both were stalking me like cunning, relentless shadows.

Desperate for relief, I finally admitted to Jason that I wasn't doing so well, and asked for help. He urged me to get back into therapy, and offered to support me to set up some initial appointments with professionals he or his friends had heard of, or others I found through the library Internet. I relented, forcing myself to get out of the house to meet each new prospect. I vigilantly interrogated each one about their approach to therapy, determined to avoid another Margaret. I soon found that none of the people I met had any training in sex addiction, and most seemed uncomfortable with the topic. Each one asked about antidepressant medication—had I taken it before? Would I consider trying it again to treat what sounded like the descent into a full-fledged major depression, the kind that could kill me?

I remember one female therapist who was a specialist in eating disorders and boundaries. She was overweight and heavily made up, which worried me. *Why is she fat? Is she binging too? Why does she wear so much makeup? Is she yet another therapist-hypocrite?* As I heard her say that more than one kind of antidepressant was available and that perhaps a drug newer than Prozac could help, I felt a steely anger rise up in me.

"I think taking a medication to change my feelings is like taking a crying baby and stuffing a rag into its mouth. It may stop the crying, but I don't want to go there."

She blinked several times, taken aback, and I sensed her fear at my outburst. That was our last session. I still didn't know why I was so depressed, but I didn't trust any of these therapists to help me figure it out. My depression shifted to agitation.

I'm done looking for therapy! They just want to medicate me, and they know even less about sex addiction than I do! But once I quit looking for help, my ruminations about suicide returned, worse than ever. A journal entry from that time read:

> Weak, stupid, stupid, stupid, fucked up stupid you'll never get it stop it you sniveling crybaby God you suck I hate you

135

weakling always in pain fucker You ruin every thing weak little shit I hate you you suck I hate you you little fucker you abuse me you are so endlessly needy hypochondriac hurting hurting always hurting endlessly needy you cost me a fortune stupid abused child you goddamned leech why don't you go away disappear forever and ever…

Painting a seductive portrait of numbness, suicide once again offered a promise of freedom from my pain and self-hatred. As I tried to stop the abuse-themed sexual images in my mind, a new obsession emerged: mental flashes of driving my car full speed into a concrete embankment. This image crystallized and shimmered at me daily, offering reassurance.

Wouldn't that be easier? Just go to sleep, blink out, go blank, be done, no more hurting. Just do it, do it, DO IT! And I did want to, even as I feared it. I was lured by the hypnotic pull of taking my life, a gasp for power in what felt like an endless ocean of powerlessness. *But what will happen to me after I die? Will I go to hell, like they said in church?*

I feel like I'm in hell now, came the exhausted response inside.

Frantic, I tried to recall the near-death experience I'd had two years earlier and the profound love I experienced then. I wanted to go back to that place of light but I couldn't bring it into focus; my thoughts were too jumbled and chaotic. Soon, staying alive became a daily struggle, like trying to find firm footing in a stinking, contaminated swamp. Surrounded by foul thought-insects, I couldn't make my way through the branches reaching out and wrapping themselves around my mind. With each step forward I seemed to sink more deeply, down to my knees, down to my waist in quicksand, my hands clawing at the hardening mud. I was caught on gray mental weeds tendriling around my wrists, up to my chin. Bogged down as if a mental weight were pressing on my chest, I couldn't breathe, even as I tried to hold my lips above the suffocation line. Without sex to buoy me up and distract me, the atrocities of 9/11 and what they reminded me of devastated me, and my desire to live dissolved with the towers. *Why should I survive when so many innocent people died?*

What kept me alive in the weeks after 9/11 was not my own mental will—which was overrun by external and internal horrors—but my autonomic nervous system's primal instinct to live. For this gift from my body and my creator, I will forever be grateful. Despite my return to suicidal fantasy, my body's beacon for life cut through the fog and sounded one last alarm deep within, even as my thoughts went under and I sought the dull rush of blackness.

This was my rock bottom, the closest I came to suicide. My body hung in there to save itself through the primal mammalian instinct of freezing when faced with a grave threat. By making me too emotionally immobile to leave the house, my body was able to avoid its murder weapon: my car. That's when life placed a gift on my doorstep: a startling visit from one of my very first friends.

◇ ◇ ◇

Erin and I met in a class for gifted children called "Summit," a new program developed for promising eight-year-olds that bussed children together from different schools once a week. She was too shy for me to get to know at first, but I figured she was smart. I don't recall the magical moment when Erin and I morphed from classmates to inseparable friends, but I do remember our laughter. We could laugh at anything and nothing, from quiet giggles to belly-aching, tearful wheezes. Time with my new best friend became a rainbow in an otherwise black-and-white childhood.

By sixth grade we were both full-time students at the same school, with different homerooms. We would meet in the hallways during breaks to pass neatly written notes and exchange small gifts wrapped in bright, delicate paper: erasers, sparkly pencils, and, most often, stickers.

When more of my childhood memories started to return, I was thrilled to recall all this and more, grateful that although I felt isolated most of the time, at least I'd had a few childhood friends. My favorite memory with Erin was a clever subterfuge we'd gotten away with in sixth grade.

Telling our respective teachers that we had to go to the bathroom at an arranged time, Erin and I secretly met in the hallway, clutching our pink hall passes, and snuck into the unlocked, darkened gymnasium. We crawled up behind a puffy, blue high-jump mat stored on-end against the wall, and hung from its top. Then we used our feet to push the mat away from the wall, flying as it dropped flat on the floor with a huge WHUMP we hoped no one could hear. We'd bounce together with hushed giggles, jumping on the mat for as long as we thought we could before being missed.

We grew apart as we grew older, and by 2001 I hadn't seen or talked to her for years. So when she called out of the blue and left a message asking if I wanted to get together, I was surprised. I told her I couldn't meet because I wasn't feeling well, but she was insistent. She said it was important and she didn't mind the hour-long drive to the mobile home. I relented, and we arranged for her to drive up the following day.

I dressed, combed my hair, and greeted her at the door with a smile, trying to act like everything was fine. She brought her toddler son with her, and we entertained him while chatting superficially. After he was comfortable and finally engrossed with his toys, Erin's congenial tone changed.

"Staci, I'm worried about you! I heard you quit your job and now you're living up here in the woods all alone. This isn't good! What's going on?"

Shocked, I tried to defend myself with the same story I told every-one, though I didn't believe it anymore myself.

"I'm up here to get a new start, to write and get to know myself!" She asked how that was going, and my bravado faded. I admitted I wasn't writing anything, wasn't really looking for a job, and had no income. I couldn't even afford utilities, but fortunately my parents were keeping up the payments for me.

"You're depressed! You need help! You need to take antidepres-sant medications to get better, and get back to living!" I tried to explain how medication and therapy didn't work for me, but she wasn't satisfied.

"How are you going to get your life back then? What are you going to do to get better, if you don't take medicine, or go to therapy?"

Today I can see that she was scared, and that her confrontation was a protective, deeply loving act. But back then I thought she was one more person telling me to medicate my feelings away. I told her I had joined a 12-Step program for healing, omitting the sexual aspect and the fact I'd all but quit. She remained skeptical. "How long until it really helps you then?"

Suddenly, her three-year-old came running up to us with a book of matches in his hand.

"Oops, this place isn't childproof," I said, as she took them from him. He then wandered off and promptly found some scissors in a low drawer, and immediately after that discovered a long fire-starter lighter that was left on the floor.

Erin decided it was time to go, and she left with a strained good-bye. But her visit was a wake-up call, a reminder that if someone was going to do anything about the mess of my life, it was going to have to be me. I wondered if I was being too stubborn about antidepres-sants, even as I couldn't bring myself to try them again. I still didn't call Diego or return any calls from Hal or Oshin, but I decided to at least go back to a sexual recovery meeting, one nearer to my new home in the woods.

It was a small meeting, and once again I was the only woman there. I wore no makeup and my now-typical uniform included a baggy sweat suit, scuffed tennis shoes, and a blue cap to cover my short, unwashed hair. This time I was too exhausted to care about the men's obvious surprise at my arrival, ignoring everyone as I sank into a folding chair. The meeting was tolerable, better than nothing, and I kept going back. After a few weeks, a longtime sober member approached me as I was leaving the meeting.

"Hey, I'm Corey," he said. I told him my name as he stuck out his hand and shook mine formally. "You need to join a book study I'm starting." His command startled me, as did his confident tone. His smile reminded me of Jack Nicholson's, disarming and slightly devilish.

"Why?" I asked, suspicious.

"Because I found this great new book called *The Power of Now* by Eckhart Tolle, and a bunch of us are getting together to read and talk about it. As a woman, I think your perspective would add to the discussion." I wanted to decline, but Erin's challenge was fresh in my mind.

What are you going to do to get better?

"Okay," I replied, and that was that. It would be painful to get to the meeting an hour earlier every Saturday for the book study, but I dutifully bought a copy of *The Power of Now* and started reading.

Tolle's story struck a chord. He felt terrible depression and had contemplated suicide. He had feelings of "absolute dread." Once I read these words, I knew he understood: "I could feel that a deep longing for annihilation, for nonexistence, was now becoming much stronger than the instinctive desire to continue to live." He spoke of healing without the use of medications, of a permanent transformation of consciousness that was available to everyone. This sounded like exactly what I needed, but more than that, it *felt right* to me somehow. In the places inside that had been feeling so awful, I began to sense a little hum of relief.

I am not just my mind. There is more to me than the part of me that wants to die, or kill me. I am more than my obsessions. Perhaps my real addiction—like Anthony once said—is to thinking?

Potent concepts, they offered a perfectly timed whisper of promise in my gloomy world. I was still vacillating about antidepressants (many men at meetings talked about taking them), when I stumbled upon Tolle's opinion of mood-altering medication, which deeply resonated with me:

> "These drugs, of course, simply keep you stuck in dysfunction. Their widespread use only delays the breakdown of the old mind structures and the emergence of higher consciousness. While individual users may get some relief from the daily torture inflicted on them by their minds, they are prevented from generating enough conscious presence to rise above thought and so find true liberation."

This cemented it. I knew I was experiencing daily torture inflicted upon me by my own mind, and I decided once and for all not to take medication as an intervention. I made a promise to myself: I would not take medication *and* I would not kill myself. Like Tolle, I would meditate, try to rise above thought, and become truly liberated. Bolstered with my new purpose, I decided to make another change, one that Diego had recommended right after we started working together, and which I'd ignored. I would move from dipping my toe in the waters of recovery to taking the plunge: I'd finally start writing on the Twelve Steps of sexual recovery.

EIGHTEEN

Step One: Powerlessness

A DYING LITTLE BIRD inspired me to begin.

It was a bright winter afternoon, and I'd just woken up from a nap on the couch. I heard my orange cat, PK, making strange meowing-growling sounds beneath the living room window. I put on a sweater and stepped outside to see what was going on. PK was crouched at the base of a tree, and I looked up to see a little bird perched on a low branch, one wing fluttering uselessly at its side, broken. I scooped up a greatly displeased cat and brought him into the mobile home, where he jumped up on the back of the couch to watch intently, the way only feline predators can. By the time I returned to the tree, the bird had fallen from the branch and now lay on its side on the ground, its wing twitching. I peered more closely to see a partly mangled face, with one eye oozing liquid that had matted its tiny head feathers, the other paper-thin lid flittering open and closed. A few moments later, there was only stillness.

Cradling its little body, I ventured into the woods to find a burial spot. With my hands, I dug a shallow grave and set the tiny remains inside, covering it with a small pile of earth.

Back inside, I washed my slightly trembling hands, while my cat protested his confinement and deprivation. Wondering why I felt so numb, I recalled a long-forgotten memory of another bird when I was very young, and then a sudden association with a horror I'd buried, until now. I sat down at my computer and started typing. *If I'm*

*going to survive, I'm going to have to try something besides endlessly
burying my painful memories like that dead little bird.*

As words filled the screen, I realized I had actually started my
sexual autobiography, the task Diego assigned me months ago as my
"First Step" in sexual recovery.

> My memory of my sexual life before age sixteen was spotty for
> most of my life. Events returned to me in rare images, which I
> ignored or dismissed as insignificant. When I was twenty-one I
> began therapy, and went weekly for eight years. I didn't begin
> therapy to get help for sexual issues, but I now believe these
> issues, and the ever-present shame and loneliness beneath
> them, have been the most influential force in my life. I am thir-
> ty-one years old. What follows is what I presently know about
> my sexual history…
>
> In my earliest memory, I was walking slowly down a pine-cush-
> ioned trail in the woods. It was summer, the breeze was warm
> and sweet and kind, tickling my little girl limbs and hair. I think I
> was about three years old. The sun winked at me from behind
> waving branches, green needles and boughs dancing with
> glee. I felt full of joy and love, following this path and trust-
> ing wherever it might take me. Suddenly I saw a dark-haired
> man ahead on the trail, and I noticed his expression. My stom-
> ach turned to lead as I absorbed the darkness in his eyes and
> sensed his plan to hurt me. I had disappeared to him, become
> a toy doll, and there seemed to be no way out. In my panic I
> found a way, becoming like a little bird. In my mind I quickly
> flew up to the branch of the tree above. I left him and the doll
> below, watching with darting bird eyes as he pushed some-
> thing into her, feeling nothing.

No matter how hard I try, I can't actually place who this person is, but I am pretty sure he is someone close to our family.

At age 13 I started staring at boys and men I saw in public. I would keep making eye contact until I noticed a reaction. I felt powerful whenever I saw a reaction of any kind, especially fear. I felt drawn to their fear like a magnet—I'd stare more and look away, confident that whoever I was looking at would continue to watch me. I became attracted to angry energy. This attention was arousing to me and I sought it wherever I went.

At age 16, going to dance clubs became the highlight of my life. I lived for the weekends, when I would take all Saturday to prepare. It was a ritual, to wash and curl my hair, take a nap, get dressed and put on my makeup. It was sacred to me, like communion preparations each Sunday. I blushed away any trace of vulnerability and drew on a mask of glamour and power. I became the woman on all the magazine covers. Once at the club I drank in the stares and comments, approaches and appeals I received. My favorite was to pick out a guy I found attractive who was dancing with another girl and stare at him, and try to get him to watch me. Then I'd dance as if it was just for him. I was careful to hide this from whomever I was dancing with at the time. It was a fun game.

The story went from there to describe my descent in college into promiscuity, secrets, lies, manipulations, and repeated patterns of self-destruction. Hurting myself, unable to stop, hating myself, unable to stop. I was amazed to find I'd written fifteen pages, and stunned to see the patterns of pain spread out over the previous eighteen years in the realm of what I once thought was a reliable pleasure: sex. And to my surprise, what revealed itself to be my biggest drug of all, what recovering people call their "drug of choice," was the "hit" of sexualized eye contact and intrigue, especially with men who were married or in positions of authority. The thrill of the challenge was an elixir that made me feel all-powerful, regardless of my relationship status, and led to betrayals time and again.

Seven months after starting sexual recovery, I had written my First Step. I called Diego to tell him, and we arranged to meet at the hospital during his lunch break. Reading the entire narrative to him seemed endless, but when I finally finished, he responded in his classically understated way.

"Clearly you went through a lot."

I was uncertain whether to read it aloud in a meeting to the bigger group, which was the custom in our recovery community. Diego cautioned against it, because I'd included memories of sexual abuse, and he said that might be overwhelming for many people to hear. I was relieved to be excused from sharing, because there were some men in the meeting I still felt highly attracted to, like the brown-eyed man, and others I felt scared of, and some, both. I didn't want those men to know so much about me.

"Congratulations," Diego said, his dark eyes meeting mine. "You're done with Step One." I sat quietly, sensing that his words didn't quite ring true; I hadn't truly accepted that I was powerless over sex addiction. I didn't feel it as a certainty; it was more like a suggestive flutter, like the beating of miniature wings in my stomach. I squelched it.

- NINETEEN -

Step Two: Coming to Believe

THE FOLLOWING WEEK, Diego sat across from me in our now-familiar ritual of discussing the Twelve Steps.

"Step Two reads 'Came to believe that a power greater than ourselves could restore us to sanity,' " Diego explained, which meant exploring my relationship with what he called "the God of your understanding," or what people in 12-Step meetings referred to as "higher power."

"Stay sober, and write about it."

Other than a desperate prayer or two in the previous few months, I hadn't thought seriously about God for a long time. On a wet and dreary January day, I sat down at the kitchen table and wrote in my journal:

> Dear God:
>
> FUCK YOU.
>
> I FEEL SO SICK OF STRUGGLING I <u>WON'T</u> DO IT ANYMORE! I REFUSE TO LIVE A HALF-ASSED EXISTENCE ANYMORE! IF I DON'T FEEL INSPIRED, I WON'T DO IT! AS FOR THE SPIRIT SUPPORTING AND LOVING ME, I SAY <u>ACTION!</u>

I read it aloud to Diego when we met at a Seattle teahouse later that week. I didn't yell the words, though I wanted to, but I proudly showed him the page with its oversized capital letters, and he got the picture: I was pissed at God.

"Good start. Write some more. Keep exploring your feelings and thoughts about God, whatever that means to you. Now that you're doing step writing, we'll meet every week."

I dutifully went home and wrote more, my rage slightly subdued this time:

> Dear friggin' spirit,
>
> I feel bubbling oceans of fear deep within me. I am swallowing sugar as a pacifier, and I know I am using it as a drug to get by. <u>May I never judge another addict who reaches in despair-ation for comfort and nurturing as they understand it.</u> I hurt, I suffer here, I can't plan fun, I can only take one day at a time and that's <u>that.</u> Okay.
>
> I feel <u>scared</u>, I feel <u>scared</u>
>
> I feel <u>scared,</u> I feel <u>scared.</u>
>
> What am I going to DO?
>
> I WAS ABUSED AND I WON'T/CAN'T GO ON WITHOUT TELLING THIS TRUTH! But what really happened? I hardly remember.
>
> My life will live the truth, I won't pretend.
>
> What does "came to believe that a power greater than ourselves can restore us to sanity" mean to me?

I put down my pen. To me, God was an old white man in a white robe sitting on a throne; I couldn't relate to him. I wondered why I felt so mad when I thought of God, where all the hate came from. My thoughts drifted back to when, as a child, mom starting making us go to Sunday Mass, and the words began to flow again.

For the first time I could recall, we all got dressed up, as if the impact of years of addiction and disconnection had disappeared beneath our shiny new clothes. I was a tomboy until age thirteen; at nine I still hated dressing up. But things took a turn for the better when we joined a small group of people from the larger church body called the Catholic Charismatic movement. Several families would get together at each other's houses for "home church." There, we didn't have to dress up, and we were welcomed with open arms. Literally, people hugged us. Since I was severely touch-starved as a kid, this new development felt awkward at first, but then pretty great. And scary, because I was almost never touched at home, and the only other touch I knew left a stain on my heart. I was afraid this kind of touch would too, but it didn't; it left a little glow I tried valiantly to hide. I was always afraid someone would take away whatever happiness I found.

Everybody brought platters and casserole dishes covered with food, and I loved to run around and play with the other kids while the grownups talked. At some point one of the dads would bring out a guitar and invite us all to sing along. No one drank alcohol, and the whole night there wasn't one fight. When it came time for communion, one of the moms handed out rough-cut triangles of fresh homemade bread from a basket, with mini cups of grape juice to drink. Everyone got quiet and a man said, "This is the body and blood of Christ," and we'd solemnly eat it, all at the same time. The bread was soft, chewy, and slightly sweet. The grape juice was also sweet, and the two combined, along with all the rest of the evening, became the highlight of my week.

148

Step Two: Coming to Believe

The regular Mass was a jarring contrast to the home church services. Annoying at best, I hated trying to sit still while men and boys walked around up on stage wearing robes and repeating the same words every week. Where were the women and girls? I also hated sitting, standing, and kneeling on cue, like a dog. I liked the music, but noticed that I felt hollow inside while singing in the big church compared to the warmth I felt during the home service songs. In the big church we sang and performed; in the smaller group we sang and smiled.

I did like one thing about the big Mass, however, listening to a singer in the choir. This woman was large, like an opera singer, with velvety black skin, and she often sang solos. Her voice rang clear—the way I imagined an angel would sound. But the way she sang impressed me even more than her lovely voice, and I was always entranced while watching and listening. She stood to the side of the altar, and it was as if she was singing her joy and longing directly into the ear of God in heaven. She seemed so in love when she sang, and that love infused her words and lifted the whole room to heaven too. Her singing was the best thing that ever happened in that sanctuary.

I was baptized at age nine, where I got a new white dress and stood with my sister in front of everybody while the priest said things and put water on my head. My mom and the others acted like it was a big deal, but I didn't feel full of anything special except nervousness. We all went out for brunch afterward, where I was given a gold necklace with a pendant shaped like a dove that I promptly lost. That was around the time I went out to the motorhome to ask Jesus to come into my heart, but nothing happened, At nine years old, I wrote off the whole religion thing off as a big nothing show, but I tried hard to be good in the all the ways I learned in Sunday School.

I do recall one thing I loved about Sundays at St. Mary Magdalen's Parish: the "Coffee-and-Donut Social" that took place after Mass. When the straightjacket of the service was finally removed with a closing song, all the kids would run to the church basement, where scents of hot chocolate and coffee mingled with the buzz of adults settling down at long tables to chatter away.

I lived for raspberry-filled donuts, and always raced downstairs as fast as possible to make sure I got one before they were all gone. With my treat safely on my plate, I'd go get a cup of hot chocolate and conduct my own personal communion: bite of donut, swallow of chocolate. Another bite of donut, another swallow of chocolate. I used to fantasize about that donut-chocolate combo to survive the tedium of Mass, enjoying that sugar rush long after we'd left the church grounds. Sugar was more of a higher power to me than anything else, until sex came along.

Even with Coffee-and-Donut Socials, I eventually grew to hate going to church. The mother of the family that inspired the home church died of cancer, and they never held them again. No one hugged in the main church, and the brief, scripted moments when the priest told us to turn to the stranger next to us and say "Peace be with you" were a pale replacement for the genuine affection I'd come to count on at the home services. My other problem was that I hated how we sat as a family (and stood and kneeled) for over an hour focused on a so-called

God, but not one person—not a priest nor a deacon nor God
Himself—ever addressed what was happening to me.

Agitated, I slammed my journal shut. Despite my conviction
to face my past, I could not tolerate thoughts of a God who could
allow me to be sexually abused, nor a church or so-called family who
hadn't even noticed.

A couple of days later I called Diego and told him I was stuck on
my Second Step and couldn't make myself write anymore.

"Be creative then," he said. "Find another way that works for you
to explore what a *caring* God might mean in your life. Throw out
everything from your past that doesn't work. You're an adult, so you
decide, not your parents or the church. And read the AA Big Book I
gave you, the chapter called "Bill's Story.""

When I did, I was struck by the story of Bill W., the founder of
AA, especially when his friend said to him, *"Why don't you choose
your own conception of God?"* I felt confused; how could a person,
not a priest or the pope, define what God was? That seemed wrong,
bad, dangerous—a sin.

Suddenly I recalled another sin I learned about as a child, the sin
of masturbation. I hadn't been to Mass since college, but I realized
that the teachings about the evils of touching myself remained alive
and well in my head, planted there by a booklet I found as a child on
our living room coffee table. Curious again, I returned to my journal
writing.

> The booklet appeared one day not long after we'd started
> going to Mass, a thin volume with a pale yellow cover. I read
> it like I read almost everything else I could get my hands on.
> Fortunately for me, dad read constantly, and shared all his

---

*Alcoholics Anonymous. Alcoholics Anonymous. 4th ed. (New York: A.A. World
Services, 2001), 12.

paperbacks about the fantasy worlds of Xanth and warrior sci-fi epics. I loved losing myself for as long as it took to get from cover to cover, searching hungrily for the next book as soon as I closed the last one. I avoided mom's books, however, scared by their ominous covers of knives and women's dark silhouettes hinting of the serial killer themes she preferred.

The new booklet, printed by a Catholic press, made it clear in black and white that masturbation was a sin. Back then I didn't know what a sin really meant, but I knew it was wrong and bad, so I concluded that all masturbation was wrong and bad. That message took hold and informed my view from that point forward; even though I tried to disregard it over the years, the shame it evoked never quite went away. But is masturbation really wrong? Is it a sin?

As I pondered the lessons of my upbringing and sex, I began to grasp the origins of some of my associations between shame and sex: sexual abuse in various forms too overwhelming for a child to make sense of, and my family and the church's blindness to it; Grandpa Westby's abuse of my sister; and then the booklet proclaiming the sin of masturbation. The denouncement of self-pleasuring became my instant authority back then, because it was the only thing I'd ever read about it, and no one else told me differently. In the absence of positive sex education, it was all I had, and nothing I read after that could fully overturn it.

Hmm…if I'm supposed to be figuring out my own definition of God, I'm not sure I want one who condemns what seems like a natural desire for pleasure. Why give me the desire in the first place, and then curse me for expressing it? What kind of God is that?

I decided I didn't even like the word *God*, but I did like the word *spirit*. It reminded me of the Holy Spirit from church, which I always liked better than God. To me, the Holy Spirit was associated with the white dove, a symbol of ethereal love, as opposed to God, whom I imagined as a mean, judgmental old man. The Holy Spirit struck me as feminine, and more accessible and inclusive than a masculine godhead. I decided I could try that as my higher power, if I dropped the word Holy, which I associated with Mass and the isolation I'd felt there.

Then it occurred to me to make a collage of pictures that represented spirit in my life. I cut a panel from a large cardboard box and glued pictures onto it: one of my sister smiling at me in front of a piece of cake, celebrating my birthday back in college; a cross; beautiful nature scenes; and a photo of a small desk, where I could study and write. I attached the pamphlet about sexual sobriety that explained how to determine healthy boundaries. *Instead of saying sex is bad, recovery teaches me to decide for myself, with help. That's the kind of spirit I want!*

Next, I glued a feather on my collage to represent freedom and the fragility of life. I taped up some pictures of me as a child, when I felt so much more innocent. Then I added a picture of no-longer-so-innocent me, taken when I was putting on heavy makeup right before going out to a club, my platinum blonde hair the color that provoked the most attention. I glued on another picture taken when I was sixteen, staring dead center at the camera, seductively. I stepped back and regarded the now-colorful mosaic.

It's not quite finished…wait…I know what it needs!

I taped a delicate dried blue flower to the board over the long blonde hair in my teenage picture, as if I were her mother tenderly tucking a pretty flower behind her ear. The last thing I attached to the collage was a recent photo of me Jason had taken, with my hair chopped short and back to its natural color. In the picture my hair was starting to grow out a bit, and I was wearing a tied-dyed shirt

I'd colored myself, blocky and unrevealing, with a peace sign on it. I had a camera grin on my face that revealed some sweetness, without seduction, and my hair was soft, without gel or spray.

There. All parts of me are included in my version of spirituality. I'm done.

Later that week I arrived at the sky blue Tudor home that Troy, my sponsor's long-time partner, kept surrounded with a meticulously tended garden. Diego greeted me at the door with a full-body bear hug. For a second I was confused—*is this sexual?* I felt some tingling of arousal as he let me go and said, "Come on in, bring your collage," and then turned to walk down the hallway. Pausing for a second, I decided the energy wasn't coming from him. I shook it off and followed.

Perched on a couch in his sitting room, I listened to Diego bustling around in the kitchen, his partner upstairs. Once we were settled and sipping our tea, I blurted out a question I'd only dared wonder before. "Why are you taking all this time to help me? You barely know me."

"Because I need to," he replied, his handsome mouth curling in a wry smile. "Helping you helps me, too."

Wisps of steam rose from my cup as I read him the rest of my writing and tried to explain what the images on my collage meant. He listened and nodded, and when I finished, Diego told me I'd now graduated to Step Three.

TWENTY

Step Three: A God of My Understanding

DIEGO'S HOMEWORK FOR THE NEXT STEP was to say a prayer every day for three months. He showed me a prayer that his sponsor had given him, but I found its language jarring; too much like church.

"This step is about getting in sync with a *caring* God of *your* understanding, so why don't you rewrite it with words that work for you?" After several attempts, I settled on something I could live with.

> Spirit,
> I offer myself to your gentle care and guidance today.
> Comfort me if I am hurting
> and relieve me of that which separates us.
> Show me how my struggles
> can help me bear loving witness to others.
> Help me be fully present to my body
> open to your truth within and without.
> Blessed be.

Diego also encouraged me to pray for help for anything I needed, whenever I needed it. The idea, he explained, was for me to explore how a loving spirit might be present in my life to help me—when I asked—to make better decisions.

Writing in my journal continued to reveal deep spiritual disconnection and rage at the idea of God, no matter what I called it. But along with the anger, I started to see deep pain reflected as well. I felt forgotten and neglected by God. *Is it possible to have a codependent relationship with God, where you do all the work in the relationship, and God seems to do nothing? It's not as if I'd never looked for God before.*

I returned to writing about past experiences of religion and spirituality. Soon, a series of forgotten memories emerged, of a time in college when my boyfriend Matt suggested we take a road trip to visit his favorite former priest. Father John had moved to a monastery in Oregon, which Matt had visited before, and he said he could arrange a quiet weekend getaway for us there.

◇ ◇ ◇

It was spring break of my junior year, and I was twenty-one. Matt and I had finished finals and were ready for something different, so I went along with his odd idea. I stocked his Subaru with fruit pies and Fritos, and we gorged and sang loudly along with Soundgarden and Nirvana during most of the four-hour drive. As the freeway finally gave way to a rural valley road, I felt myself relax as we passed rustic farms with grazing animals behind comfortably worn fences. The land opened to a pastoral green expanse on either side of us, and I spotted the rustic Our Lady of Sienna carved sign as we turned in. Once on the monastery grounds, a large, lush garden and several cream-painted buildings with neat trim came into view.

"That's where the monks live," Matt explained. "And that bigger building is the church."

Still trying to make sense of the existence of a real live monastery and the fact that I would neither be sleeping with Matt nor talking for most of the coming weekend, I felt nervous. Why did I agree to come here to be surrounded by celibate men? *To get out of town.* But I had to admit that I was curious.

I followed as Matt led the way to the guest quarters, where we were welcomed by a bald man in a thick cream robe with a darkish hooded covering that I learned was called a scapular. He was friendly as he reviewed the suggested structure for retreatants, as we were now called: silent breakfasts, Mass five times per day, hours the meditation house was available, library hours for reading, quiet times, and work hours. Work was optional, but encouraged, as a way to contribute to the community. I didn't volunteer.

We were shown to our quarters in separate buildings, mine a closet-sized room, called a "cell," with a single bed, a smallish desk, and a shared bathroom down the hall. *Aptly named*, I thought, staring at the plain wooden cross above the bed as I unpacked. Then it was time to meet Father John.

Kind eyes was my first thought when I saw him, appraising his medium length thinning brown hair, and eyes that twinkled with merriment as he greeted Matt warmly and was introduced to me. He was dressed identically to the man who had registered us.

Bizarre...like Halloween.

Father John led us on a walking tour around part of the property, which included over a thousand acres of mostly pristine woodlands owned by the monks. He told us the story of how he felt called by God, what he referred to as his vocation, to leave his position as the priest at Matt's Seattle parish and move to the monastery. Though I listened politely, I considered his life a tragedy—losing the pleasures of civilization, stuck going to Mass five times a day, speaking little, and never, ever again having someone special to curl up with. His happy tone confused me, because it seemed real.

Today I realize that there are as many ways to find serenity as there are humans, and I accept that Father John's genuine joy stemmed from finding his own form of congruence: he was living and relishing the life he wanted to live, even though it was different from the lifestyle I wanted for myself. But back then, the visit didn't make much of an impression on me, other than boredom, and I couldn't figure out why anyone would live that way on purpose. So I was surprised when four years later, after Matt and I had broken up, I felt an undeniable urge to visit Father John by myself. I must have decided I needed a change of scenery, a departure from my then full-time job as a social worker in a busy nursing home. Somehow, though I'd ended that first visit with Matt to the monastery as perplexed as I arrived, I later grew to consider the tidy buildings, carved out of the modern world, as safe places.

I'd written letters to Father John periodically over the years after that weekend, receiving nice cards occasionally from him in return, always with religious pictures on the front. He wrote in neat script, asking me how my relationship with God was coming along, and I always struggled to answer him. How could I explain in words how lost I felt, or how far I'd strayed from the Catholic teaching of celibacy until marriage? I was twenty-five-years old by then, my therapy wasn't helping, and my porn use was getting out of control. *Maybe a visit to the monastery can help me figure out why. And make me stop.*

◇ ◇ ◇

Leaving the highway on the exit toward the monastery, my eyes were drawn to a superstore's blazing neon sign: Everything Adult. An electric marquee peddled adult books, magazines, a peep show, and videos. I was driving a Toyota Tercel, which I'd bought a few years earlier, trading in my beloved red convertible Spider after one too many side-of-the-road distress calls. My little Tercel, while boring, made me feel responsible and grown up. I'm sure that Spider would have turned into the superstore, responding to the overwhelming longing that welled up in me to enter that trap.

I'd booked myself into a cheap local motel near the monastery in order to arrive in time for breakfast the next day, but suddenly imagined myself staying up all night roaming the adult store until I could find some company. Steel grip on the wheel, I made it alone to the dingy motel and watched cable reruns of a racy, late-night sex-crime show called *Silk Stalkings* until I finally fell asleep.

Arriving at the monastery early the next morning, I struggled to adjust. Images from the TV show had provided clandestine comfort, edging out the disquiet of my other urges. I suddenly regretted making the trip, and I considered leaving. What I didn't anticipate were two peculiar experiences on Sunday, the final day of my retreat, that would have a lasting impact.

As I sat in Mass listening to the sermon, I heard a priest refer to women as lesser than men and sinful by nature. A slow burn ignited in my stomach. *How dare he insult all of womankind, the celibate asshole! What the hell does he know about women? I was furious, and wanted revenge.*

After the ceremony ended, I followed most of the other retreatants to the meditation room, as was the custom, and settled in the back. Soon the monks filed quietly into the room, in front of us, and everyone knelt on wooden prayer benches facing a giant window that revealed the massive, motionless trunks of two towering cedar trees.

The view and sense of quiet reverence might have inspired awe, but I was distracted by the fire in my stomach, now boiling to white-hot rage. The priest who'd proclaimed his judgment on women wasn't there, so I picked a random monk sitting in front of me, and my wrathful gaze bore into his back. Then my rage shifted into sexual fixation and a strange, absorbing arousal, as if I might punish him by drawing out his life force and feeding on it. But this time, instead of feeling a connection to the sexual high that I usually received from such focus, the energy was somehow blocked. It bounced off an invisible shield around his body and boomeranged back at me, somehow transmuted into my own shame and despair. I abruptly fled the meditation and ran back to my room, crying so loudly that another retreatant knocked on my door to see if I was all right. I lied and she left me alone, but the tears would not stop. After several miserable hours, I finally fell asleep.

Later that day, on a scheduled hike with Father John, he took in my puffy eyes, his expression asking what was wrong. Ashamed, I didn't want to look at him, but forced myself to. His light brown eyes shone almost translucently in the sunlight. All that silence, I realized, left space for other kinds of communication—unsaid transmissions that were faster, and more heart-felt, than speech. I tried to find words to answer his concerned gaze.

"I've searched for God," I said wearily, my tears starting to flow again. "I've tried, I've looked, I've been to Mass and explored other kinds of worship, many times, but I can never connect. No matter what I do, it all comes to nothing."

"Oh Staci," he answered as he walked beside me in the woods. "Have you ever considered that your longing for God, your searching, is actually God's searching for you? That the longing itself comes *from* God, and it's *for you*?" Though not touching me physically, the tenderness of his words enfolded me like arms. Again I sobbed, doubling over in pain and confusion on the trail, as the trees and Father John stood still beside me, patiently waiting.

◊ ◊ ◊

Back at my Third Step writing, I wondered if it could be possible that God really had been there for me the whole time, searching, waiting for me, like Father John had said. *If so, how can I let myself be found?* An answer came quickly, from an unfamiliar part of my mind. *I have to start telling the truth.*

During my next meeting with Diego to read him my writing, I confessed that my attraction to the brown-eyed man, which I'd disclosed a while back, had not quite resolved as much as I'd led him to believe. Not meeting his eyes, I admitted I still occasionally felt sidetracked from listening at meetings if he was there, though I insisted that it really had gotten much better.

"Do you fixate on him in meetings?" Diego asked.

"No, not really."

"Does he notice you? Is he looking back?"

"I don't know," I said, looking away. Diego stared at me silently until I looked directly at him, and then the truth flooded from me, in spite of myself.

"Yes, I look at him. I try not to, but I can't help it! His voice gets me; he's so hot, his eyes! I love his curly hair, and how he seems so tortured, but yet he's trying so hard to recover! He looks at me too!" I felt panicked; my fixation was making life bearable these days, and I was sure Diego would try to take it away.

"Now you know what an intrigue is Staci. This is an intrigue, and you're in relapse, according to your own sobriety definition. You're not going to be sober until you can stop it."

"I've tried!" I complained. "I've tried everything you taught me. I don't look at his eyes, but I still feel him wherever he is. I try to block my thoughts by picturing a stop sign, but I don't really want to, so I can't. I haven't followed him outside after the meeting again, I don't wear anything sexy, and I don't sit by him, but it's impossible for me to control my thoughts!"

He waited for me to finish, my petulant "it's not FAIR!" ringing unsaid in the air between us.

"There is a saying in recovery, 'Are you willing to go to any lengths?' and it applies here," he explained. "You've tried to stop, and you get credit for trying. This one is tough for you, I get it. That's powerlessness. You can't change your reaction to him, so you're going to have to be willing to change something else."

I looked at him suspiciously, reminded of when I was six years old and my sister held out a glass of yellow liquid, telling me it was apple juice, and that I should drink it. I knew this wasn't going to taste good.

"My suggestion to you is that you stop going to all meetings where you might see him. You have other friends, and you're calling people more now. I think it's time for you to branch out and find another home group where you're not so tempted."

"I'll think about it," I said sullenly, intending the opposite.

"Good. Think about what you would need to do in order to be free of your intrigue with this man, who you know is married with a baby, and who you admitted you think might be violent. Pray for guidance from your spirit."

I didn't want to pray for guidance from anyone, but I was still dutifully saying my Third Step prayer every morning, so I added a begrudging request for help with my obsession. Nothing happened, no lightning or thunder, and I went right on with my intrigue—my secret thoughts and smoldering gazes—with the brown-eyed man whenever I saw him.

Not long after that, toward the end of a meeting when announcements were made, a gay man I didn't know said that he was planning to start a new group on a different night. He was looking for help, and suddenly I knew, in the pit of my stomach, that I was the right person to help him. Without needing to think any further, I approached him and volunteered. He was grateful, took my number, and agreed to call me to make plans. I called Diego as soon as I arrived home, excited to be part of a new project.

"I wonder," he said, "if this is an answered prayer?"

"What do you mean?"

"What if you help start this new meeting, and leave behind the other one? Do you think it might help with your intrigue?"

I didn't like the possibility, but looking back now I know that's exactly what happened. Since I agreed to help start the meeting, and since my new friend and I told everyone we were starting it together, everyone knew I'd be there. Those who chose to join the new meeting were men who felt comfortable around me, and those who didn't simply didn't show up. The brown-eyed man never came to the new meeting, and I stopped going to the one he attended, ending our contact, and thus our intrigue. Without the electric jolt of seeing him regularly, thoughts of him ebbed and ultimately trailed away.

I gradually realized that going to newcomer meetings meant I was constantly surrounded by men who were at their most desperate, like I was when I first arrived. I figured out that other meetings had a higher ratio of sober men who were living the principles of recovery: honesty, openness, and not reducing themselves or others to sexual objects. After leaving the newcomer meeting to start a different one, my recovery circle became much safer. I began to give back for the first time, called "giving service" in the 12-Step lexicon, by helping to set up chairs and reading the opening welcome. This change ushered in my first full year of sexual sobriety. Which brought with it a series of new challenges, now that I had sealed off my latest escape hatch, intrigue.

- TWENTY-ONE -

Lead with Your Vulnerability

SPENDING SO MUCH TIME LISTENING to longtime members talk in meetings, I began to understand that I was ignorant, at a level I'd not imagined before, about the intelligence present in this new society. I decided I needed to smarten up.

In college, I took a psychology class called Intelligence in which I learned about many forms of intellect beyond a high IQ or scholastic performance. But at five months sober, I realized that the savvy in this new culture called "recovery" still eluded me. Certainly it involved what author Daniel Goleman calls emotional intelligence and social intelligence, but there was something more mixed in, something important. This intelligence was present in the people who had been coming to meetings and doing the self-reflection exercises of the Twelve Steps and other tools for many years. These old-timers had something that the rest of us didn't, and I struggled to comprehend what it was. Wisdom? Peace? They seemed to have a deeply personal experience with some kind of inner inspiration. I started to think of the special quality they had as "inspired intelligence" or "mystical intelligence." Their serenity was not a theory, it was a fact, and I could feel it when I was near them. I could tell when I talked with them, by what they said and how they said it. And I knew I didn't have it. No newcomer did.

It was especially powerful at one meeting when a new guy showed up who was in town on vacation with his family. He shared that he'd been sexually sober for twenty-two years, his voice calm and compassionate. After the meeting, several of us gathered around him as

164

if he were a visiting sage from an exotic land. Without even knowing him, I trusted him. Self-consciously, I asked him a question.

"How do you know what to share at meetings? I always feel stupid, like I'm saying the wrong thing."

His eyes turned to me. They were dark yet soft. He had a medium-length black mullet and features that revealed a Native American heritage.

"What I do has worked for me for a long time. My sponsor suggested it when I was in my first couple of years of recovery, like you are. He said, 'Lead with your vulnerability.' " I didn't know what that meant, but he continued. "Focus on your heart. Find something trembling there, and try to say it. Say the thing you are afraid to say. Your heart won't steer you wrong."

The next week he was gone, but I decided to try his strategy. I focused my mind on my heart area, and felt nothing. I breathed and held my attention there, like in meditation, and after a while I was pleasantly surprised to notice the sensation of a faint, steady beat. As I kept this focus while listening, I felt a little flutter in my chest. All at once, I knew what I had to say, and I waited for a pause in the sharing.

"Hi, I'm Staci, and I'm a sex addict."

"Hi Staci!" everyone answered, in unison.

"In my addiction, I used to look for horrible stuff—degrading, abusive images—and I found them. I saw terrible things, and it's like they're permanently burned behind my eyes. I've been unfaithful, dishonest, and selfish with almost every boyfriend I've ever had, and I feel like a monster. I don't know why I did all that, but I did, and I'm so glad I stopped. I've been sober for almost six months now."

After the requisite "Thanks, Staci" when I finished, I didn't hear anything anyone else said for the rest of the meeting. My heart was racing and my stomach felt tight with regret for speaking up. But after it was over, a man approached me. I'd never talked with him before, but I'd definitely noticed him. He looked like an ad for the all-American male, as if he'd walked out of a J.Crew catalog.

"Thank you for your honesty," he said, his slate blue eyes fixed on my face. "I can't believe you said that. I never told anyone the specifics, but I've been doing it too." He took a breath.

"I've been looking at torture porn, and it's getting worse all the time. I need to stop, but I can't. It's killing me. What if my wife finds out? We have three kids!" He wrung his hands. "I'm gonna tell my sponsor. I figure if a woman can admit it, so can I." I nodded, well aware of how compelling the violent porn could be. I felt relieved and heartened by his admission.

Encouraged by the connection and my increasing days without acting out sexually, I was hungry for more information about what long-term sobriety might look like. I needed something to do besides pray and meditate; I wanted something I could put my hands on, and my head around. Something to help me burn off the ever-present fog and smoke of obsession about sex still crowding my mind.

Listening even more intently at meetings, I noticed one recovery author's name kept coming up: Patrick Carnes. His books *Out of the Shadows, Sexual Anorexia*, and *The Betrayal Bond* were routinely referred to as sources of inspiration, even though they were not officially part of the 12-Step literature. I found them all and began to read, engrossed. It reminded me of my college tutorial in shamanism, only this time the information was less esoteric and more practical: detailed blueprints that both defined sex addiction *and* offered solutions.

This is the most valuable form of intelligence in the world, I decided. Little did I know that within five years I'd be sober and sitting in front of Patrick Carnes himself, getting trained to become a Certified Sex Addiction Therapist.

- TWENTY-TWO -

Another Round to Sex (and Love) Addiction

DESPITE ALL MY READING, daily prayers, and attempts at staying in tune with my spirit, the antagonism between Jason and me continued unabated. I called Diego to demand why, at more than nine months sexually sober, I was almost always either sleeping or feeling really, really mad.

"It's called withdrawal. Don't worry, you're still on track," he said. "You've had a lifetime of stuffing your feelings, and they're coming up now that you're not acting them out. Keep going to meetings, keep talking about it, don't hurt yourself, and keep saying your daily prayer. Pick up the phone when you're mad, call for support, and talk about it. You need to get to work writing down your resentments and fears for Step Four. And most of all, stay sober, or you'll have to start all over again."

I put off the writing, but tried to follow his advice and reach out to my gay friends whenever I was mad. Usually the anger came on so fast and furious that I'd be past the point of caring, let alone calling. The few times I reached someone, it was helpful, but the rage started coming more quickly than I could handle. I still thought about killing myself, but remained inspired by Eckhart Tolle's story of triumph through presence in *The Power of Now*. I was resolved to stay alive and face my life, no matter what.

One day, after I'd vented yet again in a meeting, a man approached me and suggested I read a book called *Healing the Shame That Binds You*.

"When I went through withdrawal," he explained, "I felt full of anger too. But under it was a lot of shame. The physical withdrawal from compulsive sex goes faster, like a few weeks, but emotional withdrawal takes a lot longer, like eighteen months or so. Or at least it did for me."

Looking back, the eighteen-month time frame makes sense. In some ways, starting recovery was a kind of rebirth, and developmentally I felt like a toddler fast approaching the terrible twos. I bought the book and settled down on the mobile home couch to read, but halfway through the first chapter, I threw it as hard as I could across the room.

I can't do this. Eighteen months? I can't. I'll never make it. My thoughts started racing, the familiar tirade of self-hate beginning again. I tried to focus on something more positive, suddenly remembering what Jason once called this kind of thinking: a shame spiral.

"It's when you start thinking these horrible thoughts and you can't stop, each one bringing another until you are stuck at the bottom of a downward spiral and you can't get out," Jason had explained, sharing the gem he'd learned from a former therapist. "If you start one of those you gotta stop it, I mean, do anything you can to get out of it, like taking a walk or calling someone or jumping up and down, whatever. Otherwise you get stuck in despair and it sucks, big time. It can kill you."

Since attempting daily meditation, my focus had improved a little, and I became better at pulling myself out of shame spirals when they hit. But this time, with fiery rage flooding my body again, I couldn't focus. I stared at my bare arms, suddenly visualizing thin razor tracks oozing blood down them. Though I hadn't cut or even used pin pricks for a few years, the idea suddenly seemed attractive. My stomach contracted with fear.

No, no, no, some part of my mind begged me. *Don't cut.*

Then another image flashed in my mind, the face of Sally Field, with ruddy cheeks and unwavering eyes staring at me under blunt brown bangs. A few days earlier, while wandering the store with Jason looking for a diversion, I'd seen her on the cover of a video box. She was holding a girl in her arms, and the movie title in bold read *Not Without My Daughter*. The movie was about a mother trying to escape an oppressive country, but who wouldn't leave without her daughter. The storyline had stuck with me for some reason. All at once I knew why.

I longed for a mom like that, someone to protect me. And even though I'd left home years ago, I still needed help escaping a violent place: my own mind, my obsessions, and the past abuse that still had me in its web, unwilling to let go. A new determination arose.

I'm the one who has to become that mother, for myself. I have to stop sacrificing my "daughter"—my body—to escape and numb out other kinds of pain. I decided that instead of referring to myself as a sex addict, I would expand my self-definition. I would think of myself as a mother with a wounded, sexually addicted teenage daughter inside who needed a parent as strong as she was. *This wounded teenage girl is enraged, and I will become her safe mom and not let her act it out. Instead, I'll find out why she's so mad.* But as hard as I tried to think my way out of it, the destructive urge was too strong and I knew I couldn't hold out much longer without help.

I needed to find another therapist I could trust, no matter how much I abhorred the idea. My finances were in shambles, as I still wasn't working and was now charging all my expenses on credit cards. Searching for sliding-scale options, I made an appointment at a nearby community mental health center with a mental health intern. I told her everything as truthfully as I could, and at the end of the assessment she gave me a brand new diagnosis: borderline personality disorder. Later that day I complained to Jason, as I did often.

"I hate the therapist I saw, she was only a student in training. What the hell does she know? I'm not borderline, and I won't go back to see her. She wore a tight jean skirt and a little black top—she's probably a sex addict herself! I hate my life. God, do you think I'm borderline? *She* probably is. I think my last therapist, Margaret, was. *She* was the one who was so reactive, not me." And on and on I went.

"Go see Judith, Staci," Jason replied, advice he'd given me before.

"I'm sick of therapists! None of them can help."

"She's not a therapist. She's a *bodyworker*. She works miracles."

Jason loved bodywork. Neither of us had health insurance, and massage wasn't usually covered anyway, but Jason had tried acupuncture, acupressure, and other types of bodywork whenever he could afford it, and Judith—who practiced something called craniosacral therapy—was his all-time favorite.

Without a better idea, I decided to try it, and took out the last possible advance on my credit card to cover the cost. *I have to try trusting someone.*

Judith practiced in an upscale Seattle office with a waterfall sculpted in the landscaped entryway. I paused before going inside, watching silvery liquid rush over the smooth, flat river rocks and gather in a rippling pool. *Spirit,* I prayed, *please help this work.*

Judith was a lithe woman in her sixties, with gray hair pinned up in a bun and a direct gaze.

"Craniosacral therapy," she explained, "is a subtle, yet powerful, form of healing that involves gentle touch. Keep your clothes on, because I won't be performing muscular massage. The healing comes at a deeper level, the level of vital energy."

"Great," I said, trying to keep the skepticism out of my voice. "Nothing else has worked, and I'm going out of my mind. It's not just my neck, which hurts a lot, but it's my life. I'm stuck, nothing is working, I'm pretty much broke, and I hate everything." *Most of all me.*

She wasn't perturbed by my admissions. "Get on the table, face up," she instructed.

Her touch seemed unremarkable. She lightly held the upper part of the back of my neck, and I didn't feel any great healing.

She's very calm though, I thought, peeking at her quickly before shutting my eyes again. But what happened next completely changed the direction of my recovery. The revelation didn't come from Judith, but from me. As I lay there with her hands on the back of my neck, I relaxed and drifted off to sleep. The next thing I knew, I woke up with a start, exclaiming, "Oh God, I know why I'm so mad. It's the abuse. It was way worse than I thought!" My body heaved a big sigh of relief at the words, ending with a little shudder in my neck, like a twitch or mini-seizure of release. Judith gazed down at me on the table, not moving her hands from my neck.

"Sexual abuse," I said again, incredulous. "By the guy with black hair. I'm getting more images of what he did to me, and it wasn't just once, it was over and over. But I still don't know who he was!"

"Okay," she said, as calmly as when she'd explained what cranio-sacral meant. "Let's finish the session, and then I have a referral for you."

My mind reeled with confusion. *If I was sexually abused by someone, how could I not know who? How could no one in my family know anything about it?* And yet, despite the surprise of my outburst, my words rang true inside. It was as if Judith's touch helped my brain download something so fundamental to my existence that ignoring it now would be like deciding not to breathe. *But what do I do about it?*

At the end of our session, Judith referred me to a therapist named Conrad. She'd had other clients who were abused and remembered it as adults, and seeing a trauma specialist had proven helpful for them. Once home, I called the number and Conrad answered right away, as if he'd been sitting there waiting for me.

"Um, hi. I was given your number by Judith Simpson, because I think I was, ah, sexually abused, but I can't remember who did it." He had an opening, I had just enough of my cash advance left, and within twenty-four hours I was sitting on his couch answering questions about my symptoms.

◊ ◊ ◊

Conrad was a tall, lanky man with gray eyes that revealed an unusual blend of deep calm and intense alertness. I told him about the years I spent in therapy with Margaret and her diagnosis of dysthymia, the hypnosis I tried, my problems with eating and compulsive sex, and my most recent label of borderline personality disorder. He asked about my current safety and symptoms, my family history, and what I remembered about any past abuse. By the end of the session, my whole body was trembling with fear and relief. *Finally! Someone is asking the right questions!*

"What do you think?" I asked nervously.

"I think the diagnosis that fits you best is post-traumatic stress disorder, and your lack of clear narrative memory can be attributed to protective amnesia. Do you know what that is?"

"I studied diagnostics in school, but not in much detail."

"PTSD is defined by a cluster of symptoms in three categories: intrusive thoughts or sensations of past horrors, efforts to avoid those thoughts or feelings, and problems with reactivity, because your nervous system is overloaded by the stress. Given what you've told me, I'd say your PTSD is chronic—you experienced bad things repeatedly, as a way of life, and you adapted to survive. It's common in kids from alcoholic families."

I felt confused—had my relatively normal childhood actually been traumatic? Conrad kept talking.

"One obvious trauma we can start exploring is the harm you experienced from Margaret, your former long-term therapist. That was definitely a betrayal, and you remember it in detail. I find it's better to start with what you remember first, and see if insights about other kinds of abuse come out on their own. I wouldn't recommend any more hypnosis. What's your schedule like?" I explained that I wasn't working, was living off my credit cards, had no health insurance, and that I'd run out of cash advances.

"I don't have a sliding-scale opening at this time," he explained. "But I think you could really benefit from therapy to heal unresolved trauma."

Walking out of Conrad's office, I felt an uneasy optimism. I had a gut sense that he could really help me, and that somehow I needed to find the money to give it a try.

I recalled hearing about another 12-Step program for people with money problems, and went to the library to do some research. I found more info and started attending new meetings for recovery from underearning and unmanageable debt. People I met there supported me in applying for disability income due to my mood swings, and after an arduous application process, it was finally granted. When the checks started coming, I stopped using my credit cards, which were maxed out anyway. I also applied for a state grant for therapy for low-income women, and was elated when I was notified that I was funded to see any licensed therapist I wanted for a year. I immediately called Conrad and set up session two.

Thus began a new chapter of my life and recovery, one that was finally anchored by trauma therapy. I met with Conrad regularly; our sessions were tough, often excruciatingly so. We talked about how painful my therapy with Margaret had been, and I tried to trust

Conrad and not keep any secrets. Each time I risked telling him something shameful, I waited for him to criticize or ridicule me, but he didn't. Eventually, we started to explore my hazy impressions of past sexual abuse. I still couldn't see the face of the dark-haired man, but I realized through some other recollections that he was somehow connected to my extended family.

Weeks stretched into months as we talked through layers of confusion, pain, and grief. After most sessions, it was all I could do to get home and crawl into bed, but gradually I started to feel better. One day I felt well enough to imagine working again, and applied for a few jobs. After nine months on disability, I didn't yet feel strong enough to go back to social work, but I managed to find a clerical position at a small office with simple tasks and few emotional demands. It was difficult to find the discipline to get ready for work every day and to keep showing up, but having something to focus on besides my own pain brought great relief.

◊ ◊ ◊

A few months later, my parents informed me that they were selling their house and wanted to move into their mobile home. Jason and I decided to look for a place together in Seattle, but he still wasn't working much so he couldn't afford half of any move-in costs. Synchronistically, a woman I met insisted I look at her soon-to-be-vacated apartment in Fremont, one of my favorite Seattle neighborhoods. It was too small for two people, but it might work just for me. One sunny spring day, I met her at the building for a tour.

As we stood in front of a wide window, one of several lining the wall of the living room, I looked out on green, leafy trees and watched little birds flit to and fro. The front door opened onto a courtyard with a slate-brick patio, bordered by huge blackberry bushes that

174

were already showing signs of the fruit they would bear later in the summer.

I loved blackberries. I was instantly lost in the memory of picking wild mountain berries as a girl. I recalled the sweet scent of the purplish-black mound in my plastic bowl, and how it took me much longer to fill my bowl than it took my sister to fill hers, because my stained fingers would continually steal berries to my lips. Sweaty, hungry, and laughing, we'd bring our ripe bounty home, where Grandma Sprout would magically transform the blackberries into warm slices of pie with a buttery crust, topped by Grandpa Sprout's favorite, cool vanilla ice cream.

Leaving the cocoon of my memories, I turned from the bushes back to my new friend. She looked at me, and we both knew the place would be mine. But Jason wasn't happy with my decision.

We were sitting across from one another at the trailer when I told him. It led to another round of what had come to be "the fight"—the one we had over and over, the words changing here and there, but always ending with me feeling furious, hurt, and misunderstood.

"I thought you wanted to live together. I can't believe you're thinking of getting a place in Fremont without me!" he protested. "You know I can't afford it."

"I just think the change might be good! My parents are moving back and I have to go somewhere. Didn't you say Tom would let you live in his garage to save money while you grow your painting business? That's not that far."

"That's not the point! The point is, *you're* making this decision. You don't care what *I* want. You always do that, and I'm sick of it!"

And then he changed the rules of our endless circular fighting by asking a question about the unthinkable. "Are you breaking up with me?"

For a split second, the silence offered me the chance to say yes, and to end our misery. Our relationship had become mutually annoying, filled with judgments and dead habits that we shuffled through like zombies, the once-vital aspects randomly dropping off. Like how we no longer went out but stayed home and played video games, because it was cheaper.

"No! No! I'm not breaking up with you," I protested. "I love you, and I want us to be together forever. We can do this! Don't worry—I know we can make it!" Suddenly I knew what to do.

"Jason, will you marry me?"

I had no ring, and no forethought, just the desperate determination to make him feel better so I didn't lose him.

His scowl softened to surprise. "Really?" he asked. "Really, you want to get married?"

"Of course! Of course I do! This is the perfect time! We can announce it at the speaker's meeting on Saturday! Everyone will be so happy for us!" We hugged tightly, but not for long. I needed to find my phone and start letting people know the good news!

I found a plastic gag engagement ring at a magic shop, and flashed its huge "diamond" proudly at the fellowship gathering a few days later as I told everyone that Jason and I were engaged. People expressed happiness for us, and celebrated our announcement with hugs and good cheer. It was a fun evening, unfettered by worries about the future. Diego raised his eyebrows, but didn't say a word. I'd solidly ignored his and others' oft-repeated recovery advice: do not make any major life changes while working the steps, and certainly not before finishing Step Nine. Instead, I used an ill-fated engagement to distract myself from the feelings of withdrawal and grief that threatened to overwhelm me. Score another round to sex (and love) addiction, but fortunately for me, the bout was far from over.

TWENTY-THREE

Resentment and Relapse

I WAS NOW UP TO CALLING two or three recovery friends for support every day, though I didn't talk much about my therapy or the new revelations of sexual abuse. Except for telling Diego, I felt safer keeping my therapy and my 12-Step program in two separate compartments. The fewer people I told, the less real the memories seemed. I was trying to hang on to some semblance of control, and to keep what I was recalling from sending me into a tailspin.

Working again increased my confidence, as did finally getting off disability and slowly crawling out of financial crisis. I continued to stay sober from my bottom-line behaviors—the most destructive parts of my addiction—and my energy returned a little bit each day, like the light lengthening after the seemingly endless dark of a winter solstice. I finally felt ready to return to my step writing—Step Four, another "moral inventory."

"We look at our character defects because they disconnect us from other people and our higher power," Diego explained. I asked him why I had to do another inventory when I'd already finished one with Janine in my codependency program. Couldn't I just use that one?

"It's not a one-shot deal, Staci. Recovery is a lifetime process. Working the steps on different addictions means starting over."

Unlike before, Diego showed me a method for starting Step Four that his sponsor taught him, first used in AA and later applied to sexual recovery. I was to write down everyone I resented, why I was mad at them, and how their actions affected me. It felt good to get my anger out, but the hardest part came after that, when I was supposed to look at each relationship and admit my contribution to the conflict. As I went through my long list of names, it was painful to realize that, over and over, what I blamed on others always seemed connected to something I'd done to them. Continued therapy with Conrad helped me avoid becoming overwhelmed, because looking more closely at the dramatic patterns often reminded me of painful experiences I'd had growing up.

After months of agonized writing, far more detailed than the one I wrote on codependency, I finally finished my second Step Four, and was ready to read it to my sponsor for Step Five.

With sweat trickling down my spine and my stomach churning with anxiety, I read the entire inventory to Diego in a four-hour marathon. He periodically interrupted to point out how I'd caused or contributed even more than I'd thought, particularly regarding my problems with Jason. Diego was sympathetic to my anger, but repeatedly said that what really mattered was what I could learn from looking at my part of the conflicts. "That's the only thing you have the power to change," he explained. "Yourself."

Finally, after what seemed like forever, we were finished. Although I was relieved, I felt like vomiting. Then I realized I already had, verbally, for the previous four hours.

That night I slept heavily, and awakened the next morning with a warm, tingling feeling in my chest. As I wandered into the living room, my eyes were drawn to the pages of paper strewn across the coffee table, filled with the words describing the long list of people, places, and institutions I'd hated.

Something good happened last night. What was it? Why was the "my part" column so important? As I scanned months of work, my eyes landed on the source of my joy. There weren't many instances, but they were marked in the last column that Diego had spent so much time on with me. *Some of the things that happened weren't actually my fault!* I thought back to my conversation with Diego the night before.

"I can't figure out what my part is here," I'd said, "from when I was little." I'd written about my resentment at the faceless man who had sexually molested me.

"That's not your fault. Kids don't have a part in their own neglect and abuse. That's the responsibility of the abuser, and your parents, for not protecting you."

"Wait a minute...I don't have a part?"

"That's right. The only responsibility you have in that pattern is whether or not you act out any abusive behavior now, as an adult. If you keep hurting yourself or others with your sexual compulsions, because you don't work hard on your recovery, then that is your responsibility. You can't blame anyone else for that."

I was too confused and mentally fatigued to make sense of his words at the time, but with the morning sun streaming in through the windows, I read those columns with fresh eyes, puzzling over his explanations.

I was only a child, and not responsible for what other people did to hurt me, even the sexual abuse. And if my dad was controlling or mean, that was also not my fault. But if I am controlling or abusive now, say, with Jason, then it is. If my mom was passive and never stood up for herself or me, that was her fault. I was not worthless just because I felt that way when she didn't protect me. But if I'm passive now and don't stick up for myself, that is my fault, not mom's.

My head started to ache, and I called Diego and left a whiny message. "I don't get it—now I'm supposed to take responsibility for all these awful things other people taught me how to do, but I don't know how!"

He was grinning when he saw me at the meeting that night,

179

undeterred by my annoyance at having to wait all day to hear from him. "Staci," he said in greeting, "welcome to Step Six."

Diego explained that in Step Six, "Were entirely ready to have God remove all these defects of character," the phrase "defects of character" could be translated into "ineffective coping strategies." He said these were usually passed down in families, over generations.

"Working Steps Six and Seven means exploring better ways to get our normal human needs met." He helped me narrow down my list to the ten worst qualities, and we brainstormed more positive ways I could act, like being *assertive* instead of *aggressive*, and being *honest* instead of *deceptive*. Most were the same qualities I had written about with my codependency sponsor, but several were new, and specific to sex. I got stuck on what characteristic I might develop to replace *vain*, so he suggested I try *loving*. As advised, I took out a 4 x 6 card and wrote the positive qualities on one side and my negative "defects" on the other.

I dutifully read both sides of the card every few days, but then would forget about it until Diego reminded me, and I'd get it out again. It was painful to face, but at our weekly meetings I reviewed my journal writing for positive changes I'd written about, and after several months, I started to notice a few. My overall anxiety was lessening, and I really liked my cute new apartment and new job. I was being more assertive without overreacting or using sarcasm, at least sometimes. I even started dressing nicer and adding a touch of makeup and hair styling back into my daily routine. But things with Jason remained strained. I realized that getting engaged hadn't really fixed anything.

When I finally told Jason how I'd recalled being sexually abused, he didn't believe me. Still desperate to keep him, I told myself it was no big deal.

We'll work it out, I reassured myself. *After all, I've had a hard time believing it myself.* I visited him at his friend's garage, an unfinished upper loft where he'd recently moved. Shivering from the lack of heating, we snuggled together under his double sleeping bag. I pretended it was romantic, and that his meager surroundings were part of a bohemian adventure, instead of just sad.

A few months later, I attended a "birthday chip" meeting for sex addicts, disappointed that, unlike my mom's meetings when I was a kid, there was no cake. Apparently a lot of sex addicts also have problems with food, especially sugar.

"Anyone here have one year of sobriety…one year?" a man asked. I stood up and walked over to him at the front of the room, holding out my hand. He smiled, and the twenty men in the circle surrounding us burst into applause. I grinned shyly as I watched him drop a heavy bronze coin into my palm. Jason couldn't make it, but I turned to Diego and was happily enfolded into one of his big bear hugs. I felt his affection, and let it stop there.

Finally, I thought with relief. *I'm getting something right.* That is, until I saw my family.

◇ ◇ ◇

On the day of my relapse, I hadn't seen my family all together in months. Since starting sexual recovery, I'd avoided celebrating holidays with my parents; I was unsure what to tell them about it. The more I explored my past in therapy, the more I was startled by new realizations about how awful my childhood really was. I didn't know how to reconcile what I was learning with the image of the perfect family I'd always pretended I had. But getting my one-year sobriety chip emboldened me, as did the recent joyful reconciliation with my sister. During the years we were estranged, she had finally freed herself from Margaret's overbearing influence, and met and married a wonderful man. It would only be my parents, my sister, her husband,

181

and her in-laws—very low key—so I decided to give Easter dinner a try.

My parents were jovial when they picked me up, admiring my new apartment as I gave them a tour of the small, neatly organized space. To celebrate my housewarming, they offered me a present: a new digital camera. I'd heard about the latest technological advance and found it pretty cool.

As we sat on my sister's expansive back deck and made small talk over tasty hors d'oeuvres, I began to notice a strange hollowness inside. And as the afternoon wore on, a dark agitation took its place. I had a sudden urge to run out, or to violently lift the table edge, scattering the lox, crackers, cream cheese, and pink lemonade all over the deck. I felt confused and alarmed.

What's wrong with me? It wasn't anything anyone was saying or doing—people were friendly, chatting and laughing. Looking back now, I know it's not what *was* said, but what *wasn't*, by me. I was now too aware of the raw pain from my past to cover it up with a happy holiday face and no discussion, without some kind of internal backlash. I tried to smile and fit in, falling back into my coping strategy of false cheer, but I would soon get a painful wake-up call. My reaction after the visit would teach me that ignoring my true feelings to fit in with my family could no longer co-exist with a sexually sober life.

I faked my way through the dinner, but my mind was already flooding with plans for relaxing when I returned home: a date with my newly connected Internet. Thoughts of recovery were gone, as if they'd never existed. It was dusk by the time my parents dropped me off, with warm hugs that might have felt nice if I wasn't so wound up inside. I hid my growing distress from them like I always did as a child.

In the 12-Step culture, this would have been a perfect time to call and tell my sponsor or another supportive person everything that was bothering me, to problem-solve. But I'd left my recovery when my parents arrived at my door, and automatically reverted to the superficiality so well adapted to my childhood conditions. The rules that dominated my home life were the opposite of what I'd learned in 12-Step recovery. Though I'd followed them unquestioningly growing up, I would later learn from addictions expert Claudia Black that these rules—standard in alcoholic families—had words: "Don't talk, don't feel, and don't trust." My still-new recovery way of life wasn't yet strong enough to prevent what happened next.

Once home, I mindlessly fired up my computer and started looking for porn. Troubling thoughts about my family and the past receded as images of adults sexually exploiting each other filled the screen. I watched a parade of increasingly forceful sex, viewing faces contorted with pain, or pleasure, or both. Whatever pain threatened from within was quickly crushed beneath torrents of erotic adrenaline, as I absorbed the power and aggressive control I was viewing as if it were my own.

How anyone might call this feeling powerless is beyond me! I feel all the power of the universe at my fingertips. Me and Netscape, my portal to the stars. My own private web of pleasure.

But after a few hours, which passed like minutes, other thoughts, with accompanying mental pictures, began to intrude into my awareness. They seemed more like memories than fantasies, and I fleetingly recalled that I'd seen images like this before, not just in previous porn binges but in real life, as a kid. They came in flashes: a neighbor boy showing me his dad's hard-core magazines, and another magazine I'd found one day in somebody's closet while spying when no one else was around. Pictures not of sex but of sexual assaults, like these.

Immediately after my wave of arousal hit its familiar crescendo, I was wrenched out of my compulsion, sitting before the glowing screen, shaking. My jaw was clenched, and I felt a dull headache coming on.

I'd never noticed it until now, this rigidity in my mouth and jaw, a place that was typically numb. My stomach also announced itself, a leaden pulse, as I shifted in my office chair. I felt panic approaching, desperate to bury the feelings that my stomach was threatening to reveal to me. Yet I also felt more desire welling up—even as I was horrified, I wanted to start all over, to get high again and make the painful feelings go away.

No! I have to move, I have to get up, get out of this position, get away from this stupid screen full of body parts. I went out to the kitchen, grabbed some ice cream from the freezer, and collapsed onto the living room couch. My mind was racing.

I've done it again, I can't believe it! I'd fallen back down the rabbit hole, back to Internet porn, back to a place I used to need just to get through some days, but hadn't visited for over a year.

But this time, I didn't keep pretending that everything was fine. I went back to my desk, picked up the phone, and called for help. After my third attempt to reach someone for support, one of my dear gay friends answered and I told him exactly what happened. He didn't get mad, and he stayed on the phone, listening. It was bizarre to sit there alone in my apartment, staring at the computer still displaying porn, and talk to him about it.

"I'm sorry honey," Hal said softly.

"It's not your fault, it's mine."

"You're powerless. I still love you."

"I'm such an idiot. I thought I was ready to get an Internet connection again."

"You are not an idiot, stop it. You've been working really hard on this. You've been sober for over a year." A vague chest pain broke through my jumble of arousal and self-pity, and I instantly hated it.

"I don't know what to do. I don't want to stop." He didn't respond, but I could sense him waiting, holding the space. "My parents gave me a digital camera. I want to take pictures of myself."

"You could do that. I wanted to audition for a porn film—God, I wanted that so bad."

This grabbed my interest. "Why didn't you?"

"I was too scared. I wanted to, but I was afraid of what might happen if I did."

"I'm afraid. Once you post pictures, you can never get them back."

"I know."

And that was it. The urge to further self-destruct drained from me, and my recovery brain took over again. I reached over and pressed the off button on my computer. "I need to get to a meeting."

"Go tonight. I'm going. It'll be okay, baby. Bring your new camera."

Waves of humiliation flooded me as I confessed my relapse in the church basement a few hours later, but I was comforted by Hal sitting beside me, my new camera now tucked beneath his chair for safekeeping. He gave me a big hug after the meeting ended, and three men I didn't know approached me, standing in a little half-circle amidst the crowded room. One of them thanked me for my honesty.

"I know how hard it is to humble yourself like that," one man said. "After my relapse I didn't tell anyone for a month, not even my sponsor or my wife. I thought I could forget it ever happened, but not anymore. Not since recovery. Trying to keep that secret was hell." My face was flushed and I didn't say anything, but I nodded; I'd wanted to hide it too.

Then another man said, "You know that looking at porn changes your brain chemistry? It really is a drug, and for addicts, there's nothing like that rush. So take it easy now—you'll be craving it worse than before." His caution brought a memory of cravings, that achy longing I'd first noticed after finding my dad's *Playboy* in his dresser drawer when I was eight years old.

185

"Hey," the third man in front of me said, "are you going to the summer retreat? You should check it out. That could really help you get back on track."

"I'm not sure…" I replied, feeling shy, surprised, and nervously happy about their attention. The men moved on to talk with others, but their words were a comfort in the days and weeks of renewed withdrawal symptoms that followed. And despite my struggle, I didn't go back to looking at porn. Only later would I realize how pivotal this event was to my recovery.

My relapse admission marked the first time not one, but three, straight men approached me after a meeting with heartfelt, encouraging responses to something I'd said. Their attention was not prurient, they were genuinely supportive, and their group welcome was crucial. It gave me the courage to go to my first recovery retreat, which opened up a new phase of connection in the community. My gay friends had been lifesavers in their generosity and love, but, except for a few key moments, the straight men had generally avoided me.

Now I understand the wisdom of their choice to distance themselves. Prior to this disclosure, they recognized me as unsafe, and rightfully so. Even though I was showing up at meetings, had gotten a sponsor and started working on my recovery, I remained ambivalent about giving up my old ways. But by practicing my new character strategy of honesty instead of deceptiveness, I was breaking free from the sexual secrecy I'd learned in my family.

Looking back on my relapse, I now see that what I thought was power was actually powerlessness, and what I thought was triumph over my own pain was actually just another self-assault, one that mirrored what I saw on the computer screen, a reenactment of a story that remained frozen and barely recognized inside. My new fellowship was supporting me for telling the truth and, in doing so, teaching me the difference between humiliation and humility.

TWENTY-FOUR

Drum Circle

THE ANNUAL SEXUAL RECOVERY RETREAT was held in a lush forested retreat center on Puget Sound a few hours outside the city. It was organized by volunteer self-proclaimed sex addicts and their partners, as opposed to therapists or paid facilitators. As I entered the rustic wooden lodge, I was greeted with a welcoming hug by Shirley, the partner of a sex addict, and she merrily oriented me to the weekend program.

I wonder if she knows I'm a sex addict, I thought, chewing the cuticle of my right thumb. But her warmth and enthusiasm were contagious, and I started to feel excited despite my fear.

Drumming for Recovery was a workshop that caught my eye, and soon I was seated in a tree-ringed grove a small hike from the main lodge. The workshop was facilitated by Dave, a man in his sixties with chiseled features, mischievous dark gray eyes, and a salt-and-pepper ponytail. He reminded me of a wizard from an old fantasy novel, though I couldn't tell if he was a good wizard or an evil one—he seemed to possess leanings toward both. As I looked around the circle, I was glad to see another woman there, who confidently introduced herself as a sex addict named Arlene. Blonde and petite, she was holding a massive African djembe drum she had brought from home. I tried not to stare at the colorful tattoo of a snake roping around her right forearm; I didn't know it yet, but Arlene would become my drum buddy and first female sex addict friend.

"We have all heard the drum, from as far back as we can

remember," Dave announced in a low voice, his oration silencing the dozen gathered there. "It was our mother's heartbeat." With that he began to double-tap his drum, sending a low heartbeat rhythm across the grove. "Put your hand on your heart if you want. Feel your own life force there." My hand went to my heart, feeling the vibration along with his tap-tap, tap-tap, tap-tap. He continued to teach about drumming as a tool to connect with your higher power, but I'd stopped listening to his words. I was remembering the experience I'd had in college with a drum circle, wondering why I ever left that group when I'd loved the drumming so much. Was it because I had finished my school paper?

◇ ◇ ◇

In my first year of graduate school in social work, I was given an assignment to conduct an ethnographic interview by visiting a cultural setting completely outside my own experience and writing a paper about it. After a bit of research, I decided my new culture was going to be the local Lesbian Resource Center and my setting would be a gathering called the Goddess Worship Circle. I figured this was as far away from the Catholic Church as I could get.

I showed up one Sunday morning with my journal and pen in hand, posing as an interested woman there for my first time. Wanda, the leader, was a tall, gray-blonde woman in her mid-fifties with a deep voice; she wore a long, flowing rainbow robe that, though unlike anything I'd ever worn, I instantly coveted.

We met in a medium-sized room that Wanda had transformed from a carpeted recreational area to a work of art. She had pushed the furniture to the edge of the room and spread a large, brightly multi-colored quilt on the floor as a canvas for the objects she arranged into an altar in the center in line with the four directions. She sat at north and welcomed me, inviting me to follow my intuition to sit wherever

Drum Circle

I wanted. After a brief look around the circle of women sitting on the floor, I settled near a bouquet of vibrant purple irises in a crimson glass vase—a spot that would be revealed to me as between east and south. I looked around the blanket at Wanda's treasures, figurines of women—various Goddess statues, I supposed—shiny rocks and jeweled objects, feathers, a painted drum. As the ceremony started, I forgot that I was there only to observe and gather data for my paper.

I remember later writing that, despite being on different ends of the religious spectrum, in significant ways the Goddess Worship Circle was similar to the Catholic church, which surprised me. They both had ceremonies with different names, *circle* and *Mass*. Both ceremonies involved groups, had a leader, and used ritual, that is, repetitive actions with agreed-upon spiritual symbolism.

Both groups used candles, incense, music, art, and sculpture to decorate the sacred spaces where they met. Both read aloud from books they believed heralded from a divine source. Catholicism taught of a triune God that was simultaneously described as one: the Father, Son, and Holy Ghost; whereas the Goddess Worship Circle was centered around multiple feminine sources of divinity and also spoke of a triune Goddess: Maiden, Mother, Crone. Both might be categorized as polytheistic, particularly if you added the worship of the Virgin Mary, who, for many Catholics, serves as their publicly unspoken personal godhead.

Back in graduate school, I was collecting information, but my participation soon became more than detached observation. From the first prayer invoking the Goddess Artemis into that circle of seven women sitting on the colorful quilt, I felt something meaningful happen, a specialness that exceeded my everyday experience. My paper complete, I decided to go back the following week, this time just for me.

By the third week I had brought my own little pink quartz crystal

189

to add to the floor mosaic, as Wanda invited anyone to bring something special to place on the blanket altar. I loved the songs, like "Now I walk in beauty, beauty is before me, beauty is behind me, above and below me," but my favorite was closing the circle by singing something called "The Rainbow Song" and then holding hands, saying, "Merry meet, and merry part, and merry meet again. May the circle be open, but unbroken!"

Contrasting this to my Catholic upbringing, I preferred the small gathering, participation, and divinity seeped in aspects of the feminine over the large, male-dominated, disconnected experiences of my childhood Masses. But though the Goddess circle seemed lighthearted and playful at first, I soon discovered that what happened there went far beyond a group of women singing merrily on a blanket.

At my sixth circle, the setup was more ornate than ever. Wanda wore a striking, midnight blue robe tied with a silver braided rope belt. The blanket spread out before us was azure blue, and in the center she had a Goddess figure I'd not seen before, surrounded by her seemingly unending variety of crystals, feathers, and other riches. Over the previous weeks, I'd learned that there were more Goddesses than I'd ever imagined; far beyond the smattering of names I recognized from Greek and Roman mythology in school. "Pay attention to the names that stand out for you," Wanda said, "and you will find your own sources of divine connection."

The figure in the center caught my attention because she looked different from the others. She was scary: tall, muscular, and blue, with four arms, an Indian face, and large blue breasts adorned with a necklace thick with chalk white skulls.

"Kali Ma!" Wanda said grandly to the assembly of ten women after the ceremony's opening prayer. "The Goddess of darkest clarity, destruction of confusion, and slayer of impure desire." I stared at the statue, sitting in the west this time so I could see her face. Her tongue, long and red, protruded at me immodestly from her gaping mouth.

"Today we will worship with a guided journey, where you will each travel to the Goddess Kali and ask for a vision significant to you. I will drum and lead you; let your imagination take you to exactly where you need to go." The drumming started, a single steady beat, as we all lay back on the wide blue blanket and closed our eyes. Wanda called out a high battle cry that startled me, and then beckoned to Kali for help on our behalf. "Lead them, Kali Ma, to you, and let them see what you would have them see!"

As the drumbeat droned on, I found myself transported to a clear scene far from the rec room. I was me, but not me, as if in a lucid dream, welcoming a compellingly handsome man to my community through the main gate. He smiled broadly, armor and robes indicating some past century, as two men with swords followed close behind him. He praised me emphatically, and the women I led, for our charity work in the nearby town. I felt warmed by his attention, his voice like a smooth caress to my unseen places. I was drawn to his face, magnetized by his eyes, which were blue like the sea. It seemed I was some kind of abbess, and he was a visiting religious scholar and magistrate of a new wave of settlers camped nearby.

I was taking them on a tour, my women expecting this, silent or nodding as we passed. I showed them almost everything, the well-tended grounds, the wooden structures of worship and community, though I noticed no crosses or other religious symbols. "What about the sacred pool, or the holy flame? Where are they?" he asked eagerly. I frowned.

"Those places are for initiates only," I said sternly, affronted by his request. "No man may trespass and no weapons are allowed."

How had he heard of them? I wondered, for I had been careful to steer them clear of those sections of our land. It was well known that in all other circumstances, men were not allowed, except for servant eunuchs. The woman at my side shuddered slightly, but the man apologized deferentially for his question, calling it an offense and moving quickly to proclaim his gratitude for the tour.

"We do not take such a privilege for granted," he said, gesturing to his men behind him, who nodded.

The scene then switched, as suddenly as the next drumbeat, no stopping it, and I was running, coughing, choking with the smoke that filled the air which moments before had been sweet and tranquil. Women were screaming, their pale blue robes no match for the bodily violations and swords piercing them. I ran to the pool in the hidden grove, a prayer racing through my mind, *Carry me wind, carry me fast!* Yet not fast enough, for there in the water awaited more death, blood, and bodies of women I'd loved and led, petals of our order of the blue rose strewn and stained. Defeated, I collapsed by the pool and wept, lost in helpless pity, until I heard the sound of boots. I raised my head, and through blurry eyes saw the religious scholar, with even more men at his back. Once again, he was smiling at me, but not so deferentially this time.

Wanda's drumbeat ended, and I was back on the blanket, trembling from my core. I went through the motions of the rest of the ceremony, but I left the gathering deeply shaken. I was baffled by how real the simple visualization felt, and the horrible clarity of the death and destruction.

Rape! I was surrounded in that second scene by rape, torture, and murder, and it was all my fault. My thoughts disturbed me and I tried to tell myself it was only a dream. But I never wanted to feel that way again, so despite Wanda's encouragement to return the following week to discuss the meaning of the revelations we'd had, I did not go back. I was glad my initiation with Kali Ma was brief, and quite happy never to see her or the Goddess Worship Circle again. I did not yet know she would not be so easy to shake.

◇ ◇ ◇

Dave's drumbeat quickened now, five in a row, and my focus snapped back to the drum class and the warm pine scent surrounding us. After the workshop finished several of us lingered, including Arlene, Oshin, and Anthony, to talk about how wonderful the drumming was. Led by Arlene, we implored Dave to help us form our own drum circle. He cheerfully agreed, and within a few weeks we began meeting in each other's homes every Saturday to drum, share, and eat a potluck lunch.

That group became a haven for me over the next several years—my charismatic-home-church-Goddess worship-sobriety-hybrid drum circle for recovering sex addicts, where everyone had their own idea of God, or Goddess, and no one cared about the differences. Men and women, gay and straight, all single except for Dave, we drummed and talked and ate together, laughed and played, acquaintances deepening to friendships, learning to relate without sexualizing each other.

There I talked about everything, including my ongoing progress on Steps Six and Seven, the times I fell back into old bad habits, and my efforts to live a more conscious, principled life. My drumming friends taught me how to care for myself, and we encouraged each other to stay sexually sober no matter what. Occasionally, when someone faltered, they weren't judged or criticized, but encouraged to get back on track. For the first time as an adult, I'd found a sacred place of worship.

◇ ◇ ◇

Completing Step Seven, "Humbly asked God to remove our short-comings," was brief but memorable. Diego knelt next to me in his TV room and together we said a formal prayer out loud, a petition to our creator to accept us fully and to gracefully remove every deficit of character that limited our usefulness on the planet. We asked for strength and spiritual guidance, and when it was over I wondered, with a cross between fear and curiosity: *What will become of me now?*

Part Three:
Deep Spirit Dawning

"Not all those who wander are lost."
~ J. R. R. Tolkien

Top: Age 38, hiking near Ross Lake, Washington with my sponsor. Bottom: Age 40, The day my cat PK was put to sleep.

TWENTY-FIVE

Amends and Tears of Light

I'D FINALLY REACHED STEPS EIGHT AND NINE, which Diego explained involved making a list of everyone I'd harmed in my life and "becoming willing" to make amends to them (Step Eight). Step Nine involved actually contacting everyone to apologize or, if I couldn't find them—or doing so would be harmful to them—taking symbolic actions to make things right.

Make your list, check it twice, quit being naughty, and start being nice, I sang in my head mockingly, bravado papering over my terror at the reality of itemizing and facing all those I'd harmed. Still going on faith, I had no idea the total life overhaul that was coming. I didn't know how much pain that hurting others had also caused me, nor how much relief my attempts to repair my mistakes would bring.

Diego said I'd be approaching people directly, to tell them what I did to harm them and to express remorse or, if that wasn't possible, to do "indirect amends" instead. But with all situations, I had to be sure I was treating people better going forward, and that was called "living amends."

The list will never end! Everyone I've ever known will be on it! I was even supposed to include names of people or institutions I'd chronically resented, like the Catholic church, because Diego said it was harmful to hate.

"It's not being angry with someone or having a healthy conflict that's a problem," he explained in our weekly talk, "but the constant fantasies of revenge or hate. You won't tell anyone you've secretly hated them, but you need to work through it and treat them—and yourself—with 'mental respect' now. Does that make sense?" It didn't, but I plugged away anyway, using my computer to create a spreadsheet to list names, or using descriptions when I couldn't recall the name. Some were general, like "Unknown men I've objectified or intrigued with," or "Guy who knocked on the frat room door."

Looking at my list and trying to write down the harm I'd caused evoked so much defensive anger that I was venting in meetings—and in my head—for weeks.

None of my abusers have come to <u>me</u> to apologize, why do I have to clean up <u>their</u> messes? Why should I have to take responsibility for the ravages of my mom's alcoholism? For dad's raging? It isn't <u>my</u> fault I was ignored and abused! That's the only reason I acted this way! <u>They're</u> to blame, not me! No one cares anyway, no one remembers all these stupid things I did, it doesn't matter. What kind of a crazy program is this? Nobody does this—no normal person apologizes to everyone from their past. People will think I'm insane!

My mind droned on and on, minimizing the harm I'd caused, shifting the blame to everyone and everything but me, and leaving my head throbbing. To calm myself down, I tried to visualize a bright red stop sign instead of the thoughts, but it didn't work. I visualized passing clouds and attempted to focus on my breath instead of the turmoil in my head; I used every trick I'd learned for dealing with obsession, without success. No matter what else I was doing, my mind kept circling back to the anger, like a tongue continually pushing against a painfully decayed loose tooth. Finally exhausted, I complained to Diego that I was stalled again. He told me to stop working on my amends list and to go back to Step Four: writing out my resentments.

"Whenever you're stuck on a step," he explained, "it usually means you have more work to do on an earlier one." He also recommended

I read "The Promises" to myself every day to inspire me. *I should know them by heart by now,* I grumbled to myself about the reading from the AA Big Book I heard at almost every meeting.

Anthony was the recovery old-timer who first impressed upon me the wisdom contained in the basic text of Alcoholics Anonymous, and in our sexual recovery meetings he was often the one who volunteered to read aloud one of its most beloved passages, called "The Promises." As I'd gotten to know him better through the drum circle, I realized that I wasn't attracted to Anthony sexually, even though he was solidly handsome. I decided he was like the big brother I wished I'd had. In the meetings I'd grown to love listening to his Brooklyn-accented bass voice read the promises of all the good things that would come true in our lives, if only we had the courage to take action on our list of amends: freedom, happiness, love, amazement, and deep serenity.

I wanted those feelings, but although I was still sober and had finally made some real friends, it seemed like when I did feel something, it was mostly pain, without much amazement. Jason and I still fought often, our arguments bitter and stale, and we still rarely shared sexually, or even cuddled.

Support in 12-Step meetings and therapy had stabilized my mood enough so that I was able to return to work in my field, trading the receptionist job for a social work position at a community mental health center. I quit my own therapy soon after, telling myself that I didn't have the time and couldn't afford it. In truth, I felt weary and wanted a break from the painful process of exploring the past. But soon I began having problems with my new boss and her boss and, as a result, felt mistreated, bruised, and overlooked. Whenever I complained to Diego about it, or about how things with Jason hadn't improved much, he said the same thing.

"Focus on getting your step work done. That will make things much clearer. You need to clean up your side of the street before you worry so much about his."

Frustrated but determined, I wrote out my fresh list of resentments, how they affected me, and looked at my contributions. A common theme was my pattern of staying stuck in feelings of victimization instead of taking action to make things better. *Like making amends.* After reading it all to Diego, I was reluctantly ready to get back to my list of everyone I'd ever hurt.

Sitting in front of my journal, the task remained overwhelming. I tried saying a recovery prayer I'd heard someone talk about at a recent meeting: *Spirit, please help me see my part.*

Eventually, my pen started moving. First I wrote what I recalled about my childhood sexual experiences with the neighbor kids, because even though I wasn't sure if what we'd done was normal or harmful, I felt they should be on my list, just in case. Then I went on to things I'd done when I was older:

> 15 years old: Brianna's parents, for stealing their Jeep, driving it with the emergency brake on without a license, hitting a car, and then lying about it.

> Since about sixteen: Boys and men in general, for using them for sexual attention and more, without regard for their feelings.

> High school: Mr. Johnson, for cheating on chemistry test.

> High school: Man who found the mannequin my friends and I had dressed up and thrown out in the road, after he almost drove over her in the dark; for scaring him while we hid in the woods, laughing at him.

> 18 years old: Tyler, for using him for sex after we broke up and then not talking to him.

20 years old: Woman from the hotel in Paris, for opening her luggage and stealing her makeup.

21 years old: Co-volunteer Reggie at the Crisis Clinic, for cutting off all contact with him after he told me he'd been sexually abused, and never speaking to him again.

21 years old: Kenneth, for flirting with him even though he was married; for having an emotional affair.

Kenneth's wife Samantha, for violating her marriage.

Kenneth's children, for luring their father away from their mother for an emotional affair.

As I kept writing, feelings of self-loathing swept over me. Trying to stay calm, I inhaled so deeply I felt dizzy. Thoughts of killing myself resurfaced, but I remembered what Diego had said about feeling shame when working on Steps Eight and Nine, which brought some measure of comfort.

"Shame will come, and it's okay," he'd said. "It's natural to feel shame when we've hurt others—that's called a conscience; that's what keeps us from being psychopaths. The problem is when you're shameless and act it out, or so full of shame you get frozen, and then don't do what you need to do to make it right. Not dealing with shame is a big part of what contributes to addiction, and relapse. Some people kill themselves trying to escape it, but that doesn't fix anything. When you feel shame, acknowledge it, thank it even, and get right back to work. Finishing your work to make it right is what will get the shame off your back."

My hand was completely numb as I gripped the pen, but like Diego advised, I kept writing. Finally, though I thought it impossible, I was done. I read the whole thing to Diego over many weeks, and his response was practical; he helped me think through how I might begin to make things right for each situation. We divided my responses into three categories: "Money I Stole That I Need to Pay Back," "People I Need to Apologize To," and "Indirect Amends." This latter category was for people I had no idea how to find, or for people we decided might be harmed by a direct apology.

He explained that indirect amends was the category where I should put the kids from my neighborhood. I didn't know where any of them were now, and he said they might not even remember what we'd done.

"Finding them to bring it up to them now could cause everybody more harm than good," he said, "but if you really think you need to, you can make an amends to them, and to yourself, through other means."

I decided to pray regularly for their health and happiness. It felt good to do something positive, instead of feeling awful about it, and soon the sadness and uncertainty that had weighed me down for so long began to slowly shift to quiet acceptance. *We didn't know what we were doing. We were kids.*

To replace the money I'd stolen from people I didn't know or couldn't find, I donated money to various charities. It was difficult, as money was always tight, but Diego helped me set the appropriate dollar amount for each situation, and I saved until I reached it. I sighed with relief each time I sent off a check, as if something truly was being restored.

Then I started contacting the ex-boyfriends on my list, running each action by Diego before I took it. We debated about some of them, like Tyler from high school and Matt from college. I'd heard they were both happily married, and I gratefully agreed with Diego's suggestion to write them a letter and burn it instead of approaching them. We decided that any contact from me might be more disruptive to them and their wives than helpful. For one ex I did find, now living out of state, waiting for his reply was excruciating, even though I hadn't thought about him in years. Yet his return email was generously forgiving, evoking an unexpected flood of tears.

Maybe, I dared to hope, *I'm not so bad after all.*

I did feel better—lighter—after I finished each apology, like when I called a former boss to apologize for stealing from him, and he laughed at my offer to send a check, saying, "Staci Sprout, people steal from me all the time, but you're the first person to ever admit it without getting caught. You keep that money; I've just been paid by your call. You made my day." He was still laughing as he hung up the phone, and I started giggling too, my arms tingling, covered with goose bumps.

Amends to the women I'd betrayed with their partners were harder to make, because the affairs were secret, and I thought confessing would cause more injury. For those, Diego and I decided I would make indirect amends via a proxy apology at the next public speaker's meeting. I'd been asked to share my story at the quarterly gathering of recovering people from all local sexual recovery fellowships, and friends and family members were invited. I was terrified, but agreed to read the formal apology as part of my talk's closing.

The event was held in the same church basement where the newcomer's meeting took place, and the room was packed. The buzz of excitement in the air was palpable as someone called the group to order and everyone took their seats for the opening, a group reading of "The Serenity Prayer." I felt the opposite of serene, but joined in anyway. As I said the words "God grant me...the courage..." I noticed, for the first time, that they truly meant something to me. Tonight the prayer felt like a life preserver I could cling to in my turbulent sea of panic about what I was about to do.

Soon the introductory readings were over and I was standing

alone in front of sixty people—some of them married couples—
reading my story. I spoke of my powerlessness over sex addiction,
my struggles to find help, and ultimately, of finding support and sexual sobriety, to my great relief. Then I reached the part Diego and I
had prepared as my amends to the women:

> "To all the women I have objectified or competed with, or failed
> to see in my sexual addiction, and especially those women I
> violated by objectifying, flirting with, or having an intrigue or
> sexual relations with your partners, I wish to be accountable."

I paused, my eyes hastily scanning the audience, searching for the
reassurance of Diego's olive-skinned face. He was there, watching
me, his dark eyes calm. He gave a tiny nod, and I took a slow breath
inward, gathering my courage to keep going.

> "I believe my actions were wrong and harmful to you, and I ask
> for your forgiveness. You deserved better treatment from me
> and I am sorry. I have worked hard to understand the cause of
> my behavior, so that I will not repeat it."

When I finished I was greeted with applause, but it was drowned
out by the pounding in my head. I was approached by several women
in the audience, who kindly thanked me for what I'd shared. It was
surreal; I'd expected them to curse me and call me horrible names,
like bitch, slut, whore, and worse. The names I called myself in dark
moments, when I thought about how I'd acted. But they didn't. I didn't
feel worthy of their forgiveness, though I smiled and responded as
graciously as I could. When one woman opened her arms to offer
me a hug, I let her, standing stiffly, holding in the urge to weep. I was
afraid that if I started, I would never stop.

"You did well," Diego said quietly, approaching at last when the women had gone. I nodded with a little grin, still keeping my body rigid to hold in the tears as he gave me a hug. Exhausted, I went home and went straight to bed, curling up with the latest installment of Harry Potter and a pint of Cherry Garcia ice cream, until I finally dropped off to sleep.

◊ ◊ ◊

I was getting close to the end of my amends list, having crossed off name after name. I continued to be astonished by people's generosity after I acknowledged my wrongs and asked for their forgiveness. I thought back to making confessions at the Catholic church, and how much easier it had been to tell the priest everything than to face those I'd actually hurt.

This is harder, but it feels even better when it's over. I'd finished my amends actions for almost everyone on my list, at least everyone that I could find. It was now time for the last two: Jason and my family. Diego helped me craft a letter to Jason, and one evening, sitting on opposite couches in the living room of my little apartment, I read it aloud to him:

Dear Jason,

I would like to make an amends to you, would you be willing to hear me? I would like to acknowledge that many times over the course of our relationship I was sexual with you for reasons other than to have a loving connection. I believe this was harmful to you and to our relationship, and I ask your forgiveness. I'm working very hard to make sure this doesn't happen again by exploring the causes in my healing process, examining my intent when I want to share sexually with you, and stopping if I'm not in a loving place. As we've talked about, I invite you to stop sharing sexually with me if you ever sense I am not fully grounded, and if you feel comfortable, tell me directly what you are sensing. I love you.

Staci

By this time I'd learned that whenever I used flirtation and sex in certain ways, it hurt me and others: if I used it to block out pain that needed to be expressed; to cover up shame; to feel better than other people; to feel in control instead of scared; or to try to feel connected while fighting with Jason without doing the hard emotional work to regain trust with him first. But when sexual desire hit, it still felt like my thinking brain completely shut off, and I couldn't always trust my motives.

As I look back on my amends to Jason, I realize I didn't apologize to him for flirting with other men while we were supposed to be exclusive. I also didn't address the emotional harm I caused him over the years. Today, I would add remorse for my chronic criticism, my punishing emotional withdrawal and coldness, and my angry attempts to control him instead of making requests. I'd also add more to my sexual amends, including remorse that I didn't better respect his sexual boundaries; often when he told me no, I was coercive and tried to seduce him anyway. And I wish I could have been strong and assertive enough to know and say what I needed to feel safe with him, even if that meant separating or ending the relationship if he didn't agree. I would eventually learn that maintaining a respectful emotional connection and figuring out when to have sex, for the right reasons, would take far longer than simply stopping my addictive behaviors. But even doing this much of an amends to Jason was transformational, because I'd come far enough to genuinely mean it.

Jason accepted my apology and said thank you, we talked a little longer, and then it was over. *That's it, not such a big deal.* Suddenly my stomach started to feel strange, and I excused myself to lie down in my bedroom. I'd recently learned a meditation technique of focusing into sensations of pain, rather than running from them, and I decided to give it a try with my stomach. The closet doors were big mirrors, and I curled up in a fetal position on my side, turning to face them. *Ohgodohgod I hate this feeling. Here come the tears. This is gonna hurt.*

Suddenly my mind filled with images from when I was a girl and my Sunday school teacher told me about the importance of taking Jesus into my heart. I saw the little nine-year-old me walking out to the motor home in our driveway, settling in front of the full-length mirror, making my request, and nothing happening. Desperate for something to help with the pain that I intuitively knew was coming, I decided to try again. *Jesus*, I prayed, *help me now please. Come into my heart. Help me deal with this. Help me get better. I'm sorry for what I've done.*

Unlike my little girl prayer to Jesus, this time I felt something. A big something. What came in response to that prayer was a flood of energy so enormous, it would take almost a decade to begin to make sense of it.

The mirror before me shimmered, my reflection blurring, replaced somehow in my mind's eye by a visage I recalled from childhood, from a picture my mom brought home after we joined the Catholic church. It was a Caucasian face of Jesus, with full brown hair and a bushy beard, his dark eyes brimming with tears. As I focused on his eyes, I saw the tears dissolve into pure light, its bright beams streaming out toward me. The rays of light surrounded my body, warming me. My own tears came then, erratic sobs I tried to silence at first, like I always did as a child. I didn't want Jason to hear me, but soon I was beyond control, wailing like a baby, my cries bursting forth as if from every cell of my body.

Then I felt an even greater surge of pain inside, as if the light-filled gaze laid bare all my shame in an instant—all the betrayals, treachery, and abuses I'd committed in this and every lifetime, since the beginning of time, flooded me at once. I felt my gut wrenching inside out, yet the light and heat grew even stronger, a balm for the bitter burning. Somehow, the beams cauterized my wounds, easing the pain, and the deeply soothing heat gradually transformed my overpowering grief to shivering relief.

Suddenly the reflection shifted, and I saw an image of my body on a table wrapped mummy-like in a white shroud. Over my heart a sprig of a green, leafy branch was tucked into the bandage, which was sprinkled with tiny white flowers, like baby's breath. The golden-white light poured over my body, washing and purifying it, and I watched the bandages slowly fall away, disappearing one by one, to reveal a fresh face with pink, tear-stained cheeks. I was back in my bedroom, but not the same as I'd been before. Overwhelmed and unable to make sense of the experience, I fell asleep, but sadly, by the next morning it had almost vanished from my mind.

For years, whenever I looked back on the night of my amends to Jason, all I could recall was that I'd given it, felt pain, prayed to Jesus for help, and once again, nothing had happened. I didn't recall the light or the love, only the agony, and I went on feeling abandoned by Jesus like I always had. Only much later would I better understand what had occurred, and find the strength to sustain such profound feelings of divine love. I would ultimately come to accept this vision of a compassionate Christ as the granting of spiritual forgiveness, but it would take me longer to forgive myself. That would only come with more work on the shame I still carried from having been sexually abused.

TWENTY-SIX

Breakup

THOUGH I WAS GLAD to have survived my amends to Jason and the pain that followed, it didn't fix our relationship, so we decided to try couples therapy.

Our first couples therapist was a bear of a man named Garlough in his fifties, with a ruddy face and mid-length straight brown hair. He was recommended by Jason's therapist, a colleague from the same close network of professionals. Garlough's office was a converted basement in his home, with foggy windows shedding indirect light through bushes above.

"We fight a lot." I complained, once we were seated and he asked our reason for seeking counseling.

"And," Jason added from next to me on the couch, "we never have sex."

Although I didn't realize it at the time, my emotional growth from individual therapy and step writing had changed the chemistry of my attraction to Jason. As I dealt directly with resentments through my inventory and with the shame through my amends work, my old pattern was shifting. I used to seek out charming, angry men, and act out with them in ways I regretted. Now, seething resentment beneath the surface was becoming a turnoff, rather than a turn-on. This was wreaking havoc on our compatibility.

Our attempt to fix everything though couples therapy didn't last long, nor go well. It started out okay when Garlough suggested that the reason Jason and I didn't have sex was because we didn't feel safe with each other, but it went downhill after he offered to help us by watching us get started in his office.

"You would start slowly," Garlough said. "I'm not suggesting you actually have sex in here, I'm just saying you begin with simple, nurturing touch, and perhaps a kiss, and I can watch and offer ideas." Jason seemed to feel okay with this idea, but my "not sober" alarm bells started ringing.

"Uh, I don't know about that," I said hesitantly, afraid he would get mad.

"Okay, okay, we don't have to start there," Garlough said hurriedly. "What do you fight about?" I tried to explain that I didn't like how Jason was doing what he called "nurturing exchanges" with a woman, Alicia, in his therapy group, which he described as taking turns lying in each other's arms, listening to each other's heartbeat. It apparently happened regularly in their group, but they'd recently done it at her house, which I found out about after the fact. Garlough didn't seem to understand my anger about this, and soon our time was up.

"Let's give it a try for another session," Jason said later in response to my misgivings. "We can always find someone else if you don't like him after that." Our second session was the following week, but it didn't take place, because Garlough never showed up. The next day Garlough left a message of apology and said we could have the next session for free to make up for it, so back we went to the basement.

"I apologize for my mistake," he said. "And it's okay if you get angry at me." Jason said he was angry, saying it reminded him of the times he felt abandoned by his father growing up.

"Good, good, that makes sense. I'm not your father, but I am sorry. Now, Staci, how about you?"

"What's the use of getting angry?" I asked, trying to hide my annoyance. "We're here, you gave us a free session, let's move on."

"Now, Staci," he countered. "I'm concerned you're stuffing your feelings. It's okay to be angry at someone when they've set up an expectation of something with you and they don't keep their word. That's a form of betrayal."

I thought about his words for a minute. *What if I really do let it out? What's the worst thing that could happen?* "I am angry at you for something," I finally said. Garlough practically rubbed his hands together, waiting.

"I'm angry that you want to watch us touch each other. I think that's creepy, wrong, and that you probably get off by having your clients touch each other in front of you. That's supposed to be private. You got this look on your face when you asked us to do that, and it makes me think you might have a problem with your sexuality, like maybe you're a sex addict. I don't feel safe with you or want to see you for therapy. I'm glad we're not paying for this session."

Garlough's face flushed bright red. He started to reply, but I was already walking across the room to the door and heading up the steps. Jason followed behind me, but protested my rudeness once we were safely in the car. My angry outburst astonished me, but I decided I wasn't sorry. *I've had quite enough of therapists like that. I stayed stuck with Margaret for eight years, and I'll be damned if I'm going to waste a minute on another incompetent!* My anger, now unbound, didn't stop there.

The next day, I was lying on the couch reading a book titled *Goddesses in Everywoman* by Jean Shinoda Bolen, and reached a chapter about the Goddess Hera, the wife of ever-philandering Zeus. As I read a passage about how Hera was rejected and humiliated by her husband, rage started to flood me again. My face became hot, and I could hear my pulse pounding in my ears. I recalled a recent fight with Jason about Alicia and their nurturing exchanges. This time, as our familiar bickering started to escalate, he paused, closed

212

his eyes, and took a slow, deep breath. He was working on anger management in his group.

"Staci," he said, his hazel eyes searching mine. "I only want one thing from you. It's all I ask. I want you to stop asking me to change, to be different than I am. Codependents always want other people to change, and it's driving me crazy."

I had no answer for him then, but now started thinking about it. *Can I do that? Can I accept him, and quit complaining? How? I don't care what he or anyone says—what he's doing with Alicia doesn't work for me, it's too close. It makes me feel like shit. Even if they're not having sex, it still feels like he's cheating. Can I let that go? Is that recovery?*

I thought of Hera's long suffering at Zeus' infidelities and started to cough. As I stood up to get a glass of water, the coughing turned to croaking noises, wrenching from my throat. Pain cascaded over my face and down my spine, pooling in my gut with such stabbing intensity that I dropped to my knees, crouching on all fours, like an animal. The croaks turned to dry heaves until I thought I might vomit, but nothing came out except, finally, more tears. I lay on the floor for a long time, weeping bitterly, the book and my journal forgotten on the couch.

We saw our second couples therapist a few weeks later, another referral from Jason's therapist. I didn't know then that the whole therapy network was infused with an unshakable belief that as long as two adult clients agreed upon the nurturing exchange, and the therapist was aware of it, it was okay. Partners or spouses who complained were seen as resistant to therapy, and their concerns were discounted. Since that was the primary thing Jason and I fought about, I didn't realize that seeking help from yet another therapist in the same group was doomed to failure.

Not finding validation from the new couples therapist, I quit again after a few sessions, hopeless to try a third time. The flower inside me that had bloomed for Jason four years previously, and that had been wilting and straggling for years, was almost dead. I didn't want it to be true, and denied it, trying to focus on happier memories from our early romance. There were sweet moments, yet under closer scrutiny many scenes were tarnished by something painful. I remembered how special I'd felt when he dedicated a song to me at his jazz gig on Valentine's Day, but then left me alone for the rest of a long night while he jammed with his buddies. I thought of the time when we'd gotten together with friends to go dancing at a raucous Irish pub, but Alicia showed up in a tight yellow sleeveless blouse, and I was irate, competing for Jason's attention. My well of romantic past memories was running dry, its arid bottom revealing that my fantasy life had created far more of our joy than reality ever had.

Instead of trying to fix our relationship, I started investing energy in other things. I bought a pair of running shoes and started exercising. When Jason asked, I told him I wasn't ready to see another couples counselor. I kept going to 12-Step meetings and moved on to my last amends: the one to my immediate family.

◊ ◊ ◊

I called my family and explained that I had something important to tell them and it needed to be in person. Two weeks later, on a rainy Sunday, we met at the mobile home my parents had moved back into; my mother, father, sister, and I all gathered in the small, comfortable living room.

"I want to apologize to all of you," I began, as I'd practiced with my sponsor. "I've been a mostly AWOL family member for some years now, as you know. I don't always show up for family functions, and if I do I'm always late, or I leave early. I want to apologize for this, and for leaving you wondering why."

"Oh honey," my mom said, "it's okay. Anyway, we're used to it."

"No mom, it's not, and I need to say this. I'm making an amends."

She stayed silent, because she knew what an amends was from AA.

"I went to therapy to try to get help, and although I've been given several diagnoses over the years, the one that I think fits best is post-traumatic stress disorder, or PTSD, which was caused by awful things happening to me when I was little that left symptoms that haven't healed yet. I know we talked about the past endlessly with Margaret, but I never really understood what it all meant until recently. I don't like family gatherings because they remind me of drinking, secrets, and lies."

No one said anything, so I went on.

"I always tried to pretend everything was fine, but now I know I need to be more honest about things, so this is my attempt. When I was little, I was sexually abused, but not by Grandpa Westby. It was horrible, and I was too little to make sense of what was happening. I've been to more therapy since Margaret to deal with it, but I still don't remember many details. But even so, I've had classic symptoms of sexual abuse all my life. I think it was someone connected to our extended family. I always felt dread going to big family get-togethers, or going to church and talking about God, because nobody noticed what was happening to me. Now I avoid gatherings because I still feel like that, even though it's been years, and I know the abuse has stopped."

My dad spoke up then, asking why we always had to keep bringing up the past, but my sister cut him off. "Dad, let her talk. This is important."

I explained that I couldn't return to being part of the family as if nothing had happened, but I also didn't know how to get over symptoms of abuse when I wasn't even sure who did it. I asked for their patience as I was trying to figure it out, as my sponsor had advised.

"And I need to tell you something else about me I haven't shared," I said to the solemn faces. "I'm a sex addict."

"What? What's that?" My dad said, first to break the heavy silence that followed my pronouncement, his green eyes squinting at me.

"It's a person who is addicted to sex," I explained. "Like mom was addicted to alcohol, I became addicted to sex."

"How?" my sister asked.

"Well, I think it started with abuse, but I'm not sure. I've always had this really big reaction to everything having to do with sex. Either I numb out or I'm supersensitive to it, and can't get enough. I've had trouble being faithful and using porn, and I've acted out some really awful stuff. It scared me enough to make me work really hard, and I've been going to sexual recovery 12-Step meetings, like AA for sex, for years now. I don't cheat on anyone anymore, and I stopped using porn. But ever since I've been sober, I've had so many memories coming up. That's when I started to remember I was abused myself."

"Sex addict," my dad said slowly, as if the words were in a foreign language. "Now that's one I've never heard of."

My sister looked at me, her eyes suddenly narrowing. "Sex addict?" she echoed. "What does that mean for the kids?"

"The kids?" I stammered, shocked. I was unprepared for the question, though in hindsight I understand her protective reflex.

"Yes, the kids!" she replied, clearly upset. "The last thing I want is a sex addict around my kids!"

My sister had two children, a two-year-old son and a newborn baby girl, and seeing them and babysitting had been a bright, new gift in my life. I was at the hospital when they were both born, and marveled at how, even in such wee little bodies, they fiercely engaged life and toppled each new milestone that confronted them. And their joy! Witnessing their seemingly endless wellspring of delight was like a promise that my heavy existence could one day be lighter. I took care of them sometimes, but being near them took care of me too. I didn't want to lose that, but I was shaken and shamed to silence after my sister's statement.

Maybe she's right, I thought bleakly. I sat there mute and the conversation ended in extreme awkwardness. *Maybe I would be a bad influence. Maybe they'd be better off not really knowing me.*

After the talk ended, my mom, who'd sat quietly since she'd first spoken, leaned over and whispered, "I think you were very brave." I didn't feel brave, I felt terrible.

God, I thought, *recovery sucks.*

◇ ◇ ◇

A few weeks later, my mom called and invited me over for dinner, without Jason. During the forty-minute drive, I reminisced about living in the mobile home in the woods, and my former commutes to and from Seattle. I always felt some kind of pressure released as the freeway gave way to winding back roads and rows of evergreens— more peaceful. Safer.

Creamed hamburger over mashed potatoes, salty green beans, and pale yellow mini-cheesecakes revealed my mom's enduring love-language of comfort food, and my parents and I overate together, making small talk as if our recent family conversation had never happened. After dinner, I settled on the living room couch and my dad followed; he had something on his mind.

"Staci, you said a lot last time you were here. I still don't know how to make sense of it all, but I'm glad you spoke up. Do you really think you might be a bad influence on the kids?"

I'd given this some thought. "No dad, I was just surprised by the question, and I didn't know what to say. I know it's a lot for everyone to absorb. I need to talk to Christi."

"Good. Talk to her. I don't think there's anything to worry about either, but she's super-careful when it comes to the kids. You can understand why." I did. It was the only reference my dad had ever made to me about my pedophile grandfather.

"Enough of that," he said abruptly, changing the subject. "There's something else I want to talk with you about."

I waited.

"It's about Jason."

I could hear my mom busy in the kitchen, water rushing out the faucet as she filled the sink with suds.

"What about him?"

"We don't like him. None of us. I don't, and I talked with mom and Christi, and her husband too. Now mom doesn't want me to say anything—she's upset I'm talking to you about this—but I have to."

An uncomfortable heat prickled my stomach and traveled up my spine. I wanted to defend Jason, defend our love. *We're engaged to be married! How could they do this to me?* But the words wouldn't come. Dad went on.

"Neither of you has any money, but he has even less than you. He's always unemployed, he's always depressed, he acts pissed at you all the time, yet you say you're so happy. Staci, he doesn't treat you well, and you deserve better."

I began to protest, but right then mom came out of the kitchen and joined the conversation. "Barrie, I told you, it's her business! She's an adult and she has to make her own decisions."

"Okay, okay," he said. "You have to decide. I just want you to be happy."

At the time, I didn't appreciate the risk my dad took to tell me his true feelings about Jason, nor his affirmation that I was worthy of love and kind treatment by men. I dismissed his warning as irrelevant, telling myself he didn't understand, but in some ways he really did. My dad's description of Jason was an exact description of

218

his younger self; at least how I often remembered him when I was a child. Unknowingly, I'd fallen for a man like my father. He didn't know how to be kinder to my mom back then, but seeing Jason's behavior helped him realize he wanted better treatment for me. Today I believe my dad was attempting to do exactly what a father should do with an adult daughter he's worried about: express protective concern for her, have a dialogue about it, and ultimately affirm her right to make up her own mind.

At thirty-four years old, it was my responsibility to protect myself, and I'd made progress through my work in therapy and sexual recovery. Taking ownership for my mistakes was dissolving my chronic self-hatred, and my self-esteem was growing by the day. But I remained "love addicted" to Jason, because even though I frequently felt hurt by things he said and did, I couldn't set firm boundaries with him to safeguard my heart. I was convinced I couldn't survive without him, and I thought I had to put up with whatever he did. Growing up, that was pretty much how I felt about my dad as well.

I didn't tell Jason about my dad's disapproval, but a month later, we broke up anyway—initiated by Jason.

"Let's have sex," he said one night while I was visiting the new studio apartment he'd moved into. He hadn't had a chance to get a curtain for the open doorway between the kitchen and the closet-sized space where his lonely futon rested, still ripped, on the floor.

"No," I said, my voice laced with hostility. I hadn't learned how to set boundaries without rancor, but it was definitely progress for me to say no to disconnected sex. "We haven't worked out our issues. I don't want to."

"When will we work out our issues? How? You won't go to couples therapy."

"That didn't work! We tried twice. I won't go through that again!

I'm saving my money to get back into therapy myself. Doing step work is really helping me; I'm feeling a lot better than I used to."

"*You* may feel better, but nothing is working for us. We're supposed to be a couple, but you never have sex with me. You still complain about how I get nurturing exchanges with Alicia, and no matter what I say, you never get over it. You know what? I'm done. I don't want to do this anymore. It's over."

I sat stunned in the silence that followed his proclamation, his words carving out an opening to a new world. After four years of mostly tumult, I peeked in the newly created space, then quickly away.

"You're breaking up with me?" I demanded, shocked and angry. "How can you? We've worked so hard!" This was his cue in our drama for him to recant, but he didn't. And strangely, for the first time, I didn't want him to.

"Yes," he said. "YES! I'm breaking it off. It's over. I can't do this anymore."

I would not appreciate the colossal gift of his decision, nor the many other remarkable gifts Jason gave me, until years later. It was only with time that my lingering resentment would melt into gratitude that Jason had taught me the term *sex addict* and told me about codependency and sexual recovery support groups that existed to help. He gave me a place to practice talking about my feelings, however falteringly, and supported my budding recovery efforts. He tolerated my rage—much of which had been trapped inside me long before I met him—without raising his voice or reacting physically. And he stood by me when I was dangerously suicidal. Our relationship, even with its painful dance of distance and conflict, served as a vital part of the fragile umbilical cord that kept me connected to life during that dark period.

Jason also passed on many key lessons about healing he'd learned in therapy, like what a shame spiral is, the importance of bodywork for healing from trauma, and the idea that recovery from childhood neglect and abuse requires a total life overhaul, not a few months or a few years in superficial therapy. And despite the grief it brought, his final ending set me free of yet another cage of dependency and insecurity I'd crafted and could not, despite my best efforts, dismantle.

TWENTY-SEVEN

Journey to Pagan Places

I WAS DEVASTATED after Jason broke up with me. I thought my world was ending and feared I wouldn't survive the unrelenting loneliness his absence quickly revealed. It was as if a fundamental part of me had been crudely severed. My unrequited urges to be with him dangled pitifully from my heart like fraying strings. I forgot every gripe I'd ever had about the relationship and started obsessing on what I loved about him. Recognizing the return of yet another painful mental merry-go-round, I started attending meetings two or three times a week instead of my normal once or twice. Talking took the pressure out of my obsessions, but my sense of rejection remained overpowering. A few days after a meeting in which I had described how sad and lonely I was feeling, a man named Tim handed me a workbook about surviving divorce.

"Even though you weren't married, you were together for years, and the concepts in this book can still help you heal," he said. "I know, because they helped me." I was touched by Tim's thoughtfulness. He'd been through an abysmal divorce, and I'd witnessed through his weekly reports that he'd grown stronger through the process. I thanked him, and we shared a classic sexual recovery "A-frame" hug: arms circling, chests apart. By now I'd learned this lower-risk method of hugging men, though I was still careful with whom I allowed even that much touch.

Thinking back on Tim's gift, I am once again struck by how generous people in recovery meetings were to me over the years. The circles that started out terrifying became a source of constant emotional solace that bordered on magical; I'd talk about something that was bothering me, and the next thing I knew, someone would show up with a helpful idea or resource. Meetings became the reliable nurturing presence I never had growing up. I didn't know Tim very well, but the gift of his workbook was perfectly timed.

As winter yielded to a rainy spring, I began to take time out each day to read about grief and to write down my feelings about Jason. Though it was painful, answering the questions at the end of each workbook chapter revealed some startling insights, like the fact that although Jason had been the focus of my chronic complaints, in truth our relationship was the closest one I'd ever had. Reflecting, I discovered that what I missed the most was not the fireworks we'd had in the beginning, but our regular companionship; someone to be with and call my own. I also realized, with chagrin, a key mistake I had made with Jason: I remained with him long after our genuine affection was fatally exhausted. In my journal, I logged yet another pattern that I wanted to avoid in the future: "Staying too long in a toxic relationship."

On the day I completed the divorce grief workbook, I noted with a happy pang of surprise that I felt much better than when I'd started. The wrenching tear in my heart seemed almost mended, and my sexuality started flowing again, mirroring the natural flow of springtime energy humming around me. As the sunlight stretched out a little longer each day, I too felt ready to expand my horizons. I was single and free, and longed to explore a healthier form of sexuality than I'd known before. I wanted to try something wild and new. But what?

◊ ◊ ◊

I sat as usual in my Saturday drum circle, holding my elkskin hoop drum in one hand and my wood-handled beater in the other, waiting with six others on blankets spread out on the ground to cover the tall meadow grass. After the wet gloom of April and May, summer was almost here. Warmed by the dappled light sifting through tall trees, a few turtles basked *silently nearby on a log po*king out of a small pond. All eyes were on the leader, Dave, his gray brows knit in concentration. Anticipation brought tremors to my chest, though I still felt a little embarrassed by how seriously he took the drumming. Yet I was enthralled at the sa*me time. His heartbeat taps started, and we each waited for the f*eeling that would tell us it was time to add our own sound to his, as we'd been taught. When the group first started, I used to timidly copy Dave's beats, afraid to make much noise. Arlene, Oshin, Anthony, and the others were not so reticent. I smiled when Arlene began thumping her powerful djembe, imagining the turtles sliding off their log into the shimmery water, seeking quieter depths.

Over the months, and now years, since we'd first started, my caution gave way to glee, and eventually my drum sang with the best of them. Loud at times, soft at times, my bone-colored drum was ever-responsive to my urge for noise, tho*ugh I'd learned to balance it with what the colle*ctive rhythm seemed to need. When I drummed, I could stop thinking and worrying about what I was doing, what I looked like, and what everyone else thought of me. I loved surrendering to the beat, and the group sound-communion made me feel at home in a way nothing else did. Now that the weather was nicer, we met in a forested grove in the largest park in the city, choosing a spot that was tucked away from most people, a little refuge among the evergreens. We were largely left to our own devices.

Our gathering structure was simple: meet and greet, say "The Serenity Prayer," drum, and then talk. After a seemingly random amount of drum time, the sounds we created would rise to an ecstatic crescendo, or slowly ebb away, and silence would once again reign. It was a timeless dance between sound and silence, and for those brief moments, we were its facilitators. After the wild drumming, when our uninhibited cacophony would end, we'd laugh together in release, breathing heavily as we let go of our intense shared concentration and leaned back from our drums, solitary minds once more. After the slow endings, I always felt heavy on the blanket, calm and sated. We joked that drumming was better than sex.

With the drumming done, the sharing would start, and we would each take turns talking without interruption about our lives, our days, our addictions, and our recovery efforts—both failures and successes. One day, I revealed an idea that had been brewing in me since I'd finished the grief workbook.

"I'm considering going to a pagan ritual," I began, comforted as always by the fact that no one would interrupt me. "It's a gathering of people to celebrate the summer solstice, this Saturday. I'm a little worried it's addictive, because there's open nudity and the possibility of sex. But I'm not really going for that, I just want to see what it's like."

The property, about forty-five minutes east of Seattle, was owned by a nonprofit organization that held regular gatherings to celebrate the changing seasons. Their website advertised a "nondenominational pagan church," and welcomed everyone to a potluck, workshops on spirituality, and a ceremonial gathering on beautiful wetlands. I felt drawn to go, because I longed for a spiritual community that honored nature and celebrated healthy sexuality. I knew I didn't agree with the Catholic church that sex outside of legally wedded procreation was a sin. In my mind, marriage seemed to bring my parents and others nothing but misery and frustration. But even though I didn't want to get married, I certainly did want to explore sex.

I was afraid my recovery friends would not approve of my attending the solstice celebration, but when I asked Diego about it, he said it was up to me. I was thirty-five years old, but when it came to sex, I still felt like a teenager talking to a parent. Happily, unlike the directive from my parents when I was eighteen, Diego's perspective was a revelation.

"You're single now, and your boundaries are yours, Staci," he said. "They go with you no matter where you go. Just because a recovering alcoholic goes to a party, doesn't mean he's going to drink there. If you go, keep your eyes open and look for guidance from your spirit, and don't settle for anything less."

My drumming friends were encouraging after I talked about my plan to attend the solstice ritual, especially Dave, whose eyes sparkled when he said, "There's drumming there, right? What could go wrong?" I would later learn that quite a few of the others were anxious about my plan, a recovering sex addict heading off to a community with open nudity and a free-sex attitude. But they were too timid to tell me directly since I seemed so excited, and since my sponsor had left it up to me.

◇ ◇ ◇

Gripping my tinfoil-covered wild rice casserole, I looked for a place to set it down at the long, food-laden table.

"How about here?" asked a petite, grinning woman in a wispy, flowered dress. I followed her lead as she introduced herself, joining her on the tour she insisted I take when she found out *it was my first* time on the grounds. "This place is great," she said, leading me through the lush trails to the marsh pond. "Once I went out there on a little boat and it was dreamy. There's a pool though, that's better for swimming. It's clothing-optional. Do you want to go?" On the way past the indoor pool and hot tub, I glanced around trying to "look for spirit," but really just eager to get to the pool and see if people were really naked.

The land was expansive, with a lush, green lawn perfectly suited for summer play and sunbathing. I saw men, women, and children dressed in tank tops and shorts or colorful maxi dresses, talking and playing Frisbee and badminton. Some men were shirtless in the summer sun, and I practiced looking away from them instead of gawking.

Look at their feet instead of other body parts. Remember they are people, someone's husband or son, not objects. Bless them and let them go. This was a family crowd, and I didn't see any signs of drinking, or smell pot pungently piercing the air.

"*There's where the drumming will be later,*" my new sprite-friend explained, pointing out a *log cabin as we walked. "And over there is the Venus–Pan Shrine." My stomach tightened, a flush of h*eat running up my spine and coloring my cheeks, as she continued. "Sex is okay in there as long as everyone is over eighteen and agrees. There are condoms and lube and stuff to keep it safe." The shrine was a small, wooden hut with a silvery wind chime shaped in a half moon hanging over the door, swaying gently in the light breeze. Softly tinkling bells beckoned me as we passed.

"I'm going to get back to food setup, have fun!" said my new friend with a little wave, and off she went, leaving me alone near the sliding glass pool entry. Through the glass I could see that the scene looked like any other high-spirited summer swimming crowd, except for one key difference: everyone was naked.

Everyone but me, I thought nervously. I mentally recited my bottom-line boundaries that I'd recently reworked with Diego in preparation for this event. Because I said them aloud in meetings so often now, I had them memorized.

No hurting myself physically; no affairs or intrigues with men; no sex outside a mutual, caring relationship; no compulsive masturbation, with or without pornography; no creating or consuming porn, no alcohol or drugs; no willfully engaging in toxic (abuse) fantasy; no pregnancy or STD risk; no cybersex.

Taking a deep breath, I slid open the glass door.

A burst of children's laughter greeted me as two naked little ones on bright inner tubes splashed each other, bemused mom-type also nude at their side in the pool. No one seemed to notice when I set my bag *on a reclining chair an*d started to undress.

How do you strip in public? I wondered, self-conscious, my occasional nightmares of finding myself naked in a public place coming suddenly to life. Why am I doing this? This is crazy!

No, I heard myself answer, this is fun and exciting! I took a breath, unconvinced, until the breeze tickled up bumps on my newly exposed skin, and I pushed down my anxiety in favor of finding the hot tub to warm up.

Sliding into the warm water, I joined four men and two women who were already soaking. They were all in their forties or older, chatting amicably.

"Hi," I smiled, using my friendly cheerleader voice, and the greetings in return ran the continuum from polite to enthusiastic. The water line was now at my neck, and I looked down and saw the rest of my body mostly visible despite the bubbles.

Oh my God, I am naked. I smiled wider to cover my nervousness, trying to pick up the thread of conversation and join in, as if I did this kind of thing every day. As we talked, I noticed one of the men taking particular notice of me, and trying to conceal it. I could relate at first, trying not to peer under the water, wishing I had a freeze ray so I could stare at length without discovery.

Men's bodies are so awesome! But as the chat continued, I sensed the man's attention change into something else, something darker and not so friendly. It wasn't a violent energy, but I sensed a blunt force sexual desire mixed with slight contempt. I knew that energy all too well. That used to be my drug. Sex and anger, and trying to hide it.

With almost three years of sexual sobriety behind me by then, my awareness of subtle sexual energies had deepened. I was no longer gorging on all the junk sex energy I could get, trashing my senses with porn and indiscriminate flirtations or affairs. Since getting through withdrawal, my sensitivities had heightened, and I'd studied the steps to this tired dance—my addictive cycle—all too well. We'd pair off, dry ourselves, and hop in the Venus–Pan Shrine together to reenact the potent arousal-disdain of our unresolved pasts. I'd be overwhelmingly aroused, then overwhelmingly ashamed, contemptuous of us both afterward.

No thanks, I've come too far for that old thrill. Rising up out of the water, I deliberately did not look at him as I bid farewell to the awkward Jacuzzi party, dried myself and dressed, and set off to find some dinner.

The summer solstice ritual was engaging, but not transformative for me. A group of about seventy people walked in a spiral, holding hands, singing and chanting. The mood was lively, nothing heavy; it was an all-ages celebration of the sun. At one point, we were instructed to pick a card from a deck of Animal Spirits Knowledge Cards and use it as a personal guide. I liked the one I drew, a caramel lion gazing boldly at me, his fiery mane ringed by a circle. According to the description, the card symbolized courage, strength, healing, protection, and life energy. We sang a lively song as the sun set, cheering boisterously when the final glow disappeared behind the horizon.

My eyes lingered on the sex-shrine hut as I followed thumping echoes across the twilight field, searching for the drum circle. I want to go in there! What's in there? Is anyone in there having sex? I decided to wait, go drum first, and then see. Patience, I told myself, marveling at the possibility.

I was grateful that my step work and therapy had helped transform my inner battles between compulsion, self-loathing, and denial about all-things sexual into more mindful, careful explorations on the topic. My former obsessions had mostly given way to passionate curiosity about sex that was controllable, at least so far. Through recovery, the sexually addicted-teenage part of my mind had found something better, in fact, what I'd always really wanted: loving attention, nontoxic ways to release old pain, and now, an exciting new opportunity to look for an authentic, spiritually-grounded sexuality. Like any abused child or teenager who is offered nurturance, adventure, and healthy structure over time, I was slowly learning to relax and trust.

Though I still relied on my sponsor and others for help, I was also learning how to parent myself; how to listen inside and take care of my own needs, no matter how scary or painful they might be. And along with the support, I had loving accountability: I knew without a doubt I'd be telling my sponsor and friends whatever happened, and that they cared about me and wanted me to stay sober and safe. I carried them with me, along with my drum, as I crossed the darkening meadow. I wasn't free of my past yet, but at thirty-five years old, I was starting to practice sexual discernment.

The drumming was in a large living room in the cabin, and the noise loud enough that I put in earplugs as I unsheathed my drum. Several other people of various ages were standing around the room, listening. I said hello with my first beat, and joined the conversation of sounds as we meshed our creative urges. One man with a long, brown beard played the panpipes, his haunting melody dancing above our thumping, daring the rest of us, about eight male drummers and me, to follow. I watched the pan player longingly. I'd felt lonely being single for the last six months, but it had been far longer since I'd felt physically or emotionally close to Jason.

After we played for a while, a woman walked to the center of the room and started swaying, distracting me. Soon she was full on dancing, her twists and twirls spreading her purple skirt high so her bare legs revealed their muscular power. Barefoot with a sparkly tank top, her long, golden hair flowed around her as she moved to our rhythm. I became entranced watching her, her unshaven armpits peeking out under delicately swaying arms. I began playing my drum just for her.

As the music played, I realized that this woman was offering her sensuality, but not in an exhibitionist way. I recalled my old dancing days, where I used to dress in skimpy spandex at the clubs and try to magnetize all attention toward me, away from the other women. I'd soak it up like a forever-dry sponge, but that was a pale imitation of what this woman was doing. She wasn't dancing to suck up the energy of the watchers; she was dancing and emitting light for us all to see. Her moves were luxurious and generous. She was giving, not taking, and for once I didn't feel competitive or jealous watching a beautiful, sensual woman. I felt reverence.

When our session reached its chaotic upsurge, her moves grew wilder too, until our crescendo reached its summit and silence descended, random beats here and there from those reluctant to let go. She crumpled, panting, to the floor, her skirt and hair askew. The dramatic moment slowly passed, and a sweet glow seemed to take its place in the room. I felt warm, full of happiness and calm all at once.

Leaving the drum room, I made a beeline to the sex shrine and stood near it in the shadows, watching. I knew some people in this community practiced polyamory, and I wondered if having multiple partners could work for me.

I don't think so, I decided. I never did like sharing Jason, even if nurturing exchange was all he and Alicia really did. And what if that hot tub guy is in the shrine? I wouldn't want him to touch me. That wouldn't be a "mutually caring relationship"!

Hmm, another thought interrupted. How long would I have to know someone before our relationship could be considered "mutually caring"? A noise from the meadow distracted me, whoops from teenage voices, and I walked over to see flashing sparklers piercing the blackness, lighting excited faces.

"Pretty fun, huh," said a heavyset, bearded man standing nearby. He told me his name was Brad, and we fell into a comfortable chat, with him answering my questions after he learned it was my first visit to the land. Then he said something that changed my evening entirely.

"Yeah," he said wistfully, when I chuckled at the teens, who were now squaring off in sparkler-saber wars on the lawn. "They're great fun. But we had something really bad happen here last month."

"What," I asked, cautiously curious.

"A random guy sexually molested one of the teen girls, Lily. He'd been showing up at gatherings for a little while, but no one really knew him. It was bad; she's messed up." Brad explained that they'd called the police after Lily told her mom what happened, but no one could find the guy because they didn't know his real name, or have any other way of identifying him. "It really sucks, you know?"

I did. All at once the magic left the evening, even as the kids kept up their antics in the balmy night air. With Brad's revelation, the community I thought was so liberated, with skinny-dipping and a free-sex shrine, suddenly became something else: yet another place where kids were neglected instead of protected. Hearing that a teen girl was molested by a man no one really knew or could catch filled me with dread. Just like in my family.

I thanked Brad for the chat, gathered my belongings, and walked off into the night, never to return.

- TWENTY-EIGHT -

Applied Christianity

LATER THAT YEAR I started working with my first sponsee, Charlie, a happy-go-lucky gay man in his thirties. I met him through the drum circle and immediately liked him. His cheerful countenance never revealed that he'd once been jailed for molesting a thirteen-year-old boy, but he disclosed it to me right away. I learned that after jail Charlie had gone to inpatient sex addiction rehab. He said that getting caught and the six weeks of treatment had changed his life, and he'd been sexually sober ever since. He was in something called community custody in an outpatient treatment program for sex offenders, which meant he could stay out of jail if he went to weekly intensive individual and group therapy, attended 12-Step meetings, and met all the other conditions of his parole. Despite his offense history, all his healing work gave Charlie a practical wisdom I saw lacking in many people I met, sex offender or not.

Not long after that, my drum circle opened to new members, and we were soon joined by several men who weren't sexually sober. The circle that had felt so safe soon became uncomfortable for me when one of the new men sat too close as we drummed. His eyes glazed over, and I sensed pressured static around me, like needles prickling my aura. I intuitively felt that he'd lapsed into sexual fantasy, and suspected it involved me. Not knowing how to talk about something I couldn't see or prove, I quit the group. Discouraged, I decided to stop pursuing alternative forms of spirituality for a while.

In a sad synchronicity, right around this time my sponsor, Diego, called to tell me he'd relapsed. He said he needed all his energy to work his own program and was going to stop sponsoring me or anyone else until his own recovery was back on track. I was happy to hear he hadn't gone back to crystal meth or cheated on Troy, but he'd had a major porn binge and lied about it, and that meant, according to his sobriety definition, starting anew at Step One. I tried not to feel rejected again, but I felt awful about losing Diego as a sponsor. I considered a look at porn myself, but with the support of my other recovery friends, I found the strength not to.

Spirit, I prayed, *so many ways I've known you are evaporating. Please show me how to find you now.* Answers came over the next six months in the form of an unexpected job offer and a tough conversation with my sister, Christi.

◇ ◇ ◇

I'd changed jobs the previous year, landing a plum position as a mental health counselor at a thriving downtown Seattle health clinic for homeless and low-income adults. The place was all heart, and I grew to love working near the bustling Pike Place Market in a miniscule office I decided was cozy rather than cramped. Around that time Charlie was starting to backslide, his erratic phone calls alerting me that unless things turned around, he was going to end up back in jail with a parole violation for viewing pornography.

As his sponsor, I offered to attend a care conference with Charlie, his therapist, our friend Anthony, and the owner of the sex offender/addictions treatment clinic where Charlie was a client. I showed up not knowing what to expect, and discovered a nondescript building that looked like a dentist's office. I never would have guessed it was devoted to treating sex addicts and sex offenders. The pair of professionals impressed me; they obviously cared about protecting the community and preventing Charlie's descent into mania and relapse. We made a plan that ultimately led to Charlie's turnaround, and though it involved him doing most of the work, I felt grateful to have been part of the solution.

With a lot of work and the right help, it is possible to prevent senseless destruction from mental illness and sex addiction! But meaningful as it was to help Charlie, when the owner of the clinic called a week later to offer me a job, I was less than enthusiastic.

"You're a licensed social worker and a recovering sex addict yourself, and a woman—that's a powerful combination," he explained. "You seem to understand what we're trying to do here, and I wonder if you'd consider joining my team." My no came immediately, as I told him I was happy with my current job. I thanked him for the compliment of his offer, not adding that I absolutely did *not* want to work as a therapist with sex addicts, let alone registered sex offenders.

No way. I'm not strong enough for that kind of intensity. But a tearful reconciliation with my sister changed my mind.

◊ ◊ ◊

Christi had sent me a letter after my family amends and admission of what I'd realized about abuse and sex addiction, but not knowing how to answer, I'd put off replying; this kicked off another period of estrangement in my family. I took it out and read it again, her neat script detailing her care and concern for me, along with her overriding obligation as a mother to protect her children from any possible risk of abuse like we'd seen in our family. The letter ended with her restating her position: no contact with the kids.

I tried to sympathize with her perspective. Even though I was now years into sexual recovery, she was startled by my recent admission and was seeing me exactly as I'd seen Jason when he disclosed his sex addiction on our fourth date—as a sexual threat.

She's seeing me like Grandpa Westby, but I'm not a danger to kids.

Sex addiction and pedophilia are not the same! Many pedophiles are not even addicted to sex; they offend for other reasons. I have to at least <u>try</u> to help her understand!

After exhaustively debating the issues with my friends in recovery, I worked up the courage to call her. I was relieved when she agreed to meet me at my apartment. She sat stiffly on the edge of my couch as I bustled about in the galley kitchen to make her tea, as others had done for me. I sat across from her and, before trying to make my case, thanked her for coming. Neither of us bothered with small talk.

"Christi, I read your letter, and I understand that you have concerns about me being around the kids because of what I shared about my sex addiction. But I want you to know I'm not a bad influence on them, and I would never hurt them."

She peered at me, unmoved. "That may be true; I hope it is true. But that's not a chance I'm prepared to take. Not after what happened to me." Her voice was low and deadly—mama bear in full protective mode. I felt my shoulders slump. *C'mon spirit,* I prayed. *Give me something here!*

After what seemed like forever, words came.

"Okay. It's up to you. I'll respect whatever you decide, but please think about this some more. Sex addiction is <u>not</u> the same as pedophilia. Every sex addict has a problem with sex, but that's not the same as being attracted to children. I definitely don't have that problem, and never will. I struggled with porn and affairs, but I've been sober for years now."

She blinked, taken aback at my directness, and I continued.

"Look, by cutting off contact with me, you think you're protecting the kids, and you might feel safer. But if you do this, you're choosing another risk, which also has consequences, and that's having them grow up without really knowing their loving auntie. I actually believe keeping them away from me will make them *less safe*, not more."

I took a slow breath, gaining momentum. "I know my experiences messed me up, but Christi, the buck stops with me. I have worked hard for years on my spiritual growth in 12-Step groups and therapy, and I can reassure you I am not a danger to other people, especially children. Because of everything I've been through, I've learned to *protect* children. I want to help raise my niece and nephew, and I want to keep them safe. What I know *can* help them, because I have no illusions about what this world is like, and how dangerous some adults, and even other kids, can sometimes be. I'm not in the dark about the risks. I can stand up for them like I wish someone had stood up for me!" I was crying now and could see through my tears that she was softening too.

"I'll think about it. That's the best I can do, I will think about it and pray about it. I cannot let anything happen to them. God, I was so scared when you told us all that. It's just so much."

"I know, I know. I'm sorry you're having to worry about all this; I'm sorry we all do. But we can make it different, I know we can. I promise."

Within a week she sent me another letter—one I've cherished ever since as a symbol of her courage and love. She accepted what I'd said and agreed that I could see the kids as I had before. I was elated, calling everyone to share the happy news.

Fortified by my success in speaking up, and Christi's change of heart, I decided that perhaps I was strong enough to consider that new job offer at the sex offender/addictions clinic after all. I called to see if the position was still open. It was.

TWENTY-NINE

Certified Sex Addiction Therapist (CSAT)

I WAS SURROUNDED by over a hundred other therapists in a conference room in Hattiesburg, Mississippi. Sent by my new employer, I was receiving training from, Patrick Carnes, a key founder of the sexual recovery movement, to become a Certified Sex Addiction Therapist, or CSAT.

In my previous twelve years of attending trainings in mental health and elder care as a social worker, I had never heard a professional teach the way he did, sharing intimate stories from his life to perfect strangers. I was riveted. He was slightly taller and huskier than I'd expected, with short brown-graying hair and blazing blue eyes that moved steadily around the room. Though his topic was dead serious, Carnes was a funny and endearing speaker, with a habit of periodically reaching up and tugging on his left ear as if to balance out his painful self-disclosures.

The researcher-scholar-psychologist-author spoke openly about how he dealt with the demons of his sexual addiction, and how none of his many prominent therapists had been able to help him in any lasting way. He talked about the terrible consequences to his life, how his sexual compulsions caused him to stack his problems atop one another like slippery rocks waiting to tumble, and yet he kept acting out, kept piling on more problems, precariousness growing, while he remained numb to the risks. He told us how his pile did finally topple, nearly crushing him and his family, and yet he resumed his craziness, and the rocks once again trembled on their growing cairn.

One day, inspired by witnessing the camaraderie of a 12-Step meeting for alcoholics and their family members, Dr. Carnes thought of creating a similar kind of meeting for people addicted to sex. He drew together men who struggled like he did, eventually a woman joined, and they started meeting regularly to share their stories and get better. Their support saved his life and, more than that, his soul. He described how the new idea grew and inspired other meetings to form.

The part of the story he didn't relate, however, was how the new fellowship gained momentum. The gatherings multiplied across the world, and found their way to Seattle, where I discovered them twenty-three years later.

His honesty emboldened me, and I decided to be direct in return. At the first opportunity, in front of the whole room, I asked Dr. Carnes about something that had been bothering me since I started offering therapy to sex addicts three months earlier.

"I'm a recovering sex addict, and I found help in 12-Step meetings. I refer my clients there, but most won't go. In your inpatient center for sex addicts, you require people to attend sexual recovery 12-Step meetings or you won't accept them into your program. But can I do that as an outpatient therapist? I mean, just because 12-Step programs worked for me, does that mean I can require others to adopt my practice? What about free will, and honoring the client's freedom to choose?"

The room fell silent as he considered his reply, and I was completely unprepared for the impact of his answer.

"Your story, your experience as a recovering sex addict and how meetings helped you get sober, is the most powerful thing you have to offer any client. More powerful than any training or clinical skill. You want to help your clients? Tell them your story."

I don't know how anyone else experienced his words, but to me they felt powerfully amplified. They reminded me of times in my life where an everyday encounter with someone was transformed into something extraordinary. This happened mostly while working in hospice and nursing homes as I sat with elders in their final days and hours. Sometimes they spoke with a kind of raw authority that made my hair stand up on the back of my neck. Whenever I heard that kind of voice, I paid attention, and this was one of those times.

After he spoke, the training came to a sudden break. Disoriented, I stood up on wobbly legs and fled the room. I headed outside to the back patio of the conference center, leaned against the stucco wall before my legs gave out, and slid to the ground. It was a bright, sunny Mississippi day, and I gasped the thick air. I felt like a thin wire flooded with electricity that was ready to blow. I forced myself to focus on the heat on my face, and used techniques to get grounded that I'd learned over the years. My mind struggled to figure out what had just happened, even as my trembling body knew it was something of great significance.

I sat on the ground trying to deepen my shallow breaths and collect my thoughts. I had expected the training to be powerful, but I didn't expect that the first words to me from Patrick Carnes would be advice to tell my own story! It seemed impossible: too intense, too vulnerable, and too discrediting. Yet as I sat on the sunny patio, my body trembled in reaction. The raw power of his message was undeniable.

Still overwhelmed, I decided I didn't have to make sense of it right that minute. Filing the whole thing away in a mental Someday drawer, I took a breath, stood up, brushed off my clothes, and headed back to the training.

Certified Sex Addiction Therapist (CSAT)

◇ ◇ ◇

Gaining a clinical perspective from Carnes and other experts on the treatment of sex addiction was satisfying and revealing. All CSAT candidates had to take the same tests we would later administer to our clients, and reading my results validated the progress that years of healing work had yielded.

It's right here in black and white, I noted happily. *I'm not so crazy anymore!* Except for some lingering post-trauma symptoms and residual anger, I no longer met the criteria for any psychiatric disorder, because my life and level of functioning had reached an all-time high. I was happy being single and spending time with my recovery friends going on hikes, holding barbecues, and gathering at holidays. I saw my family occasionally, but limited contact to tolerable doses. And I grew passionate about my work.

As a social worker, I'd always loved the clients I'd worked with over the years, but to my surprise, I especially enjoyed my new role as a CSAT. The addicts and partner clients I treated were generally highly intelligent, well-resourced, and deeply motivated to work on personal and family growth. I began to witness transformation taking place at a faster pace than at any other job in my career, including hospice. If people worked hard in sex addiction therapy, I discovered, they resurrected to a new life before they died.

I was working less, earning more, and absorbing volumes every day from my boss and the clinic treatment team. I learned about the ten types of sex addicts, and more about how to distinguish people addicted to sex from sex offenders (those who commit or are accused of committing illegal, intrusive sex acts). One difference was that sex addicts came to the clinic voluntarily, whereas sex offenders were court-ordered and forced to choose between treatment and jail. But some sex offenders, I learned, were also addicted.

I didn't love the loss of my 12-Step sexual recovery meetings, however, but since many of my new clients attended them, I felt an ethical duty not to confuse our relationship by having two roles: a therapist *and* a fellow 12-Stepper. To keep my support network strong, a few other professionals and I started an invitation-only house meeting, and I picked up the slack with meetings in my financial 12-Step program. I also started recovery for compulsive eating, with erratic progress.

But as the novelty of discovery and growth gave way to familiar routine over the first two years on the job, the stories of sexual intensity I heard day after day began to weigh me down. Constantly witnessing others' suffering exacerbated pain from my own unhealed past abuse, and my old depression returned. I arranged my work schedule to start at one in the afternoon and end around nine each night, because I had started watching movies until two in the morning. I was back to using sheer exhaustion to avoid nightmares, but it wasn't working. Soon I knew I needed more help, because no matter how late I stayed up, the bad dreams with themes of sexual exploitation always reappeared. Tired and desperate, I called Conrad and got back on his schedule.

With no mental health care coverage or grants available to pay for my therapy, the cost of weekly sessions was almost as much as my rent. Anxiety about money soon drove me to a frank conversation with my boss: could he think of a way I could earn more besides providing therapy to sex addicts at the clinic? His answer was immediate and positive: he needed help on the court-ordered side of the clinic. Would I consider conducting psychological evaluations on people, usually men, accused of sex crimes?

These Sexual Deviancy Evaluations were forensic records that summarized the findings from an exhaustive battery of written tests, polygraphs, and verbal interviews of the accused. They were lengthy, and netted the clinic thousands of dollars each. If I wanted, I could earn a chunk by contracting to administer and write a significant portion of them. My part would involve reading all the court documents and other records, conducting in-person interviews, and making detailed mental health assessments to determine whether or not the test-taker was a psychopath. Treatment was inappropriate for psychopaths, my boss explained, because they used all the psychological savvy they learned to become more skilled at manipulating and exploiting others.

I thought I knew what a psychopath was from watching slasher movies growing up; I'd seen my first one, *Halloween*, at age eight at a neighbor's house. Afterward, I could barely sleep for a week, imagining the shadowy outline of Michael Myers standing in my bedroom doorway, holding a gleaming knife. I would grab my pillow and quietly tread into my parents' room, finally falling asleep on the floor on my mom's side of the bed. It seems poignant to me now that I never woke them up, yet understandable; by age eight, I'd long since stopped considering them a source of comfort for any painful feelings, at least not while they were awake.

Noticing my hesitation at his idea, my boss reassured me that the clinic did not evaluate violent sex offenders; they only worked with first-time or low-risk offenders who had a likely chance of being awarded community custody. If convicted, these clients could live outside of jail as long as they complied with every mandate of their intensive treatment and didn't violate parole. I was only slightly reassured, but without another good option, I agreed to the new role. It would start with another specialized training, this time on psychopathy. The next class available was in Montreal, Quebec in Canada, so one rainy November morning I boarded a plane and off I went.

Looking back, this seems like an ironic and possibly disastrous way for a survivor of sexual abuse to earn more money to pay for therapy: evaluating those accused of sex crimes. But at the time, it's what life offered, and I can now see the synchronicity as a wake-up call that further propelled me to face my abuse history head on.

I'd always heard sex offenders never got better, but I would learn from Charlie and my subsequent work at the clinic that this is not actually true. If they are not psychopaths, people who commit sex offenses can benefit from skilled treatment and, like the proverbial light bulb in a therapist's office, if they want to change, they truly can. A typical length of intensive treatment at my clinic was seven years, but many stayed longer than that. At formal graduation ceremonies, I saw some men leave that I highly respected. In fact, some of America's pioneering work on family reconciliation after sex offenses was created at the very clinic where I worked.

If only such a program had been around when Grandpa Westby was caught; our family could have used the help.

THIRTY

Monsters and Magic in Montreal

My trip to Montreal seemed charmed from the start. The rental car company made a mistake, and I was inadvertently awarded an upgrade to a white Ford Edge, a vehicle I decided was totally sexy. My first time driving an SUV, I enjoyed the higher visibility as I sped down the Canadian freeway in search of my hotel. A friend had taught me how to get a great deal through the Internet on a four-star hotel, so I settled into my modern, spacious room and ordered room service. My employer was splitting most of the travel costs with me, making this kind of luxury possible for the first time in my life. I felt like a queen looking out over the city, eating savory roast chicken accompanied by plump mushrooms sautéed in butter.

The two-day training was grueling: in addition to learning the psychological qualities of people whose behavior revealed them to be psychopaths, we also watched videotaped interviews of imprisoned psychopaths so we could learn how to conduct our own assessments. As I navigated the strange freeways back to the hotel after the first day of class, I barely registered my surroundings. I was no longer in a new city on a travel adventure; I was in the gray box of my mind, with narrow tunnel vision. Triggered by the horror of the videos, I'd involuntarily dissociated, switching into survival mode. I became single-mindedly focused on the safety of my hotel room, only stopping briefly at a convenience store en route to buy a bag of greasy cheese puffs and a big box of Toffifay chocolates. Since starting food recovery, I rarely turned to junk food overloads, but I was desperate to numb myself out.

Day two of the training was also painful, but recalling my food hangover that morning, I decided to avoid the convenience store and take a different route back to the hotel. Once in my room, I tried a tool Conrad had recently taught me to use when intrusive thoughts or images hit. He called it the *containment space*. Closing my eyes, I focused on putting my overwhelming feelings about the psychopaths into an unbreachable vault; I pictured my horror as a grayish-black fog being sucked into this imaginary space, not to be opened again until I was sitting with my therapist. It actually worked, and my dread gradually shifted to excitement as I changed my clothes and set out on foot to explore the downtown charm of Old Montreal on a Friday night. I'd booked the hotel over the weekend to have more time to see the city, and planned to fly home Sunday afternoon. Still sponsorless, I hadn't made a sobriety travel plan, but when the urge to have random anonymous sex visited, I tried to put it too in my imaginary vault.

I fell in love with the city immediately, surprised that I'd found someplace I liked almost as much as Seattle. If Seattle was the Emerald City, I fancied Montreal and its lovely water's edge as a sapphire, sparkling in the night. As I walked along the Saint Lawrence River, I felt alive and happy, although extremely cold. I needed a better coat. Two hours later, I'd spent almost all my extra money on a white down jacket with a faux fur-lined hood and a thick book about human trafficking. Snuggling back in my room under a cozy comforter with the rest of my chocolates, I carefully avoided the porn channels on the fancy flat-screen TV. Instead, I read about how girls around the world were tricked into becoming sex slaves and forced to make exploitive media, and how much money their captors made off their misery.

The next morning I strolled through the Notre-Dame Basilica, marveling at its intricate stained-glass depictions of the city's history. The hushed cathedral reminded me of my Catholic roots, and I felt comforted by the ornate beauty of the cavernous building.

I still don't agree with Catholic shame about sex, but there is something spiritually alive in this place. My old resentment at Catholicism had diminished, and in its place I felt some peace. *Is it the Holy Spirit? Was it there all along?* As I pondered this and other questions of faith, I shuddered to think about what my teens would have been like *without* my church-influenced determination to save myself for marriage.

On my to-do list that day was to call a man named Alec, a Montreal native my friend Oshin had put me in touch with before the trip. Alec was a serious Buddhist who'd stayed at Oshin's apartment when a Buddhist dignitary had visited Seattle.

"You have to call him," Oshin had said. "He's amazing! He's kind, thoughtful, and funny. I loved having him stay with me. He'll show you around Montreal." I'd e-mailed Alec before arriving and he'd seemed nice enough, offering to give me a little tour of the city in the afternoon. "Oh," Oshin had added, "and he's gorgeous." Stepping out of the church, I took a breath and called Alec, and we agreed to meet nearby.

"You have very good posture," I blurted out after introductions were made and we were walking toward a tour of the local botanical gardens.

"Thanks," he said, a smile in his brown eyes. "When I was fourteen my parents were divorcing and they sent me to a therapist, who told me that girls liked guys with good posture. That's the only thing I remember from therapy." Embarrassed by my comment about his appearance, a no-no in the "How to Maintain a Friendship and Avoid Flirtation" column, I realized I liked his proud, erect stance.

Wait, don't use the word erect. *Don't go there.* It had been so long since I'd been alone with a single, attractive man! I focused on the natural beauty around me as we finished our tour and headed back towards the river.

Strolling around downtown Montreal with Alec was delightful. Leaves blew at our feet and clouds roiled overhead, the dropping temperature justifying my purchase as I nestled into my puffy new coat. I told him about my work and reason for visiting, and Alec was curious about sex addiction and the spiritual implications of psychopathy. As we walked, we discussed the different perspectives of good versus evil and well versus sick, casting for something bigger to explain the unexplainable. Afterward, we stopped at a small café for hot drinks, the humidity of the busy espresso makers steaming up the window as our conversation wove us together.

I learned he'd recently returned from a spiritual quest to Vietnam, and he talked about how scary it was to be constantly showered with attention by women on the street—he'd felt lonely as a single man, yet sensed their interest was more opportunistic than genuine. Alec disclosed he'd been divorced for two years, and admitted that his immaturity was a key factor in the demise of his marriage. The painful divorce had motivated him to deepen his spiritual journey. His emotional insight was endearing.

Alec had a late afternoon commitment, so we agreed to part ways and reconnect for dinner. Once back at the hotel, I tried to take a nap in the freshly made bed, but what came instead were deep, shuddering sobs. My numbness from the training gave way to raw grief, surprising me. The vault of my containment space had opened, perhaps because of Alec's kind attention and our intimate day together, and was coaxed out further by my solitude and rest.

I buried my face in the soft pillow and howled out my horror at the men I'd seen interviewed. The things they said, and how they said

248

them! When asked about their crimes, each one displayed callousness and sadistic pleasure as they bragged about the suffering they'd caused. In my grief, I pictured their faces again, their eyes staring into the camera, filled with suspicion and hatred as they detailed their sexual and physical assaults. But as I kept crying and breathing, I visualized more than their surface appearances. In my mind's eye, I could see their energetic presences, like gaunt wraiths with hollow dark sockets for eyes. Each man was surrounded by a Swiss cheese aura of dark, sucking shadows that rivaled any horror movie killer I'd seen as a child.

I know a man like that, my mind told me in a thought that felt quiet but true. *He was a relative. That's who abused me. He was like that. A psychopath. But who? Which relative?! His face is always a shadow.*

No answer came, and I gave up trying to figure it out, but my tears kept flowing until they were spent. Soon I drifted off to sleep, cozy and warm, and I awoke later feeling lighter.

I wonder, came a dreamy thought, *where Alec and I will go for dinner.*

◇ ◇ ◇

We chose a neighborhood Italian bistro with petite tables and a festive atmosphere. The weather had turned even colder, rain mingling with soft flakes of snow starting to flutter as we sat down. Our conversation still flowed easily as we devoured crusty bread and creamy, salty butter and, later, several courses I barely tasted. By this time, I was smitten.

Toward the end of dinner, the snow had developed into a flurry, and we ran like children down the slippery sidewalk to my SUV, our breath fogging the windows as I blasted the heater. Our laughter settled to silence as we waited for the windshield to clear, and I became acutely aware of heat rising in my body too from sitting so close to him in the compact cab. Alec stared at me, his handsome face grinning beneath his navy woolen cap.

"Let's go dancing!" he said, to which I happily agreed. We headed back to his place to check the Internet for options. Alec was staying with his parents in a classy high-rise condo not far from downtown Montreal, though they weren't home. We considered finding a party, but decided instead to tour a downtown art gallery before hitting a funky bar nearby to dance.

I didn't realize I'd left my bag at his place until much later—after the art, after the dancing, and after our first touch on the dance floor. His touch left such a strong sensation it was as if his hand had stayed on my hip, swaying with me. He ordered a cocktail and offered me one, but I declined. After my first three months without alcohol, I'd decided to continue abstaining, and was happy with my choice. I had no desire to drink; I was intoxicated enough by the music and Alec. When we left the bar, I pulled my coat around me as we stood on the sidewalk with the snow collecting around us.

"Let's go back to your hotel, and I can walk home from there," he suggested. I nodded, not wanting our night to end, and not wanting to fly back to Seattle the next morning. Alec was true to his word as he opened his arms for a close hug in the hotel parking garage and thanked me for a wonderful day together. I wistfully watched him walk away, amazed. How was it possible that I was free of the compulsion to take our night further than one sweet date? How could it be that I could let him go, content without so much as a kiss? I thought back to men and bars, and drunken sex in public places that left me ashamed to see sober faces. My sense of Alec lingered like a fresh scent, and I fancied our connection like a little flower still in its bud. In the past, I would have clawed open the petals one by one, devouring. I smiled to myself as the elevator pinged its arrival at my floor. I drew a bath in the jetted tub, and was adding pink bubbles to the swirling water when my phone rang.

"Staci, I have your bag," Alec said. "You left it by my computer desk." A sudden thrill ran through me, because my bag contained my passport, which I needed to fly home the next morning.

"I'll drive over and pick it up now," I said, quickly putting on my coat. I met him minutes later in his lobby, the doorman watching us curiously as Alec handed me my bag with a smile and another warm hug. As I drove off after our second good-bye, my body was humming with arousal.

How I want to be with him! It's been so long! I sighed, putting the car in gear. One-night stands had been too destructive for me in the past; I didn't want to feel that way again. I was sad, but still in awe that I had learned, despite my body's deep longing, to say no to sex.

Halfway back to the hotel I glanced over at the passenger seat. There, half folded in the crease, was a navy wool hat.

◇ ◇ ◇

After that, the night went from enchanting to sublime. From the call I made to Alec, to standing in front of him and the doorman once more holding out his navy hat, to Alec saying, "Do you hear what song is playing?" and me noting that the lobby music was Paula Cole, one of my favorites, singing:

> I don't want to wait, for our lives to be over
> I want to know right now what will it be
> I don't want to wait, for our lives to be over
> Will it be yes or will it be, sorry?

And from there to Alec saying he wanted to stay with me, wanted to come back to my hotel, to me replying that I needed to sit and talk about it first. We sat on a lobby couch; both of us agreed we didn't

251

want a long-distance relationship. When Alec reached out to hold my hand, his touch was so distracting I told him I needed to take a walk to cool off. I ran to my car, called Oshin, and said a prayer of thanks when he answered my call. I poured out my situation, and then asked in a rush: what on earth would a sober person do?

"Staci, forget your judgments about what someone else would do! What is YOUR definition of sobriety?" The answer came to me, memorized after repeating at meetings for years:

"No willful physical self-harm; no sex outside a mutual, caring relationship; no porn—creating or consuming; no willfully engaging in toxic fantasy (abuse); no alcohol or drugs; no pregnancy or STD risk; no cybersex."

"Well then, what do you think? Is being with him sober?"

"I can't think! I'm so attracted to him, it's been eons, every fiber of my being wants this man, there isn't a brain cell left to think anything other than that!"

"Okay then, let me tell you what I think. I think Alec is a wonderful, spiritually principled man. I think you are both single, adults, and even though it's only been a day, it sounds like you both care about each other. I think if you can figure out how to not get pregnant or an STD tonight, the rest is up to how you feel. Connect with your heart. What does it tell you?"

"It tells me I want to give it a try and see what happens. I trust him. I think it will be okay." Relief and joy washed over me as I said the words; I thanked Oshin and hurried back inside. Paula's song was no longer playing, but mine was just getting started.

Not long after, I stood before Alec in my hotel room. We'd embraced and undressed, and then paused without touching to look at each other. I didn't realize I was trembling.

"You're cold," he said, softly.

"I'm not cold," I said, despite my nakedness. "I don't know how to

252

describe what I'm feeling." Alec suddenly leapt onto the king bed and playfully patted the fluffy white comforter next to him.

"Come here," he said. "We went too fast. Let me wrap you up like a special present, and I'll unwrap you more slowly." And he did.

We did not have sexual intercourse that night, but we enjoyed slow, gentle physical love, me for the first time in my life. I later realized that the trembling was revealing my vulnerability; I never understood before how powerful nakedness or touch could be while being fully present with my mind, heart, and body. And when our passionate touch came to a mutual end—strangely complete without either of us reaching orgasm—Alec held me and stroked my hair.

"I am so grateful, Staci. I was never able to be like this with my wife—I was too young and eager and stupid. I feel like I've been given another chance with you. Thank you."

I couldn't find words to answer, but snuggled closer to him until we fell asleep.

THIRTY-ONE

Dating Disclosures

THREE DAYS AFTER I ARRIVED HOME, my mind was still in Montreal. Alec and I had exchanged affectionate e-mails about our day together, and memories of our tender night sustained me as I prepared for my new role as a sex offender evaluator. I was amazed that I had been able to feel close and connected to Alec that night, yet as I understood it, we hadn't actually "had sex." I savored the memories of being lovingly held after being single so long, and noted the contrast when it was over with how I'd always felt after being with a man before—empty and sad. I saw that past sex with men seemed more about mutual taking, but this time it was as if we were both giving generously to one another. *I never knew sex could be like that.*

But my afterglow proved temporary, because pleasant thoughts of missing Alec started to turn to obsession, circular and pressured. I was back on the mental hamster wheel, and I reached out again to Oshin for help. He was supportive, but it would take something else to teach me that even this joyful sexual awakening had left emptiness in its wake. It was only when I took a long weekend off to watch the sixth season of *Six Feet Under* that the bottom finally dropped out of my joy.

I loved the whole series, the first I'd seen to feature a female sex addict and bluntly show sexual compulsion beyond its glorification. The graphic scenes skimmed the edge of my sobriety definition, but the characters charmed me, and I was both excited and sad to reach the end of the show. I loved the Sia song, "Breathe Me," that played during the finale, serenading scenes of the main characters dying, one after another, being greeted with love by those who'd crossed over before them. But watching so much death brought back memories of my near-death experience years before, and I suddenly remembered my brief contact with the spirit of Grandpa Sprout. A wave of grief engulfed me, and I wept more violently than ever before. I felt enraged, lost, and beyond lonely—I felt utterly abandoned. I longed to see Alec again and be held, but even more, I longed for the love I could barely recall in that place of light during my near-death experience.

I need love now, while I'm alive. Why is Alec so far away? I stumbled to the computer on wobbly legs and e-mailed him: I'd changed my mind; couldn't we try a long distance relationship after all?

Alec's e-mail reply was mercifully quick and kind. He said he'd tried it already, before his trip to Vietnam, and decided it was too painful to try again, no matter how much he would want to be with me if we lived closer. I knew he was right, but felt overexposed, achingly raw from our physical tenderness, yet unable to nurture it in his absence. The brief happiness of our interlude seemed to have hooked into a trove of deep pain that was now being tugged to the surface of my heart with each word Sia sang:

> Help, I have done it again
> I have been here many times before
> Hurt myself again today
> And the worst part is there's no one else to blame
>
> Be my friend, hold me
> Wrap me up, unfold me
> I am small, and needy
> Warm me up and…breathe me

I downloaded the song and played it over and over, my sadness shifting to confusion. *How can something that felt so good leave me feeling so broken?* No answer came, but after what seemed like hours of crying, anger took its place. *I am sick of grieving! I don't care if it was sober or not, I never want to feel this bad again!*

I decided I needed to find someone in recovery I could talk to, someone who could understand and help me figure things out. I knew Diego wasn't available to sponsor me again, though we remained friends. He'd recently returned from a week-long therapy intensive for sex addiction and was busy with his new therapist and current struggles. Realizing I'd been waiting for him, I decided it was time to find another sponsor.

And even though I love gay men, this time I want it to be a woman.

◇ ◇ ◇

Selena was a stunning beauty in her forties, voluptuous with long, glossy blonde hair. She reminded me of a mermaid. I'd met her the previous year at a recovery conference, a cheerleader type who told the group she prayed to the Goddess instead of God or spirit, and had first gotten into sexual recovery when she was eighteen. She lived in another state, but phone sponsoring was common because so few women were available. I loved that Selena had experience with sober dating in recovery, and that when I'd first called to ask, she'd said, "I'd be honored to be your sponsor."

Right after she agreed, I became so shy I didn't pick up the phone for weeks—I was terrified of rejection by a woman! I finally found the courage to call and talk to her about Alec to see what she thought. I'd already read her my sobriety definition.

"Do you think I relapsed?" I asked, fearful of her answer.

"Do you feel powerless?"

"No, I just feel super sad, and frustrated."

"Is it unmanageable?"

I thought about her question for a minute, relieved by the answer that came.

"No, but it hurts a lot. I think I can deal with it without going crazy."

"Then there you go! Trying to be healthier sexually means taking some risks. It sounds like what you're learning is that you want someone with Alec's qualities, but someone you can have in your life for more than one day."

I agreed, admitting to her and to myself that even if Alec lived closer, it probably wouldn't have worked. I'd decided that I really wanted someone who didn't drink or smoke, both of which he'd revealed that he sometimes did.

"Good to know," Selena said. "Think about what else you might want or not want in a partner, and write it all down." She went on to teach me how to create something she called a Sober Dating Plan.

My obsession now turned to working on my plan. I found a book called *If the Buddha Dated* that advised me to write down every quality I wanted in a mate and then divide the list into three categories: must have/deal breakers, high priorities, and nice but nonessentials. The idea of being so deliberate about choosing someone to date was new to me, and quite bizarre. My previous selection criteria had boiled down to two major points:

1. I want him

2. I can get him to want me

When I reviewed the draft of my plan with Selena, she offered suggestions and coached me to always pay attention to how I feel when I'm with a man, beyond sexual chemistry.

"You can get a lot of information from your feelings. Knowing yourself is the most important dating skill of all!" She shared a story about dating without a plan—she was now in a happy relationship but had paid her dues before finding it—and then suggested five simple rules that are common in sexual recovery dating to help me avoid a similar fate:

1. No sexual intercourse before ninety days of dating, to get to know someone first.
2. Go slow with other stages of sex—one at a time.
3. Talk about sexually transmitted diseases before sex, and what you'd do if you got pregnant.
4. Get tested so you'll have current information on STDs to share, be honest about the results, and get his.
5. Tell him you're a recovering sex addict before going any further than kissing.

She reminded me that being with a sex addict is a risky proposition, so telling people about it before they make a commitment was the honorable thing to do.

I hated the idea of admitting I was a sex addict to someone I was just getting to know, which I hadn't done with Alec. Unexpectedly finding new empathy for Jason and his effort to be honest with me years ago, I noticed my first positive thought about him in a long time. *He was a lot more courageous than I knew. Maybe following a plan will make things turn out better this time.* I was scared to try dating again, but having a plan helped me to feel hopeful too.

◇ ◇ ◇

Ron was a professional athlete, with a boyish face and sandy blond hair that always seemed tousled by the wind. His blue eyes smiled across the table at me in the Starbucks, where we'd arranged to meet via an Internet dating site. Computer dating was a new experience, and I chose Ron because his gentlemanly replies to my get-to-know-you questions were refreshing in their candor. In the section of my profile where I was asked to list the most important character quality in the person I was seeking, my answer was honesty. It took six months for me to realize that Ron was a failure in that regard and, in fact, was a sophisticated liar. That first day he was disarmingly likable, and I happily agreed to see him again.

On our third date, he took me out to a steakhouse near my work. I ordered a raw oyster appetizer, not a good idea considering how nervous I felt; they sat untouched on ice in front of us.

"Ron, there's something I have to tell you."

His eyes grew curious, but didn't lose their smile. I hesitated, thinking back to the guy I'd dated before Ron, and how I'd told him about my sex addiction during a walk around Green Lake in Seattle. *God I hope it doesn't go like that.* I recalled how enthralled he had been as he asked me to describe exactly what I did in my addiction, with particular emphasis on whether other women were involved. It was a long walk back to the car, and a terse ending on my part before anything really began.

This might be bad, I fretted, looking at Ron. *I should have waited to bring it up 'til dessert!*

"Um, when I was little, I went through some really hard times. Was abused, actually. It really messed me up, harmed me. I got mixed up about sex and pornography, and used it to feel better. Too much. Okay?"

Oh God I should have rehearsed this with Selena, I thought miserably. Ron's expression looked slightly bemused, emboldening me to go on.

"I don't do that anymore, haven't for some years. Use sex or porn to numb out, I mean. I get a lot of support with the past now, so I don't have to keep reliving it or anything. But I wanted you to know."

259

After a brief pause, Ron said, "Ah, okay."

I looked at him, waiting for something more.

"Thanks for telling me." He held my gaze and smiled. Relief was instant: *no creepy questions!* I felt only a tiny twinge that I hadn't actually used the words *sex addict. Did that matter? Had I really told him? Close enough,* I thought, raising a quivering oyster.

Six months later, after returning home from a long weekend apart, I was ready to make another revelation. Ron and I had moved through the usual dating milestones, except for two: I hadn't met any of his family or friends, and we hadn't said we loved each other. I'd followed my dating plan, with lots of support, and we'd had "the talk" about STDs before doing anything risky. And although I thought it might kill me, I was quite proud that I actually waited ninety days before having sex. I felt closer to Ron than ever, and had realized during the weekend away that I missed him terribly. I decided I was ready to tell him I loved him.

Praying for courage, I invited him to my cottage on Sunday. There was a slight bite in the air as the bright summer sun waned in the approach of early autumn, but my new realization of love kept me warm. I paced the hardwood floor until I heard his knock.

He looks odd, I thought as I opened the door, noting the paleness of his normally tanned face. I could immediately tell something was wrong. After settling on the couch, he opened our conversation with his own revelation.

"Staci, I need to tell you something. I'm embarrassed to say it, but you deserve to know."

The warmth that had filled my stomach chilled with fear. "What?"

"I had another girlfriend, um, after I met you. We'd been seeing each other but it wasn't really going anywhere. I tried to break it off, because I really fell for you, but then her mom died and I felt sorry for her, so I waited for a better time. It was after we said we were exclusive. It's over now, but I was too afraid to tell you until now. I didn't want to lose you. I'm sorry."

"When did you end it with her?" I asked, stunned, trying to get my bearings. "Was it before or after we had sex?"

"I can't remember when I broke it off. It was definitely a while ago, though. I mean, I've seen her since then, just as friends. I was helping her out with a few things, but it wasn't a big deal. Nothing romantic. Don't get mad."

Suddenly, I found myself shifting gears from girlfriend-newly-in-love to sex-addiction-therapist, as my professional brain recognized exactly what was happening. This was an infidelity disclosure, the kind I helped clients navigate day in and day out. I knew that these kinds of disclosures were predictable: tell the person the minimum possible incriminating evidence to feel like you were honest, but not the whole story, because they'd get pissed and might leave you. I was mad all right; my cheeks were now hot and my stomach was frozen into a block of ice.

I flashed back to the day I told Ron what I did for a living. When he'd asked what kind of therapy I specialized in, I'd said I worked with people with sex and love addictions. He'd laughed like a teenager. When I'd asked him why, he'd said, "I'll bet you hear a lot of strange things!" I'd told him I did at times, but usually I heard a lot of sad things, at least until people started making progress. Now I wondered if his laughter had been about something else entirely. *Was it because he knew he was a sex and love addict, and I, the so-called professional dating him, was completely clueless?* I turned up my interrogation a notch.

"Exactly *when* was the last time you saw her, and what exactly did you do together?"

My quest for specifics was fruitless as he gave vague, rambling answers. And then I knew for sure: he hadn't ended it, he'd never ended it. As his calculated story continued, I felt the urge to float out of my body and watch from a safe distance. His lies were ice picks to my stomach, but I forced myself to not dissociate. Instead, I breathed more deeply. With effort, I held my hands still to keep from curling them into fists, ready to punch. *Stay here. You can do this.*

I thought of the partners of sex addicts I worked with at the clinic, and how I encouraged them to hold on to their dignity no matter what their spouses or boyfriends did, realizing with dismay that this was my opportunity to practice what was astoundingly easier to preach. I then thought of Selena and her encouragement when I'd called her, feeling crazy after being physical with Ron the first time—sexual abuse memories had flooded my body, and I couldn't grasp what it all meant.

"Your body never lies, Staci. If you are ever forced to make a choice between what your gut tells you and what else you think might be true, always side with your gut, always choose your body. At least that's been my experience. The times I've ignored my gut messages, I've paid dearly for it."

I wondered if the cluster of uncomfortable body sensations I'd noticed back then had actually been wise warnings to slow down. I'd been torn between Selena's caution and the possibility of more pleasure, unsure what to do. Then I'd dreamed that Ron had cancer, which made no sense because he was an athlete and very fit. Two days later, my friend Oshin had called and told me *he'd* dreamed that Ron had cancer. I hadn't told him about my dream, and when I did we'd both deliberated the coincidence. Could there be something sick about Ron, we'd wondered, and we were picking up on it somehow in our dreams?

No, I had decided, *he's healthy and fine. It's my abuse stuff again. I'm so out of practice with sex after all these years in recovery. I just need to get used to it again. I need to quit reacting to my past and get on with a normal life.*

Yet here he was, admitting he'd been lying the entire time. Had I chosen another sex addict? *If so, he has a long road ahead of him.* This thought was followed by a surge of hope that we might be able to heal together, if only he could get into recovery. *I know about recovery. I can show him how! I can teach him!* But, after a pause, an answer came from a much wiser place. *Too much work after only knowing him six months. I don't have the energy. I can't be a partner and a therapist.* I knew this to be true, and my hope faded into resolution. I'd promised myself after Jason that I wouldn't stay stuck in a bad relationship again, and I intended to keep that promise.

"Ron, it's over. I was going to tell you I love you tonight, but I can't be with you now."

Part of me wanted him to protest more forcefully, to try to convince me I was overreacting, but his reply seemed obligatory. His mouth said, "I started seeing a counselor; maybe we can work this out." Yet I could tell he was relieved as I led him to the door and bid him good-bye.

Four hours and seven support calls later, I finally fell asleep. By the next day I had changed my mind, sure we could somehow work it out. A parade of glorious memories from the past six months flowed through my head, and I barely made it through the workday—I should have called in sick. Longing, hurt, and disappointment wrestled inside, wringing me out. I set up an emergency massage for the following morning with my massage therapist, who I was now seeing at least once a month. I soaked in the loving touch as I told her the whole story. In response, she taught me a prayer to use with impossible desires, and I went home and added it to my prayer journal, reciting it as earnestly as I could.

Spirit, I ask you, could you please make this work with Ron, if it's right for me? And if it's not, I ask that you please let me know absolutely. Don't be subtle; if it's over, could you please make it very clear to me, so that I don't need to go on missing him for months and months? If he's bad for me, I will accept that. I surrender him to you, I surrender my desire to you. Thank you, and blessed be.

Within three hours I received an e-mail from Ron's girlfriend of two years, the one who knew his family and friends, the one who'd been waiting for his imminent marriage proposal. She was kind and extremely hurt, and my role in his secret scenario had been the unwitting other woman. After getting a strange feeling about Ron for a few months, she'd finally checked his e-mail and text messages and discovered our exchanges, and though they weren't sexually graphic—thanks to my "no cybersex" boundary—she'd seen enough to figure out he was cheating. She'd then called Ron's sister, who admitted he'd been reenacting the same drama over and over with other women ever since high school. The family had hoped he'd gotten over it now that he appeared to have settled down with her. And apparently, Ron's father had done the exact same thing to his mother, over and over, throughout their entire lives.

THIRTY-TWO

Lifespan Integration Brings Empathy

RECOVERY IS SUPPOSED TO BE about living in reality, no longer using "misery-postponing behaviors," a description I heard therapist Terrence Real use to define all addictions. But the reality after discovering Ron had another girlfriend was that I felt terrible, and I endeavored once again to stuff down my feelings. I crawled into bed, propped myself up with fluffy pillows, and tried to read without success. My mind was preoccupied, insisting I eat something salty and something sweet. I chose rice cakes for their crunch and dried mango slices for sugar, overeating both. This wasn't working; I needed to get out of my bedroom.

Too many ghosts in there.

To cheer myself up, I decided to treat myself to a movie, Avatar, in 3-D. The movie and giant bag of buttery popcorn obliterated thoughts of my breakup and missing Ron, until the credits rolled and I pondered the story line—soul mates who overcame betrayal and worked together to save the world. My heart sank, and then some punishing thoughts crowded in. *I'm a Certified Sex Addiction Therapist who was dating a sex addict and didn't even know it. How insanely stupid, how utterly ridiculous of me...*but I stopped this thinking. I'd practiced freezing harmful sexual fantasy and self-hating judgments in my meditations over years of recovery—not daily, but often enough—so that by now my mental muscle was pretty strong. I'd learned enough to know that thoughts like that, rage turned inward, kept me stuck in the pain. *I want to get through this, and fast!*

I tried some replacement words: *I forgive myself for my naïveté, innocence, sadness, imperfection, not knowing. He's responsible for his lies, not me.*

The thoughts didn't feel quite true, but they were better than condemnation. Then another thought popped up, and stark fear along with it. *I went on the pill and had two months of unprotected sex with a liar.* What could I replace that with? It was simply true.

In addition to the STD talk, I'd followed my sober dating plan to the letter with Ron, even though it felt excruciating at times: go slow with calls, texts, and dates (take turns, don't see each other daily, and wait for my turn to communicate), build up to being more sexual (one base at a time), no actual intercourse before 90 days of dating, no risk of unwanted pregnancy (which meant taking responsibility for effective birth control), and a talk about what we'd do if we became pregnant. I recalled being touched by Ron's conviction that if we did, he'd want me to have the baby, saying abortion went against his Christian values. I'd told him I wasn't sure what I'd do if faced with that, but promised if it happened, I'd work with him to figure it out.

All my planning and his Christianity didn't change the fact that he'd had another girlfriend, or maybe several, the whole six months we dated, and never mentioned it! In light of his lies, I went to Planned Parenthood for a new test. When the results came, I was massively relieved to find nothing new, but bristled at the doctor's warning that I would need to retest in six months to rule out HIV, which could take a while to show up. How I hated Ron then, and the uncertainty his lies had created in my life! But I missed him too.

I decided to send him a written request that he take an STD test and send me the results, so I could have peace of mind. My deeper motives were murky to me. Did I just want contact again? Within a few days I received a letter back, jarring my heart. Ron was a lovely writer, poetic and elegant. He had a photographic memory and recalled any activity I mentioned, wanting every detail about how I'd enjoyed it. He always made me feel important, and his reply to my curt request for the test was no exception. His card contained an apology, with lyrical reminiscences of our time together in my cottage over the summer. I struggled to remember his recent disclosure, the talk with his concealed girlfriend, and what it all really meant. I longed for relief, rereading his letter and caught up again in being romanced.

Talking it over with my therapist, I realized Ron's words reminded me of the charm my dad and other men in my family turned on full blast when they wanted something from me. As a child, I was too young to recognize the difference between truth and manipulation, but not anymore. I did not reply to Ron, nor would I see or speak to him again, but my grief work was far from over. His betrayal stirred up every loss I'd ever felt. Or more accurately, every past loss I'd never felt, numbed out instead by my compulsions. As if on cue, my protective denial melted into stage two of the five classic stages of grief: anger.

"Do an inventory," Selena said in response to my rant about Ron's treachery. "Get it all out so you can be free, and learn from this." I procrastinated, deciding instead to read a new bestseller called *The Girl with the Dragon Tattoo*, about a young girl who was raped and ultimately exacted brutal revenge on her attacker. Finishing that book was all the inspiration I needed to start writing about my rage. Ten minutes later I read over the gouges in my journal. *Okay then. Get in touch with anger—check.*

I made a list of all the men and boys I could recall throughout my life who had sexually harmed me in any way, and everyone I could think of who didn't protect me. When I reread the list, I noticed the name of an extended family member, someone I hadn't thought about or seen for years. Suddenly my fury exploded, as if every cell of my body was electrified, expanding and imploding at the same time. It was *him*—finally I knew it, after all this time—he was the one with dark hair, my primary sexual abuser, whose face I could never quite see, until now. *He repeatedly raped me, and he was in my family!* I put my pen back to my journal and scribbled out his name in dark circles over and over, and then added:

> I FEEL SO ANGRY AT HIM, AND MY FAMILY FOR NOT FIGURING IT OUT, AND SOCIETY WHO DOES NOTHING ABOUT CHILD SEXUAL ABUSE!!!!!!!!!!!!!

Punching his name in a Google search, I decided to find him and confront him. Instantly an obituary came up, revealing his death less than a month before. I read a few sparse facts about his life: he was a war veteran, he worked in a factory, he left behind several distant relatives I'd never met. There was no mention of me, or the misery he'd subjected me to that was rapidly connecting in my mind, like long missing pieces of an intricate puzzle. Overwhelmed, I shut my journal and called Conrad, requesting an emergency therapy appointment.

◊ ◊ ◊

A few days later I woke up feeling acutely lonely, shaken by a vivid dream-memory of my cat PK's death the previous month. Overcome with the loss after eighteen years, I'd pushed it out of my mind, but now it flooded back in detail.

The vet had told me his kidneys were failing, so I'd called three close friends to be with me while a mobile doctor came to my home to give him the fatal shot. I remembered his orange furry body quickly stiffening in its stretched out pose on my bed.

I heard my friend Oshin asking if I was ready for him to carry PK out, wrapped in a fuzzy blue blanket, and how I'd said yes. Oshin held him gently, respectfully. He was so focused, his breath steady, his tender gaze meeting mine until my fear and sadness melted into love for my dear cat, and for the sacred process of dying that awaits all living creatures. Oshin turned and walked out of the room, and PK was seen by me no more. Looking back, I knew I'd let him go too quickly. I should have stayed with him longer, stroking his pumpkin fur, letting myself cry. But I was afraid; I couldn't bear the pain.

I *could* see him that morning after the dream, as if he hadn't died but was still stretched out, sleeping, at the foot of my bed. *Here,* my mind suddenly grasped. *His body was right here on this bed! He's dead, he died, he's gone!* And then the tears came. *My beloved PK abandoned me!* Sobbing, my mind railed. *He left me, like Ron did, like grandpa did; like all those I let comfort me have always left me.*

On some level I knew this wasn't the whole story, but right then, as I vaguely recalled once sitting on my good grandpa's lap in total safety, the world became very small. I felt pain like a knife sliding into my stomach. I held myself there and cried out, grateful I was living alone so I wouldn't disturb any roommates. After more crying, I finally fell back asleep.

Upon awakening later that morning, a clear thought rang through my mind: *it's all about the trauma.* Hearing this, I thought again of Ron. Every secret he kept was a child's broadcast of his own over-whelming hidden pain. I knew this as a professional, working with sex addicts day after day, but did I have the courage to apply it to my private life, when I was the one betrayed? If I did, forgiveness might come easier—easier than the angry mental rants about him that were still clouding most of my days.

My sponsor was sympathetic, but urged me to write more in my inventory, to get my part in things going wrong. Another hurt, angry journal entry read: *What did I do to Ron? I didn't deserve his betrayal!* I wrote and wrote, reading my journal to her and, later, to my therapist. It was a time of introspection; I hardly left the cottage, except for work and essentials. Grief, in the form of more deep, knife-wound stomach pain, seemed constant. As I fought to fully grasp the details of my own sexual abuse and its horrific reality, I alternated between wailing, binging on chips, and finding the strength to set them down and call for help. It was exhausting, but I comforted myself by deciding that as soon as I finished my inventory, I would return to the Internet dating site and find someone else to love. *This time, I'll be more careful!*

My sponsor encouraged me to wait a while, to take some time to be better prepared. She advised that I write out the way I'd like to feel with my ideal partner, and what we'd enjoy doing together. Reading this to her offered a small sliver of hope as memories of Ron still haunted me. I prayed constantly for relief.

And relief *did* start to come, slowly and surely, sparked by Ellen, a new friend from my financial recovery group, who insisted I get out of the house and join her for a drum and dance performance by a visiting troupe from Africa. The pounding rhythms and beautiful, writhing bodies stirred a primal, earthy arousal and longing in me to be like them and fully inhabit my body again. I began jumping on a mini-trampoline while listening to happy hip-hop songs. I read a biography of Frankie Manning, founder of the Lindy Hop, and signed up for a beginner's class. I kept going to sexual recovery meetings, calling for support, and praying for guidance on how to heal without going back to my addictions. And one day while journaling about what I'd learned, I wrote an oath to myself:

> I will NOT allow myself to be used for sex. I am a channel of
> divine feminine sacred sexuality. Period. I will protect this with

my last breath! I will not open my sexual field with someone who chooses to use other women, even pictures of them, for sex. I can protect my boundaries with clarity, gentleness, and love.

As summer yielded completely to the wet, gray darkness of autumn in Seattle, most mornings I began to notice a new and beautiful pattern: right as I awakened, I'd hear a different encouraging thought or insight, like a message from a loving mother whispering in my ear. I started writing these thoughts in my journal, and one morning the message was: *The shadows that I saw around Ron were exquisitely familiar.* I thought about *familiar*, and how its root word was *family*. My thoughts turned to my own family and what I'd learned from them about romance and love, honesty and trust.

I realized that although I was unconscious about Ron's deceit, I was quite *familiar* with it from childhood. It felt right, instead of wrong, because that's what I was used to on levels I was still trying to figure out. Sure, I'd talked in therapy about my difficulty building lasting intimacy with men, but talking apparently hadn't been enough to change the pattern.

Why didn't therapy with Conrad help me avoid this? Frustrated and in pain, I decided to switch to a female therapist. I asked around until a coworker offered a persuasive recommendation about something called Lifespan Integration.

"You have to try this new technique for clearing trauma," he gushed. "It's taking off in Europe, and it works faster than anything else out there!"

Research revealed that Lifespan Integration, or LI, was a relatively new therapy technique developed for clearing the pain of traumatic memories without having to relive their every detail. I signed up for an LI training, where I met Karen, an LI specialist, and was soon sitting in her comfy office as a new client.

I admired Karen's style, her bright expression and colorful outfits becoming a welcome introduction to each session. I also liked how, at her suggestion, we meditated together briefly before we began to talk. She was openly spiritual, yet respectful of all religious views; I still wasn't sure what I was but had come to find strength in heartfelt prayer and meditation from any religion.

"LI involves creating a timeline, or list, of brief memory cues from each year of your life that you can remember," she explained. I told her about my recent breakup and concern that my past abuse might have set me up for yet another heartbreak. As we created my timeline together, I was happy to note that from age three forward, I no longer had any obvious breaks in my memory. *My last therapist may not have protected me from Ron, but all that work exploring past trauma with Conrad really did help me fill in the gaps.*

Karen read me the cues while I let my mind briefly focus on each one, before moving on to the next. She kept a steady pace even when feelings came up—this was not traditional grief or feelings work, so we didn't stop to discuss them. And unlike therapy with Conrad, where we dug into traumatic scenes from the past, linking the series of known memory cues helped me realize I had survived everything, and now resided fully—and safely—in the present.

After several sessions, something strange happened. As I focused on each memory and more details per memory started to emerge, I noticed that a cloying black smoke surrounded each image in my mind's eye. Memories that took place in my childhood home revealed a shadowy substance wrapped around me and our entire household, creating a palpable, inescapable thickness.

When we finished the timeline, I described the blackness: "It was toxic, dense, and everywhere, but I was used to it, so it felt normal."

"What do you think it means?" she asked.

"I have a sense it was my dad's sexuality, his leaky, shameful sexual energy. It was real, not just in my imagination! It clogged up the whole house." This thought felt true, yet no memories of physical sexual abuse by him had emerged. The smoke was associated with a more covert, creeping kind of energy. All at once, I knew I needed to talk to my dad, to tell him about the painful impact his sexual immaturity had on me growing up. And my mom too, for not noticing it or protecting me. After reading about no-touch sexual abuse in a book called *Silently Seduced*, I decided I'd start by writing them both letters.

◊ ◊ ◊

The next therapy session I focused on Ron again, angry and seeking sympathy for my victim story: Ron was a liar and a cheat, and it wasn't fair that I would have to anxiously wait four more months until my next HIV test…but Karen interrupted my rant. She reminded me of the journal entry I'd written and copied to her, as guided by my sponsor, about what I'd said were my responsibilities in the matter:

> › I was impatient physically and sexually. Dating plan or not, three months isn't really that long to get to know someone before bonding at the deepest level. The less time I know someone, the more risk if it doesn't work out, and I had been willing to take that risk. Most people can be on their best behavior for about six months. We hadn't even made it through a single conflict.

> › I didn't really assess Ron's character before starting to date him; I relied on the dating site to screen him for me.

> › I didn't listen to my gut as my sponsor advised; I put it to sleep in the intoxication of romance and Ron's formidable attention. I ignored the red flags, like the dreams

273

Oshin and I had that Ron had cancer, and the practical fact that he would never introduce me to his family or friends.

> I was naïve about what I really needed in a partner. I need someone in recovery, who has had therapy, and who is willing to heal and grow with me, since that is such an important part of my life.

> Ron wasn't the only one with secrets. I told him almost nothing about my past abuse, my 12-Step involvement, or even that I was still in therapy.

I reluctantly agreed to return to the conversation about my past, the letters to my parents, and my nightmares—although since I had recalled which relative had abused me, my sleep had actually gotten a bit better. I was willing to focus on the deeper issues, but at the same time, felt slightly disappointed to quit talking about Ron. *It's so much easier to focus on what he did than try to deal with the past abuse. And I still miss him.*

One day, I received another card in the mail from Ron. I'd promised my sponsor I wouldn't open it unless I was with someone, so I tucked it in my bag for later that night, when I was meeting friends at a local ballroom for a swing dance. I didn't feel pressured to open it; in fact I felt relieved to put it off. It was a Hallmark envelope, thicker than a card. My stomach felt spacious and vulnerable, and a little cold. To warm up, I breathed in slowly, and then tried to bring air up from my diaphragm to my nose.

He is not my source for love and kindness, I told myself. *I have many other, more reliable sources for that.* I called a friend but was sent to her voice mail. I tried another, and again received no answer. I'd learned to keep calling until I reached someone, and it helped. Later that night, surrounded by happily swinging couples, I opened the card with a sigh of relief. He'd sent his STD results, and I was all clear!

◇ ◇ ◇

The following month, I flew to Colorado for a high school friend's wedding. I was entranced by the beauty and jubilance of her October celebration. Inspired, a new vision came to me: *I want to get married someday, to a man who is honest and faithful.* I thought back to the bridal magazines I used to look at as a teenager, and impulsively bought one to dream with on the flight home.

After landing, I immediately came down with the flu. Captive in bed, I again felt overwhelmed by sadness and shame from the past. Even though I'd completed all my amends, a backlog of dark feelings that still felt stuck in my body emerged whenever I let myself really dream of a joyous future.

Exhausted, I fell asleep and had a happy dream of my cat PK, but the second I awakened my joy plummeted once more to shame and sorrow, my stomach wrenching with pain. I moaned and cried, hating the pain while trying to love myself out of it. I drifted off again, dreaming once more of PK purring happily, young and spry again, rolling about in the sun as cats do. In the dream I lovingly petted his soft, orange fur again and again.

Journaling later, I puzzled over a suggestion my therapist had made to write about any positive results of Ron's betrayal. I found one: I didn't miss him as much anymore. In fact, my sadness at his loss seemed to free up grief from so many other losses, which was helping me release and heal at deeper levels than ever before.

I think LI with Karen is really helping me. And like she says, the more sadness I get out, the more room I'll have inside for joy.

Soon, my journal writing revealed yet another gift from Ron's infidelity: a mirror. As I read over my angry scribbles about his betrayal, I suddenly saw myself in his actions. I had been exactly like him, someone who had thoughtlessly cheated on boys and men throughout my life, hurting them and their girlfriends and wives, never feeling the pain I'd caused. Like Ron, I'd always moved on and never looked back, until I found recovery. But even after finishing my amends, I hadn't really *felt* the pain I had caused others. *At least Ron had the decency to send me his STD test results!*

I thought back to my college boyfriend Matt—how I'd cheated and then only admitted it to him in a partial disclosure, just like Ron did to me. *This is probably how I made Matt feel! And the emotional affair Jason had with Alicia from his therapy group; how I hated him for that! Yet I did the same thing to Matt with Kenneth, and kept it all a secret.*

It was painful to look at my own past betrayals, but somehow it seemed fair. The people I hurt hadn't deserved it, and neither did I. *This pain is good for me, like touching a hot stove. It hurts, but it's instructive. I wouldn't want to make anyone else feel this awful. This is empathy.*

Wrapping myself in a blanket, I stepped out of my bedroom into warmth, despite the chill outside, basking in the sunlight through the kitchen windows. I glanced around in gratitude for the sweet, sacred space to live, remembering the book *A Room of One's Own* by Virginia Woolf that my recently wedded friend had given me. I spent a quiet day resting, reading, and regaining my strength.

THIRTY-THREE

Confronting Dad's "Silent Seduction"

MY DAD WAS WILLING TO LISTEN while I read my letter. I suggested we set up a session with his new therapist, Linda, who insisted that mom also be present. Dad had started therapy a few months earlier to talk about stressors with mom over her anger at his playing an online computer game almost all day, every day.

His status as an Air Force veteran qualified him for free therapy at the Seattle Veterans Administration hospital. As always, the VA was crowded and busy, an anthill in full swarm. We filed into a weathered room decorated only with a small circle of government-issue chairs and a blank dry-erase board. Linda seemed seasoned and a bit tough, with a good sense of humor. *You'd need to be tough to survive at the VA.* I could tell immediately that my dad trusted her, and it seemed like she cared for him too, in a good, professionally detached way. My mom sat quietly at his side.

Linda turned to me. "So, what would you like to talk about today?"

I told her I wanted to read a letter I'd written to my dad, and she asked how many pages.

"Eight," I said, and she shifted in her chair, saying we only had fifty minutes. Could I summarize the letter so we'd have time to process it? I automatically focused on my gut, which I had noticed recently was the place I consulted for the best response in difficult situations. It was hard as granite; there was no way I was going to skim the letter I'd been working on for weeks, and for a lifetime. I choked out the words "I'd rather not," and added that if I couldn't finish today I'd be happy to come back for another session.

My dad, bless him, said, "Let's go ahead, Stace, go ahead and read it." And so tough Linda capitulated, and I began to read. I chose not to reveal the relative who had sexually abused me physically, because I didn't want that disclosure to distract from my confronting dad's covert sexual abuse. Partway through the letter, my voice faltered, but I pushed through the pain that threatened to close my throat:

> My specific examples of ways I believe I was covertly sexually abused by you are: I believe you became sexually attracted to me as I developed from a pre-adolescent to a teenager, and I felt the unspoken energy of your sexual attraction. I have felt it on and off throughout my life. Just because you have denied it was there, that does not mean that I did not experience it. As you know, I am very sensitive to others' feelings, even if they are unspoken. Your unwanted sexual attention in our home when I turned about age 15 made this gift of sensitivity feel like a particularly cruel curse.
>
> You took an unhealthy interest in how I dressed, and would often make flirtatious, sexualized comments when I dressed in a way you found attractive, or when you happened to catch a glimpse of me naked or partially naked, for example, saying, "Hubba, hubba, ding, ding, baby you got everything" to me in a sing-song voice.
>
> You took an unhealthy interest in my developing body and commented about how I looked often, criticizing my body shape and comparing my body unfavorably to Christi or saying it was "just like mom's" as if we were cattle on an auction block and you were the rancher. You acted as if my body was an

object subject to your judgment and approval instead of a special miracle and wonderful part of me. At times you praised my body in ways that were inappropriate for a father to his daughter. I recall a comment you made about my breasts being the perfect size, when you said, "Anything bigger than a handful is a waste." And you sometimes talked with my friends and me about sex with graphic detail that made me feel uncomfortable, even though I never asked you questions about sex....

Most of all, I feel protective of my niece and your granddaughter. Your behavior toward her is an important part of how she develops, and I will do everything in my power to prevent her from being subject to your sickness. I am grateful that although I did not learn much protectiveness from you or mom, I have learned enough from other sources to be protective of children. As long as you are unconscious about your behaviors, as you have demonstrated via your continued comments and your minimization with me, you will be unable to stop acting out the same destructive cycle with the next generation. As she grows up and her sensuality develops, I believe your inappropriateness will emerge with her even more. I want us to work on this directly now to prevent this from happening. And I want us to have a clear conversation now so that you will know what I am referring to if or when it happens again, because I intend to address it directly at that time. I do not want my niece to be confused or think it is her fault that you are acting strangely around her.

I'm also aware that your grandson/my nephew learns how to be a man in part from you. I do not want you passing along these behaviors to him.

I hope you can consider the things I have said and that you choose to pursue healing in these areas. That is your choice and I cannot control it. But until I can see evidence of this maturing in your sexuality, and the resulting ability to have boundaries in what you say, do, and how you handle your attractions, I will continue my distance from you. I'm sorry to say that even now I think about Thanksgiving and partially dread the occasion, because I fear you will make a comment that reveals your immaturity. I truly hope, for the sake of our relationship and because you deserve it, you become willing to work on this in your therapy.

For now, if we are together and I hear a comment or for any reason feel uncomfortable with your actions, I will do my best to address this directly in the moment. I would like help from your therapist today to discuss and perhaps role-play how I might respond to any comments I might feel uncomfortable about.

Thank you for being willing to listen to what I have said today. I will leave a copy of this letter with you and with your therapist for your chart, in case you wish to refer to it in the future. On the last page I have written down a book I request that you read, called *Silently Seduced*, to get a better idea of what I've been talking about today. If you do get and read this book, I request you let mom read it too, and afterward I would like us to have another therapy session to talk about it. I would like our family to heal this dynamic, and I believe we can. The generation before us did not do so, which I believe is why you did not learn healthy boundaries. I believe Grandpa and Grandma Sprout were sick in these areas, as were Grandpa and Grandma Westby, and the harm they caused you contributed to your actions. But I think we can do better now. I am open for feedback if you want to respond.[*]

After I finished, everyone was quiet for what seemed like a long time. Then something startling happened: when dad started to reply, adamantly insisting he'd never felt attracted to his own daughter, Linda interrupted.

"Barrie, I want you to consider that even though you were not intending to harm Staci in any way, she may have picked up on something you did not mean to do. Can you imagine that could be possible?"

Dad took a breath. "I never sexually abused her, or her sister. I would never hurt my granddaughter. I know I did not do that."

Linda's reply was gentle. "It's very important for you to make sure she understands that you never touched her sexually and would never want to harm her, or your other daughter and granddaughter, is that right?"

"Yes, yes," he said emphatically. "I never would...I mean I never thought the porn mattered. The kids were too young, and anyway I got rid of it, Lani made me. I guess I could see how my dumb jokes would have made her feel uncomfortable."

I was holding my breath, energy buzzing through my whole body as if I would evaporate or fly out of the building at the speed of light. My mom reached over and patted my knee, and I started breathing again.

---

[*]For the full version of this letter, see Appendix F, "Full Letter to My Father About Covert Sexual Abuse."

Linda tried again. "Barrie, can you understand how she might have felt you were sexually attracted to her, given what she said?"

"I wasn't. I never was."

"Do you think it could be possible that you weren't consciously aware of it, but on a subconscious level, you might have been attracted to your daughters? And that came out in your comments and jokes?"

Finally dad let out a big sigh. "I suppose. I guess that's possible."

That moment was so important to me, his admitting the possibility of a covert attraction, which made my painful experiences seem real, like I wasn't crazy. I felt a wave of love and gratitude sweep over me, and blinked back tears.

"Let's read that book she mentioned Barrie," mom said. "We can talk more about it when we have more time." The session ended, my life rotating on its axis. I had finally spoken up. I was heard! And we were going to talk about it further.

◇ ◇ ◇

A week later I listened to a voice mail from my mom. "I've read the first few chapters of *Silently Seduced* honey. Call me." On the phone she said she had recognized herself in one of the stories in the book, and realized that emotionally she'd been leaning too much on my sister and me.

"I know you tried to tell me this before, but sometimes reading it from a book, a professional outside the family, helps it to sink in better," she said. She apologized and affirmed her commitment not to burden me with her anger at dad, adding only half-jokingly, "and his fucking World of Warcraft!" Mom's status as a video game widow remained one of her more vitriolic rants.

"Your dad and I haven't worked everything out," she added, "but I can get support from other sources besides you." Mom thanked me again for having the courage to read my letter and said she planned to talk about it in their next session with the couples counselor they'd recently started seeing. She asked if she was going to get a letter too, and I told her yes, but I was still working on it.

"I know you're not going to be there this time," I explained, "but I'm meeting with dad and Linda again Wednesday and I'll finish your letter after that. Would it be okay if I mailed it? All these appointments are getting overwhelming." Mom agreed.

◇ ◇ ◇

Dad greeted me in the hectic VA waiting room and said there was a mix-up in the therapy schedule. It turned out our appointment wasn't even on the books that day.

"What should we do?" he asked, looking as nervous as I felt. We decided to find the cafeteria and try talking, just the two of us. The silence was awkward as we made our way through the teeming hospital halls. We'd barely sat down before he had a correction to make from our session the previous week.

"I need you to know I never was attracted to you, no matter what I said last week. I wasn't. I'm sorry I was a jerk sometimes, but I didn't sexually abuse you or anyone."

My face flushed, but I forced myself to sit quietly, my mind racing. *He's taking back what he said! He's refusing to be accountable! He hasn't even read the book, and he's...he's...*the angry thoughts continued, but I tried to focus my awareness deeper, as I'd practiced so often in meditation. I noticed a myriad of emotions pulsing inside: shock, bitterness, confusion, frustration, resignation. Then I felt chagrin.

I was the one who agreed to meet without a therapist to mediate— what did I expect? And yet I also realized, having had him corroborate my feelings for even a week had been long enough. Whether or not he agreed now, I'd grown to believe myself, and consider my experiences valid. I didn't need a therapist to make him see or make

283

me believable, *I* believed me. And then, as I looked at his angst-filled face, another thought came. *He wants to be believed as much as I do.*

"Okay dad," I said. "I get it. You have your experience and I can have mine, and we don't have to see things the same way. And I know you never physically sexually abused me. But if you say anything I feel uncomfortable with, any lewd jokes or comments, from now on I'm going to speak up, right then, no matter where we are or who's around. I need you to know that."

"Sure, fine, tell me." He sounded annoyed, but I ignored his tone and poured honey into my mint tea, watching the thick, golden stream wind into tight curlicues as it sank into the steamy liquid.

Dad tried again. "Look, I love you. I'm sorry. I want us to be friends. What can I do?" After a long pause, I made up my mind. I told him what I'd come to know about who *had* sexually molested me; how it had been vague for so many years, but that finally my memories had clarified. In the chaotic clamor of the VA cafeteria, I told him which one of mom's relatives it was, and some of the awful details of the abuse I'd recalled so far.

When he reacted, I was grateful for three things: one, he instantly believed me; two, in a grizzly bear voice, he stated his intent to kill this relative; and three, that this particular relative had recently died, which he hadn't known about.

I think it worked out fine that his counselor wasn't there after all.

THIRTY-FOUR

Letter to Mom:
I Needed You

MOM'S LETTER WAS SHORTER, flowing off my fingertips, through the keyboard to the pixel screen, to the printer and onto a piece of folded white paper, then into a stamped envelope, and dropped into a mailbox with a quick prayer: *Spirit please help her hear me.*

Dear Mom,

I needed you.

I needed you to be there, come hell or high water—turns out both did.

I needed you to see me, to see that I was a child, and that Christi and I were not dad's little spouses, made so because neither of you had the maturity to create a loving, balanced relationship with an adult.

I needed you to physically protect me, to kick someone in the head who might threaten me, and to be physically, mentally, and emotionally prepared to do so at all times. I needed you to be skilled with words, so it never came to that, and even more important, skilled with common sense, gut impressions, and prayer that you used to keep us safe. I needed you to have picked a partner who would protect us too, from the outside world and each other when we needed it.

I needed you to teach me to know the divine in me and to support me to see it everywhere. I needed you to give me words to describe the auras I saw, the conversations I had with trees and bees, and the feelings that flooded my body when I was in nature. I needed you to teach me about feelings in general, how to understand and regulate them when I needed to. I needed you to honor my feelings as part of what I had to say in the world, even if I was so sensitive that I was a pain in the ass sometimes. I needed you to believe me if I cringed away from someone, not to dismiss my reactions but ask why I was cringing and what I needed just then.

I needed you to have your own spiritual life, to show as much of it to me as you could, and to practice it devotedly.

I needed you to love your work, be exhilarated by it, and regale me with success and challenge stories of your work world. I needed you to be creative in some way, exuberantly so, so much that sometimes I felt jealous of your art and tried to tear you away from it, sometimes successfully.

I needed you to get to know what kind of food I needed in my body, by watching me and keeping track. I needed you to feed me balanced, healthy food on a regular schedule, and to teach me to avoid junk foods because of how they decreased my energy and dampened my spirit. I needed to see you with your trusty water bottle because you so valued living water, and to model the benefits of drinking enough water every day.

I needed you to have your own money, an abundance of it, and to enjoy your money, and to teach me the containers for money and what money is useless for.

Letter to Mom: I Needed You

I needed you to laugh, every day, to look for things to laugh at and with. I needed you to laugh so hard sometimes I got scared and you had to reassure me that you were perfectly healthy in wild guffaws, your unbridled uproar.

I needed you to be sensual, and unabashedly so—to love what you loved with a passion so wild it bordered on recklessness, though did not go past...except that one time, which we all laugh about now, and you tell me the stories to teach me what not to do.

I needed you to love your body, and mine. I needed you to exercise as play, to see you return home in your workout clothes with face flushed, saying "I'm starving!" as you ran to the shower.

I needed you to have your own friends, women friends, who loved you passionately and would do anything for you. Women who told me in one million unsaid ways that their love extended to me, and that as long as they lived, they would be my mothers too.

I needed you to love sex, and teach me about sex with delight at each stage of my development, as I was ready to learn. To teach me when and how to say yes to ecstasy in all its forms.

I needed you to know how to say no to sex you didn't want, in its myriad of forms, and to see you say no unashamedly, brutally if needed, my whole life long. No to dad if you hated him just then. No to pornography in the house in any form. No to leering, creepy neighbors, no to teachers with crushes on students. No to boys who would pressure me to be with them, and touch me when I was sleeping. No to Grandpa Westby who abused Christi. No to grandma who knew what was happening and said nothing. No to dad who would flirt with me and my friends. No to the Catholic church who would infect me with their misogyny and shame of sex. No to me who would punish myself for other people's actions, over and over. No again to me, who would go on to hurt others.

And most of all, I needed you to be imperfect, and to know it, and if you couldn't give me what I needed, to get help for you and for me. I needed you to never give up on me, even in our biggest defeats, no matter how long it took.

Staci

The next day mom called to apologize, her sadness transmitting through the phone as clearly as her voice. My response surprised me: I heard myself tell her that it was hard enough to write and send the letter, and I wasn't ready to talk about it yet.

I've carried her sorrow on some level my entire life. I can't bear to witness any more. Besides, talking hadn't worked out so well before. I recalled our last attempt at counseling, just the two of us five years earlier. It was a painful memory.

◊ ◊ ◊

It started after I gathered my mom, dad, and sister together and apologized for being an absentee family member, admitting what I knew about my abuse and sex addiction. For the next year, mom's functioning steadily deteriorated. She started forgetting small things, and then bigger ones. Her driving became less coordinated, and after a minor fender-bender, my sister expressed concern that if she got much worse, it would no longer be safe for mom to watch the kids. Mom agreed her memory and concentration were getting pretty bad, and we feared early-onset Alzheimer's or some other form of dementia. She went to the doctor but they didn't find anything wrong—she was only sixty-three years old.

It came to a head while mom and dad were babysitting at my sister's home, when mom began acting disoriented and suddenly fell to the floor, her body jerking and her eyes rolling back in her head. The ambulance was called and mom was rushed to the hospital, where doctors ran a full battery of tests searching for the cause of her seizure. Turned out it was a reaction to her prescription pain pills.

After that, I became determined to help her sort out her medication mess, feeling guilty I had not been more involved. With her memory loss she'd been having trouble tracking everything, so I asked her to sign a release of information so I could talk to all her doctors—she had quite a few—and coordinate who was prescribing what, to make sure everyone had the big picture. When mom was defensive, saying her medical care was her private business and I had no right to interfere, I figured she was resisting the reality of her loss of function and the fact that she needed help. I reminded her that her seizure almost killed her, and reassured her firmly this was for the best. She finally relented.

Within a few days, mom called a family meeting, gathering us together in their mobile home in the woods. My dad, sister, and I sat there in the country-cozy living room as the bomb dropped.

"I need to tell you what has really been going on." She was silent a minute, gathering her thoughts, courage, or both. "I don't have Alzheimer's." Another pause. "The truth is, I got addicted to my pain pills. I never went back to alcohol, but I got hooked on tramadol."

After that, the story came out in a rush: after I left for college and she and dad were empty nesters, she was prescribed the opiate for a minor surgery, and later found ways to get more. She drifted away from AA and stopped calling anyone for support. Mom said sometimes her use was heavy and sometimes it wasn't, depending on stress. Whenever symptoms of intoxication became noticeable, she blamed her psych meds to keep us from asking too many questions. She had several doctors we didn't even know she saw, and none of them knew about the others. She'd apparently spent some of her retirement savings on the sly, and even hocked her jewelry to buy more drugs. Mom closed her confession by saying she thought she'd take the secret to her grave, until dad started asking questions after her seizure and I pushed to talk with her doctors to get a list of everything she was taking. She figured she owed us the truth, and had decided to check herself in to an inpatient treatment center for drug addiction.

Holy shit. Images of Scooby Doo, my favorite childhood cartoon, flashed before my eyes, with the villain, unmasked at the end of the episode, muttering, "And I would've gotten away with it too, if it weren't for you meddling kids!"

Mom was true to her word and went to inpatient treatment, but I was so mad at her I wouldn't attend family week with my dad and sister. The professional in me knew it was a lifetime opportunity, but I was resolutely resentful.

I refuse to give up a precious week of my vacation to slink about the halls of a rehab center, once again supporting her, the one who'd never tucked me in at night, never told me bedtime stories, but instead was passed out on the couch, needing help herself. I thought I'd worked through my past resentments, but mom's relapse and chronic deceit had tapped into a level of anger I hadn't even known was there. Listening to me vent about it over the phone, Oshin urged me to reconsider.

"You need to go, if not for her, *for you*. Don't you see what an incredible chance it is to have a mom in rehab and get to work on healing *with her,* instead of after she dies from her addiction like my mom did?"

I couldn't see anything except betrayal, but I let him talk me into a road trip on the weekend, where he and I could at least have a fun drive down together; I'd visit mom briefly on Saturday.

Waiting with Oshin in the visitor's room, I felt sullen. When mom came in to meet us, she was wearing a black down vest with a tan lining that I'd never seen before. She loved reversible clothes, and I found myself distracted, trying to figure out if the vest could indeed be worn either side out. We made small talk for a few minutes, until mom excused herself to go to the bathroom. Oshin turned to me, his dark eyes blazing but not unkind.

"Staci, you need to look at your mom, really look at her. I know you're mad, but she is radiant. She is shining with such light and love! Do not miss this chance to see her here. It may be the first time you ever have." Confused, I watched her return from the bathroom in her puffy vest, wearing no makeup, her short, curly white hair more flat than usual. Oshin asked her a steady stream of questions about rehab life, laughing at her anecdotes and recounting his own from two stints in inpatient treatment where, right after he'd been admitted, they took his shoes.

I stared at her face as they talked, trying to figure out what Oshin was talking about. Then I saw it: behind her eyes, there was something new. I saw mom, yet I also saw someone there, beyond her role as my mom, alive in a way I'd never noticed before.

For the first time in her life, she feels safe.

Catching me staring, mom said, "Honey, I'm so grateful you came to visit me here, I know it was a long drive. I'm sorry I lied to you for so many years, that wasn't fair of me. I've been working hard here on my Fourth Step, finally writing a letter to my dad." Then she laughed ruefully, adding, "I had no idea how angry at him I was!" I blinked back tears, trying not to cry.

I know why you're angry at him! My whole life I'd suspected that, like my sister, mom had also been molested by Grandpa Westby. But whenever the topic came up, she'd denied it.

"I think he abused Liz, but my father never touched me," she'd insist. Elizabeth was her older sister, the aunt I'd never really known, reputedly a wild, wicked alcoholic who could be lovingly kind when she was sober, which was rare. Liz perished in her fifties from cirrhosis, leaving my sister and me beautifully etched gold rings and infinite unanswered questions. "When I get home," mom continued, "can we go to counseling together?"

We did go for one session, to an addictions specialist who challenged her to stay sober and *really* look at the history of sexual abuse in our family. In the session, I told her I'd felt harmed by her hatred of sex throughout my life, and all the messages she'd given me that she despised her body and the idea of dad touching her. I asked if she would read a book about sexual abuse so we could talk about it, but she never did. As the months and years went on, she returned to AA and stayed off the pills, but she never went back to her step writing. Our discussions about the past trailed away. The luminescence I'd seen in her while in treatment darkened after she returned home, turning to irritability and seething anger, especially toward my father. Her past compliance or passive-aggressiveness was replaced by outright hostility, and every time I visited my parents they fought about everything and nothing. Though never physical, their banter was emotionally ruthless; I cringed inside whenever I heard it. It was exhausting.

◇ ◇ ◇

Five years later, I'd spoken up again, and this time, she wanted to talk about my letter. I'd dreamed of her caring, prayed for this moment, but now that she was actually ready, I couldn't bear it. I found myself mute.

Looking back, I understand that of all the abuse and losses I'd suffered, the hurt from my mom was the worst, safely frozen behind a locked vault with the combination long stowed away. I had a vast military-industrial complex inside to deal with my lifetime of mom's absence, and such protection would not so easily stand down.

"It's okay if you don't want to talk now, honey, but will you let me know when we can? I'm so sorry, and so sad I hurt you."

"I know, Mom, thanks. I'll let you know."

Three weeks later I was repainting my cottage bedroom walls a soft white, freshening up the dull gray that had surrounded me since I'd moved in. Taking a break, I turned on my phone and noticed I'd missed two messages, one from dad and one from my sister. I soon learned that each had left the same dire message: Mom had gone to the ER the night before with complications from a voluntary surgery, she was in an emergency repair surgery now, and could I come to the hospital right away? The doctor didn't think she was going to make it.

THIRTY-FIVE

Mom's Near-Death and New Beginnings

DR. ROBERTSON LOOKED TIRED AS HE SPOKE to my dad, my sister, and me in the deserted waiting room. He'd been up all night. His blue surgery scrub cap was pushed back on his head, the matching shirt revealing strong, tanned forearms. I stared at his hands; they had just been used to cut open my mom.

"Mr. Sprout, it's good you brought her in. She was highly septic, and would have died very soon if you hadn't. But I need you to prepare, because we did everything we could, and we're still not sure she's going to wake up. She's out of surgery, but she's not out of danger."

Mom's elective surgery had been a few days prior, a remedy for severe acid reflux gone awry. Somehow the wall of her stomach had been perforated, and the resulting seepage had caused a near-fatal dose of toxins to poison her entire body.

After the doctor left, we sat speechless until my dad said, "Can we pray?" We held hands and he prayed that God might restore mom to us if it was his will, and that no matter what, mom might be surrounded with love and protection. He ended his prayer "In Jesus's name" and we all said amen.

We then had a deep conversation about what it would mean to us, both emotionally and practically, if mom died. I was teary and grateful for our little family, amazed that after a lifetime of addiction, stuffed feelings, and secrets, we could talk openly about something so vulnerable, important, and real.

I'd brought extra clothes and overnight necessities and called in sick to work, saying I wasn't sure how long I'd be off. I made up a little nest of blankets and pillows for myself on the built-in mattress next to the window in her room and posted a message on Facebook asking people to pray for mom. The caring wishes that poured in from friends and family helped buoy my vigil.

For the first time in my life I felt calm at a hospital, fueled by single-minded determination to be fully present for the woman who had, in a hospital room similar to this one, given birth to me. The next few days were touch and go for mom, as we weathered a roller coaster of health crises and resolutions that included an adverse medication reaction and a collapsed lung requiring emergency inflation surgery. As often as I thought of it, I prayed for her recovery.

It's hard to sleep in a hospital room at night, and I had many long hours to think. Mostly I thought about mom. *What if I lose her now, when we haven't really talked about my letter, and I haven't even told her I remembered who abused me? She said she was sorry—can I forgive her? What if I told her right now, even though she's out of it? I remember from working in hospice that people can hear things even when they're not conscious.*

I was torn. A part of me said no, I couldn't forgive her—there were too many unresolved issues from the past that she seemed to have no recollection of, important things she'd never addressed. But another part of me said yes, I could. This part told me that no matter what influenced her to take up addictions and how many mistakes she made along the way, at least she'd gotten into recovery.

A warm feeling filled me then that began to melt a hidden trove of deep bitterness, like bright sunshine on the last hard crust of winter's ice. All the nights mom was gone after she started AA when I was nine—missing my school events, not cooking dinner or asking about my day—she'd been at recovery meetings. Her therapy sessions with Barney, her efforts to stabilize her mood with medication, and her search for God through the church were all part of her love, not just for herself but for me, too. I thought she'd left me behind, useless and unimportant, but in reality she had given me the greatest gift she had: her recovery. A gift her alcoholic mother had never been able to give her. *What if I let that be enough?*

My heart softened further as I realized that mom had done her best to break our toxic family legacy of alcoholism, mental illness, and abuse. She'd found a new family—a new tribe—in addiction recovery, which had paved the way for me to later find mine. She'd given me life not once, but twice, because for an addict, getting into recovery *is* being born again. Though I hadn't been conscious of it, she was my role model. And like my mother, I'd had relapses too. When she'd finally admitted her relapse with pain pills, she took it seriously enough to do something I'd never done: she checked herself into rehab. I thought back to the timing of her relapse; it had happened right after I went away to college. What if her sadness from missing me had been part of the pain she had been trying to escape?

And how about the pain she probably feels now, after reading your letter? I winced when I heard this small voice inside me. Mom was never slow to get to the doctor when she had the slightest pain, yet she'd apparently suffered for days without telling anyone while deadly bile was leaking inside her. My father was finally able to make her go to the ER, but it might not have been in time to save her. *Had she neglected to get help because of despair after receiving my letter? When I wouldn't listen to her response, had she finally given up?*

All my life I'd fantasized about having a perfect mother, but how fair was that? What did I really know about her life, or what growing up under the shadow of her own sick father—and absentee mother—had been like for her? Even if her father had never touched her sexually, being spared such a horror did not mean there was no impact, if he was molesting her sister. Such secrets damage everyone in a family.

And what kind of mother would *I* have been if, during one of my episodes of mindless, risky sex, I'd gotten pregnant? If I'd had a daughter before recovery, how much love and constancy would I have been able to give her? And what kind of man would I have chosen as the father of my child?

My thoughts went to my father, and what his life would be like without mom if she died. He had no friends except fellow online gamers who lived far away; without mom he'd be lonely. *Would I care for him, bring him dinner, keep him company? Would he even survive long without her?* I knew he still wrestled with the heavy burdens he'd carried all his life that no medication could fix: a depressed mother incapable of providing loving care, and a violent, alcoholic father who only got straight in time to dote on his grandchildren, leaving a damaged son in his wake. My father chose a beautiful, alluring young woman for his wife—a women with her own demons who turned to alcohol and pills, and who rejected and eventually hated him.

Could I forgive dad for his immaturity, his anger, and his inability to fully contain his sexuality around his two teenage daughters? Could I hold him solely accountable without considering the impact of his parents' neglect, and the influence of a culture that had handed the scorned, sexually rejected husband the instant fix of pornography? A society that gave him easy access to captured images of seemingly shameless nubile women who never said no, and never looked away?

And for all his issues with women and sex, dad did something that tectonically shifted the reality of our family: at key times when it mattered most, he believed his daughters. He came back to therapy with Margaret when he sensed I was in trouble, even though he couldn't stand her. He called the cops on Grandpa Westby and rescued my sister from a lifetime of feeling crazy. He was enraged and protective when I finally spoke the name of my worst abuser. When he could, he stood up for his children in their times of need.

And though they were almost seventy, both my parents still aspired to grow, seeking counseling, showing up for me when I asked, and listening as best they could. They provided material comfort for me as a child, and gave me shelter in their mobile home when I bottomed out in my addictions and couldn't provide for myself. They'd given me what they could in the ways they knew how. They loved me. I hadn't always been able to see or feel it, but it was there.

Yes, I thought, tears flowing down my cheeks. *I think I can. I can forgive them both.*

On the third night, I heard mom's voice call out to me in the dark, a strained, hoarse sound that seemed to come from someone I'd never met.

"Hello? Is someone there? Can I get some water?"

"Right here, Mom," I said, pressing the call light button I'd kept next to me, hoping for this moment.

"Staci, is that you?"

"Yes, Mama, it's me. I rang for the nurse, she'll help you."

"Oh good," she said. "I need a pain pill."

Mom was given her pain pill, but she didn't relapse. I called my dad and sister with the news of mom's awakening, and we celebrated on the phone together, giving thanks to God, Jesus, and spirit—according to our respective higher powers. It was another sacred moment, with more to come.

Mom was surprised she was out for so long, and was too tired to talk much. She gently held and patted my hand, thanking me for staying with her. Right before drifting back to sleep, she gave me what I would later learn was a "mother's blessing," one I've kept close to my heart ever since. "I love you honey," she said in her raspy voice. "I'm so glad you are my daughter."

First thing the next morning, mom insisted on seeing the doctor. She told him she was a recovering addict, and that she needed to be careful about drugs. The staff flagged her chart but seemed to keep her comfortable, administering not too few or too many meds. And then another miracle happened, one I had not even thought to pray for.

Mom's breakfast tray of liquids sat before her on the bedside table. She was sitting up in bed, slowly reaching for a strawberry milk-shake, when dad walked in. Hearing the door open, she turned her head, and at that moment I saw something happen between my parents I'd never seen before.

"Barrie," she whispered, her frail, betubed hand shifting directions from the milkshake toward him. "Come here." Her face transformed in that moment from pale and haggard to soft and open. Her eyes were bright as he came to her side and took her hand in his huge one, enfolding her slender fingers.

"Hi, hon," he said quietly. "Glad you're still with us."

"So am I," she said, glancing at us both, smiling. "So am I."

Seeing my mom look at my dad this way was like the first dawn after a dark lifetime lit only by artificial lights. Her beckoning him to her side was infused with vulnerability, gentleness, and tenderness. *It's love. After forty years, I'm seeing my parents' love for each other. For the first time.*

My parents had come together in youthful infatuation, unaware of the generational legacy of pain they each carried inside. They didn't know how to work through anger, grief, and betrayal, or that by withdrawing into addictions and taking their stress out on each other, they were adding more to the pile of misery. They created and raised children, a gargantuan task even for the healthiest of couples, but were unaware of the optimum conditions necessary for their little ones to thrive, because their parents had not known how to teach them. We all survived, but the battle zone of my childhood lacked even the smallest expressions of love: greeting each other with genuine happiness, sharing gentle touch, talking with tender, affectionate voices, and connecting through deep, soulful looks like the one I was witnessing now. How I'd longed for that precious gaze all my life, between family members and directed at me. In its absence, I'd settled for the lustful stares of multitudes of men, and the empty pleasure of sex without love to fill my aching loneliness.

Could I forgive myself for my mindless searches and exhibitionist grasping? For focusing on empty sex instead of love because I had no concept that true love existed or, if it did, that I was worthy of it? For acting out my pain and causing harm to others? *Yes, I can forgive myself.*

I finally understood that, in my authentic heart, I hadn't meant to hurt anyone. I wanted to feel special and find a way to make the pain go away, and I didn't know any other way to do it. The sexual violations to my innocence had impacted me beyond my comprehension, and I hardened into someone who could not be crushed. But I'd done my best to find my way out. That had to be good enough.

And for all their flaws, my parents had stayed together to raise their children, and now here they were, looking with love at each other, and looking out for each other. By insisting she get to the hospital, my father had saved my mother's life.

Hmm. Maybe there's something to this lifetime commitment thing after all. After seeing the splendor of my friend's celebration, I'd begun to dream of a wedding, but now I wanted more than that. I wanted a marriage. I wanted a soul mate—someone to gaze at like my parents were gazing at each other.

After a moment, mom turned to me. "What are you grinning about, little one?" I noticed my legs were swinging under my chair, my feet taking turns kicking out.

"You," I answered. "Both of you."

THIRTY-SIX

What All the Fuss Was About

Fifteen months later

WHEN HE HANDED MY RED OVERNIGHT BAG to the seaplane pilot for my surprise birthday getaway weekend, I was giddy with delight. I'd always wanted to fly in one of the tiny, yellow-and-white planes on Lake Union and jet to the San Juan Islands, and here I was doing so with a man I adored. *So many dreams are coming true this year,* I marveled. *How did I get here?*

I'd met him the previous year, five months after my mom's brush with death and full recovery. In the aftermath of that experience I realized I'd outgrown my clinic job and wanted to open my own private practice in downtown Seattle. The new business took off immediately, and for more support, I invited him and another clinician to join me in a therapy consultation group for sex addiction specialists. He was well respected in the community, and I was grateful when he accepted my invitation to meet regularly to review our cases together. I'd never met another practitioner with values so similar to mine, and listening to him describe the care he offered his clients made me want to get to know him better outside the group setting. I knew he was single, but I kept my desire to myself. During a conversation right after we first met to discuss the structure of our consultations, he'd made it quite clear he was unavailable.

"I want this relationship to remain strictly collegial," he'd said, "not romantic. I haven't always done well with that boundary in the past, and I don't want to make that mistake here."

I was slightly taken aback by his frankness, although since I knew he was also a recovering sex addict, I wasn't completely surprised. And he'd been true to his word, never flirtatious, never pressing me for details of my private life, nor sharing much about his own. The closest we'd come to an intimate exchange was sharing our success at balancing our workload with caring for ourselves outside the therapy office. But after five months of meeting regularly, something shifted.

It was a rainy November evening, and we were meeting in his comfortable office. Joe, the third member of our consultation group, was absent again, leaving just the two of us. Neither of us had a pressing case, so he suggested we get better acquainted by sharing our recovery stories. We settled into facing brown leather chairs, and he began talking in his deep baritone voice. Listening with my ears and eyes as well as from a deeper place—a place I now trusted to tell me the truth—I saw into the heart of a man unlike any I'd seen before. Tranquil and gentle, yet fierce and powerful, he spoke of his life's journey: growing up on a farm under brutal criticism and physical abuse from his father and idealized by his overbearing mother, he'd emerged as a rising star in international evangelical Christian ministry. A charismatic leader of a charismatic movement, his addictive behavior had repeatedly broken trust and hearts, and finally his own, until despair drove him to seek 12-Step support and therapy for alcoholism, sex addiction, and codependency. His missionary work had taken him all over the world, but his recovery had grounded him in a private therapy practice in Seattle not far from mine.

As he detailed his repeated experiences of public and private failure, he bowed with grief at the mention of the pain he'd caused, especially to his children. Yet I could see he'd used these experiences to grow when many would have stayed stuck in bitterness and resentment. He'd learned the value of sobriety and of receiving reality checks from others through regular therapy, 12-Step meetings, and a weekly men's prayer support group he had started in which they held each other accountable for sexual sobriety. He'd made amends to those he'd hurt, and his children, now grown with families of their own, remained bright spots in his life.

"My life isn't perfect," he said, a wry sparkle in his sea blue eyes. "In fact, it's pretty mellow compared to my old standards. Being a therapist, reading a good book, watching movies, doing service in recovery. I haven't gone back to church, but I do feel the quiet presence of Jesus guiding me and loving me, despite my flaws."

As I thanked him for his honesty, the attraction I'd kept at bay for months slipped out of my careful grasp, deepening as I witnessed his compelling balance of strength and humility. I admired how he had used steadfast recovery to shift devastation into quiet wisdom, and then offered what he'd learned to help others. He was handsome and magnetic, and I loved being near him, even though we hadn't yet touched.

At least not physically.

Then it was my turn to speak, and when I was through I was trembling, amazed that I'd told him my story at a greater depth than I'd ever told anyone before. I claimed it all—the lies, hurting others, and my battles in recovery to get sexually sober and make it right. Harder even than admitting that, I spoke of the sexual abuse I'd suffered that was still slowly revealing itself.

The intense compassion of his response calmed me, and we sat in silence gazing into each other's eyes, being together. When our conversation resumed, we found even more common ground in gratitude that the pain of our addictions had led us both to recovery, and a healing process that had relieved us of our worst and given us back our best, despite everything we'd been through.

"Hey," he finally said, when the conversation had ebbed once again into intimate silence. "Do you want to go get something to eat? Just as friends."

I said yes, and that first night out I laughed more than I had in as long as I could remember. I was careful not to flirt, calling my sponsor immediately after dinner and, over the next few weeks, detailing each moment of the conversation with close friends. They urged me to go slowly, considering his earlier "no romance" boundary, and watch what unfolded. Over the next several weeks, there was no overt romance, not even a hug, but we went out to eat a couple more times after consultation group. I went out on a few dates with other men, but in my head I compared them all to him, and each fell short.

Two months later, after yet another jovial dinner together, I couldn't hide my feelings anymore. I was tumbling down into mysterious new territory that felt far more terrifying and exhilarating than any I'd known before. I was starting to notice signs of affection from him I didn't want to ignore, and I realized that after a lifetime of false starts, this might actually be the real thing. At my sponsor's urging, I asked him to meet me in a coffee shop near the University of Washington to—she helped me write the script—"talk about the nature of our relationship." I was relieved when he agreed, and after an awkward start, both of us shyly admitted we had feelings for each other beyond friendship. Later, we walked around the picturesque campus and wandered into the sanctuary of the Suzzallo Library's reading room, its walls lined with stained-glass windows reaching up to the vaulted ceiling sixty-five feet above. As we sat in silence, I prayed that this relationship might be divinely guided. It was a wonderful beginning.

We met later that week for one more discussion before we officially started dating, in which we explored the boundaries we felt comfortable with around physical affection. It was strange to be so mature and deliberate, trying to cover all the bases before we even stepped on the field, so to speak. I might have thought such conversations would diminish the power of my attraction by removing all the suspense, but to my surprise our talks only increased it. We hadn't covered quite everything, however, which became clear during our first formal dinner date.

We were seated at a candlelit table by bay windows overlooking the darkening Seattle waterfront. I was watching two distant ferries slowly intersect across the cobalt surface, their golden lights glinting at me like jewels, when he broke the news.

"One thing I should tell you, and like most of my boundaries, I've learned this the hard way: I don't want to have sex before I'm married. Not to be presumptuous, but since we're dating now, I thought you should know."

I fumbled with my water glass, trying to appear calm. The intense pleasure of being near him collided rudely with this new fact, and I tried to fathom how waiting that long might be humanly possible. Since admitting my feelings for him, they had grown exponentially, to levels I could barely comprehend with my conscious mind. *That's crazy! I know I want to get married someday, but when? How on earth could I hold out that long?* Yet the idea of letting him go seemed even more painful.

Welcome to the world of sexually sober dating, I answered myself. Where people tell each other the truth about who they are and what they want. Better keep praying. And I did.

In this new kind of dating, I learned that sexual chemistry was not inflamed by secrecy, but tempered and deepened with honesty and directness. Eventually, I met his family and friends and he met mine. We had conflicts, and we resolved them one at a time and felt even closer. And for the first time, I worked together with a man to build a hearth for our flames of desire, instead of flash burning the

306

whole house, leaving nothing but euphoric recall and smoke on the barren horizon. I would eventually discover that sex really could be making love: creative and passionate and tender and transcendent. And I would learn the incredible truth that the more intimacy grew, the more wonderful lovemaking became. But before all that, my husband-to-be gave me a beautiful gift: the opportunity to further practice the grace of patience, and how exquisitely worth it waiting could be.

◇ ◇ ◇

The day of our wedding a year and a half later was the closest I've come (so far) to the heaven I'd visited during my near-death experience. My sister, Christi, serving as my loyal matron of honor, gracefully coordinated our celebration plans behind the scenes, and kept me sane when the pressure mounted. Almost everyone we knew, from near and far, was able to join us. My fiancé's adult son and daughter from a previous marriage flew in for the event; his daughter would be reading the "love chapter" from 1 Corinthians 13 in the Bible, and his son was the best man. The whole wedding week was a kaleidoscope of beauty, effortlessly intimate connections, and whimsical laughter, all nested in thriving, loving community.

Our ceremony and reception were held on the same land where my drum circle used to meet: the beautiful Seattle Native American cultural center called Daybreak Star. It was a stunning August day, not a cloud in the sky, and bright sunlight poured through tall cedar-framed windows into the two-story room surrounded by colorful native art. As I stepped into place at the top of the stairs to make my entrance, the guitarist concluded his acoustic melody in the chamber below. In the ensuing silence, over a hundred people in the audience stood, in unison, to look up at me.

What do they see? I'd let myself thoroughly enjoy being pampered by a series of beauty appointments, including a professional updo, makeover, manicure, and pedicure, choosing a sparkly nail polish that matched my coral bridal bouquet. The white chiffon gown my mom and sister had helped me pick out was a halter sheath that reminded me of Hollywood in the fifties: elegantly sultry. It was delightful to reclaim the joy of dressing up in celebration of the occasion.

I blinked back tears as the smiling faces of friends and family briefly blurred into a sea of love and light. Oshin stood proudly, ready to sing "Amazing Grace" and "Bless the Broken Road" during the ceremony. Next to him was Anthony, my fireman friend who had inspired me in meetings over the years, and who would be reading a passage from the Big Book of Alcoholics Anonymous. Charlie and Arlene, two former drum buddies, were in charge of the send-off at the end of the night, where they would be handing out two-foot-long sparklers for a festive adieu. Laura, my hair balancer, was there with her husband, as were Hal and his new sweetheart, and my oldest friend Erin next to her once-toddler son, who had grown to basketball-star height. Several sponsees beamed up at me, and even Kenneth from the Crisis Clinic was there; we'd reconnected as intrigue-free friends following my formal amends to him, and he'd started his own sexual recovery not long after.

When the music started playing a Hawaiian rendition of "Only You," I took a breath and began my descent, careful not to misstep, keeping a firm grip on the railing for support. As I looked from face to face around the room, each one brighter than the last, warm love filled my chest and poured out of me, expanding as it went. My eyes found my sister, waiting for me at the front of the room by a pink, rose-covered archway. She looked beautiful and grounded in a coral dress stitched with delicate white beads. My sweet niece was a flower girl wearing a white tulle ballerina skirt she'd happily picked out herself, and my nephew stood by her along with my brother-in-law, as dapper ushers.

My parents awaited me at the bottom of the stairs like spruced-up sentries, their expressions a mixture of pride and tenderness. After all we'd been through, it meant the world to me that they could be there, standing by me on this day to wish me well. My father hadn't made a single inappropriate comment since the day I read him my letter at the VA, and I'd met with my mom and my therapist to share more with her about the past abuse. To my relief she'd listened, validated my feelings, and been loving and kind. Their relationship had stayed strong, and I was proud to link arms with them and slowly walk together down the satin runner.

Then I saw my fiancé waiting, tall and gorgeous in his immaculate black suit. As I reached him, my parents embraced me with happy smiles. I turned to face him, the best man I had ever known, and was overcome by wonder and gratitude that this moment had finally arrived. As I prepared to pledge my love and fidelity before those gathered around us, I felt a kind of nakedness that was altogether new: a raw, intense vulnerability that was completely free from fear. I'd written my vows myself, and after more than a decade of hard work, support, and grace, I knew, one day at a time, I would keep them.

The End

(But Really, a Whole New Beginning)

Top left: Age 43, A playful moment during wedding photos. Top right: Whimsy with my sister Christi during reception dance. Middle: Age 44, A happy moment with Pat after a talk I gave on healing from sex and love addiction. Bottom: Mom and Dad walking me down the aisle.

Author's Note

I HOPE YOU HAVE BENEFITED from reading this book, and that it might inspire you to claim and achieve your own best vision about sex and love, whatever it is. If you need a suggestion until you come up with your own, feel free to borrow mine:

> May you discover and fully enjoy your sexuality in a safe, honest, loving relationship, starting with yourself! If you want a sexual relationship with another, may you completely choose your partner, and be fully chosen by them. May you say what you want, feel, and need directly, without shame, in a million loving ways, and may you be fully heard. May you make sexual choices by respecting your true desires and the true desires of others. And at the perfect time, may you enjoy lovemaking in all its physical, mental, emotional, and transcendent glory!
>
> As you create pleasure and joy through sex, may you be free from harm in all forms, including the transmission of infection and any risk of unwanted pregnancy. If you want the sacred duty of parenting, may you conceive or adopt with love. And if you've been hurt sexually, like so many of us have, may you find all the help you need to heal quickly and completely.
>
> Your sexual creativity is a vital, beautiful part of who you are, and deserves protection. May you keep it in balance with all your other values and desires, including your physical and emotional well-being, your spiritual or religious practices, your friendships, school, work, or other forms of creativity, your family and parenting responsibilities if you have them, and your service to the community. If you desire it, may you fully explore the safety and wild joy of sacred sexuality!

And as your own sexual visions come true, perhaps you will join

311

me in helping to make my global dream into a reality for the next generation:

> I have a vision that as young people journey in sacred sexuality, they will be surrounded with love, empowerment, support, and protection. And I dream that one day soon, they will no longer need so much protection.

Please join the conversation at www.facebook.com/staci.sprout, www.stacisprout.tumblr.com, and www.twitter.com/stacisprout.

Gratitudes

OF ALL THE PARTS OF THIS BOOK, this one is the most humbling to write. For my words to truly convey the feelings of my heart, I would have to write epic poems, but I'm no poet and will have to fall back on simple thanksgivings and hope they suffice.

My gratitude to my dear sister, Christi Zellerhoff, whose love and support elevated this project exponentially. You read every word and *still* gave your consent, though this story exposes some of your pain too. The spirit of service that motivated you shored me up on difficult days; my truth on those days was that if you could stand behind me, then I could keep going. Your suggestions of family stories, emphasis, and details I'd forgotten were crucial to the finished product. I love the confidence and vulnerability you have shown to me throughout our lives. You are beautiful inside and out: a professional model *and* a role model to me of loving character and faith.

To my memoir writer's support group (aka "The Memoir Mafia": Abby Smith, Helen Wattley-Ames, Mercedes Nicole, Linda Lockwood, Julie Bjorklund, the late, great Don Normark, Angela Gillium, and honorary members Jennifer Hopkins and Roz Duavit Pasion), I offer you my deepest thanks. Week after week, you listened to me read and shared your beautiful writing with me, modeling how to be courageous with my raw attempts. You heard words I'd never shared with anyone and kindly encouraged me to share even more. You told me what worked for you and what didn't, never shirking your role of helping me hone my craft. Whatever is still not silky smooth in this book is surely something you pointed out that I did not listen to! You also showed me that real writers live well and die well, through your wild dancing at my wedding reception and, later, by Don's most amazing exit—reading us an excerpt from his memoir, from his hospital bed, hours before his death, surrounded by love and Mercedes' uplifting music as we sang along.

Many other generous souls took time to read my early drafts and offer feedback via pen or keyboard. My four beta readers, Maia Rose, Ben Black, Leila Kubegusa, and Carmen Holiday, each slogged through my many messes and handed me back brilliant ideas for cleaning things up. They prevailed over sadness and confusion, sharing concern and even loving confrontation when this first-time writer was being stubborn and blind. I knew that when I heard the same comments from multiple people I trusted implicitly, it was I who needed to yield. To my betas, I thank you for being the kind of friends and writers who graciously tell the truth. From you I learned compassion for myself and my family at levels I didn't know existed. May you receive back the kindness you offered me a hundredfold!

My later draft readers were invaluable, each suggesting improvements to the manuscript the rest of us had somehow missed. To my sisters in recovery who told me to include more hard details to better represent the horror of sex addiction for women, and to those who shared where they had to stop reading because the words hit too painfully close to home, I thank you. You know who you are and I love you. The women of the sexual recovery movement are amazing graces, and I feel blessed to be among your company.

To my friends Kim Kubal, Diane Schwartz, Jeannie O'Gorman, Cheri Cox, and Jim Hustad who each gave stellar detail, fine copy editing, content polish, proofreading, and encouragement, I thank you for taking your valuable time and energy on my behalf. It takes a village to raise a book, and you are my book-mamas (and papa) too!

To my compassionate colleague and friend Robbin Wolf, LCSW, CAP, Sexologist, CSAT, I offer my deep gratitude for your generous consultation on the project. You helped me sort through my childhood sexual experiences to determine what they meant and what to include. Your direct and fair witnessing was healing for me, as was your expertise about resources for sexually abused children, and the impact such sexualization can have on later compulsion for children and adults. I eagerly look forward to reading *anything* you write on this subject.

I'm also grateful for my writing coach M.J. Schwader, whose mentorship on writing memoir steered me away from using my annoying know-it-all voice to cover up painful realities, and to whom I was accountable for writing weekly. M.J. was often more of a skilled therapist and magician than a writing coach, helping me push past blocks to write about what was true, and then rewriting what was even more true. M.J., you are awesome and I can't wait to read your memoir on your transgender adventures!

I thank my dear therapist (who will remain anonymous) and my magnificent massage therapist, Cypress Mendoza, for being safe harbors where I could get help to make sense of the feelings that emerged throughout this process, along with the memories of abuse that were further unearthed as I tried to find my authentic voice. Jackie Stratton was a loving energy healer and midwife to this first soul-baby. Jeffrey Serage, your feedback as a colleague and enduring friend has been invaluable. Betsy, your loving guidance has been a vital part of the happy ending of this story, thank you! Maria, my star translator and fairy godmother, I adore you! And to the pioneer CSAT, author, and role model Marnie Ferree, your guidance over lunch was instrumental in empowering me to throw the dice with self-publishing and claim ownership of my story.

To my UK recovery brother for your feedback: the depth of your perspective dazzled me (as always). Your gentle questions about the man behind the shadowy figure of my abusive relative in this story reminded me that *all* humans deserve compassion, perhaps most of all those who wear such distressing disguises. And to all those who gave their permission for me to write about you—and even picked your pseudonyms: muchas, muchas gracias!

I am also grateful to my support team during the final two years of writing and editing: the luminaries Trish Fotheringham, Leila Kubegusa, and Melisa Noel. Our weekly gatherings were sanctuaries, and I will always cherish your time, your loving attention, and the way you shared yourselves so generously with me. You understood like no one else, and I thank you.

To my copy editor, Lea Galanter: your finesse with words left me in awe as you pruned away the unnecessary clutter so the story could simply be. Your speedy returns of chapters edited were awaited with great anticipation, like Christmas every few days! One regret I have about finishing this project is that I won't be getting shiny new chapters from you anymore…but I think there are a few more books inside me, so I hope you'll keep some space on your dance card for me. And thank you Laura Sullivan, the hair whisperer, for connecting Lea and me at the perfect time!

I am grateful for PatP, Gary and Sara, Lisa Marie, Linda and Jinpa, and all the other inspired financial advisors and friends who guided me over these years to make sane, solvent decisions about this project.

To my oldest friends and Summit Sisters Erin Earle, Kat Anderson-Wolff, and Julie Wahlstrom-Zavala, you weathered my disclosures about my past and supported this project as you have always supported me: unconditionally. How lucky and blessed am I to have lifetime friends like you!

To my parents, Barrie and Leilani Sprout, I extend my love and heartfelt thanks. Despite the brutality handed down from generations of alcoholism and other addictions, mental illness, and abuse, you gave me your full permission to trust, feel, and share in this book, and that has been tremendously healing. May the tide fully turn with us.

Gratitudes

To my husband, Patrick Means, I offer my eternal gratitude. What kind of security—on all levels—would a husband need to support his wife in publishing a memoir about her sex addiction recovery? What kind of strength would he have to be blessed with to brave the challenge of sifting through some of the details included within (and many more that ended up in that dark space where deleted words and phrases go)? Pat, your dedication to helping me carry the message of hope to those suffering from sex addiction has proven unshakable. Many a time while writing, my courage wavered and I wished you would ask me to stop, to not publish, but you never did. I can still hear the words you earnestly repeated from the beginning, "I believe in your story one hundred percent, and I *know* it will help a lot of people." Your love inspired me to get serious about writing, and sharing your astute ideas and experience as an author (*Men's Secret Wars, The Boundaries Book*) were priceless gifts that helped make the manuscript better. Our passion was my muse, and I found healing in your love during those dark days when it seemed like the pain and shame of revisiting the past would never fade. I love you, honey, and I thank you for your steadfast love and inspiration. It is not an exaggeration to say this book would not exist without you. You are my treasure beyond measure.

And, finally, to my creator, by the many names and faces I have come to know you: the divine feminine spirit in all her forms; Jesus; my helpful ancestors; all the patient and kind angels, guides, and human souls; Gaia-Earth, and the animal spirits and faerie folk who have supported this endeavor; I thank you. I honor you, I love you, and I respect you. What a magical adventure it has been! Thank you, thank you, thank you all for your assistance in placing this story into the hearts and hands of everyone who may benefit from it.

★ ★★

Appendices

"Every great dream begins with a dreamer.
Always remember, you have within you the strength, the patience, and
the passion to reach for the stars to change the world.
-~ Harriet Tubman

Appendix A:
Am I a Sex Addict?

ASK YOURSELF THE FOLLOWING TEN QUESTIONS to help you decide if you are a sex addict. For each question, answer Yes or No for the sexual or romantic activity that affects you. This test was adapted from the ten clinical criteria, developed by Patrick Carnes, Ph.D., which are used to help therapists and their clients assess for sex addiction.[*]

Am I a Sex Addict?	YES	NO
1. I can't stop some kinds of sexual or romantic behavior, even though I want to stop.		
2. I do it more intensely than I want or longer than I want.		
3. I keep trying to stop, reduce, or control it, but I can't.		
4. I spend way too long seeking it, doing it, or recovering from it.		
5. I can't stop *thinking about* seeking it, doing it, or recovering from it.		
6. I do it instead of things that are important to me, like work, school, home, or social commitments.		
7. I keep doing it, even though I know it's causing big or repeat problems in my social, financial, psychological, or physical life, or making the problems worse.		
8. I'm building up a tolerance—I need more intensity of what I do to get the same effect.		
9. I'm giving up or limiting social, work, or fun activities because of it.		
10. I feel bad, scared, restless, or irritable/angry if I can't do it, or if I try to stop.		

If you answered Yes to three or more of the ten questions, you may benefit from consulting a professional trained in sex addiction therapy to help explore whether or not there is a significant problem and, if so, what you can do about it. Sex addiction ruins and ends lives; it is not something to ignore or minimize. Like any addiction it is progressive and can be fatal. If someone you love has a problem,

---

[*]Patrick J. Carnes, Ph.D., "Sexual Addiction and Compulsion: Recognition, Treatment & Recovery," CNS Spectrums 5, no. 10 (Oct. 2000): 4

getting specialized therapy to help you navigate your own journey can make a vital difference. You can find a Certified Sex Addiction Therapist (CSAT) in your area, or arrange distance therapy, through the Find a Therapist page on the International Institute for Trauma and Addiction Professionals (IITAP) website at www.iitap.com, or by calling 1-866-575-6853. You may also take more comprehensive self-assessment tests at www.sexhelp.com. See the Resources section for more information.

If you suspect you are a sex addict, you may also find help by attending several 12-Step sexual recovery meetings to see if you can relate to what you hear. If you suspect a loved one is addicted to sex, you can attend an open 12-Step meeting in a sexual recovery fellowship to learn more; there are fellowships for partners and families of sex addicts to get more support. See the Resources section for a list of some 12-Step fellowships; many have their own self-assessment tests on their websites.

Appendix B:
The Twelve Steps of Sex Addicts Anonymous

1. We admitted we were powerless over addictive sexual behavior—that our lives had become unmanageable.

2. Came to believe that a Power greater than ourselves could restore us to sanity.

3. Made a decision to turn our will and our lives over to the care of God as we understood God.

4. Made a searching and fearless moral inventory of ourselves.

5. Admitted to God, to ourselves, and to another human being the exact nature of our wrongs.

6. Were entirely ready to have God remove all these defects of character.

7. Humbly asked God to remove our shortcomings.

8. Made a list of all persons we had harmed and became willing to make amends to them all.

9. Made direct amends to such people wherever possible, except when to do so would injure them or others.

10. Continued to take personal inventory and when we were wrong promptly admitted it.

11. Sought through prayer and meditation to improve our conscious contact with God as we understood God, praying only for knowledge of God's will for us and the power to carry that out.

12. Having had a spiritual awakening as the result of these steps, we tried to carry this message to other sex addicts and to practice these principles in our lives.

Appendix C:
Are Women Safe in 12-Step Sexual Recovery Meetings?

WHEN I TEACH health care professionals about identifying and treating sex addiction, I am often asked the following questions about women and sexual recovery:

> › What about female sex addicts? Should I refer women to 12-Step meetings for sex addiction?
>
> › Won't there be mostly men?
>
> › Won't there be sexual predators there?

I can understand these concerns, because although my journey in sexual recovery has been overwhelmingly positive, I know that not every woman looking for support has had the same experience. To broaden my perspective, I requested feedback from the first woman member of a large 12-Step sexual recovery fellowship—a wry, witty, effortlessly loving retired schoolteacher I'm grateful today to call my friend. Her answer:

"For women, I think starting sexual recovery surrounded only by men is like wading into the ocean: some can swim, others are devoured or drown, and others leave the water before getting very wet. The overwhelming stigma, secrecy, and shame women sex addicts face creates a different entry-level experience than men. Certain 'tough cookies' like you can make it, but it's not for everyone. There is still tremendous attrition for women seeking help."

She said that in her experience watching women get started in a fellowship of mostly male sex addicts, two things seem to make the difference between their staying or going. The first is access to women-only groups, and the second is whether they had already found stability in another 12-Step fellowship before starting recovery for sex addiction.

Women-only groups, she said, or groups focused on GLBTQ members that include women, can offer havens for women who need to express vulnerability and come to terms with their experiences of victimization by straight men, but who feel unsafe doing so in regular men's meetings.

"One of the reasons women stayed in our early fellowship was that eight or nine of the pioneers had recovery elsewhere to build on, and were strong. They were able to transfer what they learned from other 12-Step programs to sex addiction, and then gently help new women demystify the 12-Step culture so they could get traction. Not everyone feels okay about higher power or God issues, and not all meetings are healthy. Some are dangerous, because some members are predatory. Many meetings do not have the gentleness that women often need to learn to be gentle with themselves."

I could relate. At times I felt preyed upon by both men and other new women during my search for help in 12-Step meetings for sexual addiction.* I remember getting a "program call" from a man I was sure was masturbating while we talked, and another from a man who called to talk about his addiction, but who seemed more into phone sex than phone support. One newcomer woman to whom I offered a ride to a meeting asked me to come into her apartment first, and then undressed in front of me, saying she needed to change. I recall her smirk when she noticed my discomfort, which was cruel. But I also recognized her intent to shock because, before recovery, I'd also often misused the power of my nakedness.

While these experiences were uncomfortable, when I consider the big picture of my journey, the occasional intrusions in the sexual

---

*Attempting to seduce a vulnerable new addict seeking help in a 12-Step fellowship is called "13th-stepping." It is exploitive and, in every instance I've heard about, extremely damaging to the newcomer.

recovery fellowships were minor compared to the transformational culture I found there. But they can happen in an all-volunteer community of self-identified sex addicts, particularly with newcomers, and are worth taking precautions to avoid. I've occasionally heard stories of unscrupulous therapists attending 12-Step meetings to attract or control clients, and of meetings ruled by one or two charismatic leaders who used shaming, ridicule, and in-group/out-group fear-mongering reminiscent of harmful cult dynamics. These types of controlling behaviors are outside the traditions of 12-Step programs, but the bottom-up, democratic nature of the 12-Step fellowship structure means it's up to the groups to police themselves.

To avoid a negative experience, it can be helpful for new women to call a designated meeting contact person before attending to ask questions about the meeting, to get an idea of what to expect about how the meeting works and how receptive the group might be to a woman attending. Women might first want to attend an "open" meeting where they can bring a support person with them who is not a sex addict, as opposed to a "closed" meeting where only self-identified sex addicts are invited (meeting schedules usually designate open versus closed meetings). Having someone trustworthy to discuss experiences with before and after meetings can be helpful as women learn to discern their own safety.

Women can also try attending multiple meetings to get a sense of connection or discomfort with each one, and try phone meetings instead of in-person meetings to minimize risk, especially women-only telemeetings. Telephone meetings were not yet in place when I began sexual recovery, but they have become an incredible resource for women, who can now call in multiple times per day to listen or participate in the audio gatherings.

More memorable to me than awkward or scary moments in recovery are the times I've been nurtured, supported, and taught important insights from men about men: their hopes, dreams, failings, and triumphs. I have seen male beauty that outshines the flashiest superheroes, not because of big muscles and feats of daring, but through daily acts of heart-centered courage and integrity, built week after week. These men taught me true character, regardless of gender. All genders and sexual orientations are welcome in sexual recovery, though specific meetings are only as welcoming as the people who happen to attend them. In my experience, most people who have admitted their own powerlessness over sexual addiction were less judgmental about others' sexuality in general, but not always.

I look back fondly at an early meeting I attended in a rural area where one man was so shocked to see a woman there that he launched into a soapbox testimony about how men *must* stop objectifying women, *must* quit seeing them as "only tits and ass." I was instantly irate, reactive to hearing the words "tits and ass," and interrupted the meeting in protest.

"How dare you talk that way in front of me?" I roared. "Tits and ass? That's insulting!" I reacted to only those words and missed his underlying sentiment, which was actually nobler. The fifteen or so other men in the room rallied, led by the longest-time member, and explained gently to me that my concerns and feelings were valid, but that the protocol of the meeting was "no cross talk," which meant that everyone listens without interruption. The man in question apologized for causing insult, and the group held a special "business meeting" after the regular meeting to hear more about my feelings, the intent of the man I'd reacted to, and generally discuss what it was like to have a woman appear at what had been an all-male meeting for years. After that discussion, I always felt at home in that group because we set a precedent of talking through conflict safely, in a way that honored everyone. (In my experience, sharing in meetings doesn't usually include provocative language.) This pattern, where I would express frustration or offense about something and have the men with me in recovery remain patient and present during the dialogue until we worked things through, was priceless to me. It was a key part of my starting to learn how to turn conflict into deeper intimacy.

I created five techniques to successfully deal with being stared at, which happened occasionally, or to replace my compulsion to stare at others in meetings, which happened a lot, especially at first. These mental/visualization skills translated to my daily life outside of meetings with great success:

> The *Fermé Figure*, which means "Closed Face"

> The Nod

> The One- and Two-Way Mirror

> The Breath

> Becoming Shimmeringly Present

In case you want to try them yourself, I describe them in more detail in Appendix D, "Skills for Dealing with Unwanted Staring (Theirs or Yours)."

And then there are the women of sexual recovery. It's important to note that there are at least five different 12-Step sexual recovery fellowships, and some have more women attend than others. The fellowship I felt most at home in had very few women members. Though my experience of women at my various stages of recovery has been mixed—it is a wounded population prior to serious healing work—my most lasting impression is of the women who have been working in recovery for many years, like my sponsor. There is an intelligence and kindness in this "elder women" population that defies imagining, considering the brutal life circumstances that often brought them into the rooms of recovery. These women glow with love, humility, humor, and tender caring. To this day, I can never seem to get enough time with them; I feel like I'm sitting at the feet of the Goddess incarnate, soaking up their wisdom and thinking: *someday I want to be just like them.* They are all races and creeds, all shapes and sizes and sexual orientations, and their life circumstances range far and wide: teachers, nuns, writers, hippies, entrepreneurs, former sex workers, welfare recipients (so many struggle financially, at least at first), computer techies, accountants, and more. Yet their enduring recovery lifestyles unite them in a single word that universally applies: grace. Best modeled by my sponsor, she and other recovering women sex addicts taught me how to love and embrace all parts of myself, no matter how wounded I was and what damage I did in my addiction.

In addition to the love and support from men and women in recovery, I also believe I've been kept safe by forces far larger than myself, and random good fortune. I'll summarize this belief in one anecdote:

During my first year of recovery, a burly black man approached me right before a meeting was getting underway. He had a serious look on his freckled face. I'd seen him in the meetings but we'd never formally met or talked before.

"Uh, hi. I'm Cliff. You're going to think this is strange, but I want to tell you something."

"Okay-y-y," I said, bracing myself a little. *I hope this isn't another intrigue confession.*

"As you walked down the stairs into the meeting just now, I saw two angels at your back."

"What?"

"Two angels, like, you know, beings of light. I can't explain it, but

I saw them. I think they are protecting you. They were right behind you, at your back."

"Uh, thanks." I was dumbfounded. What do you say to something like that? I thought of it all meeting, barely hearing a word said. I was curious, doubtful, and hopeful all at once.

So that's why no one sits next to me on either side, I mused. *Those seats are taken by my angels.* I decided I liked the idea of two angels at my back, and named them Chip and Chet, after two characters in a fantasy novel I loved as a kid. Even today I smile, thinking of this brief conversation, the risk that lovely man took, and the angels who had my back. I think they always have.

Appendix D:
Skills for Dealing With Unwanted Staring (Theirs or Yours)

THE FOLLOWING TECHNIQUES are not intended for situations where you suspect you are in danger of a physical attack, though they may prove helpful in self-protection.

The *Fermé Figure* or "Closed Face"

The French women I met while studying abroad in college were masters of this skill, and generously taught it to me. The *Fermé Figure* involves focusing your imagination on creating and holding an impenetrable mental wall around your face and body. When this wall is in place, it is as if nothing around you exists, including any man (or person) who might want your attention. If you imagine yourself in the center of a personal web of energy, it's as if you shrink your web to a miniscule point in the center of your solar plexus, so that none of your "tendrils" reach out anywhere to anyone. Instead, you imagine you are enrobed in granite or some other impervious substance, and nothing from the outside can breach it. All stares, approaches, and comments are ignored completely, without exception. When I first tried this tool, I felt quite rude, which was interesting to explore. I had to ask myself: why is it my obligation or responsibility to engage anyone or everyone? Shouldn't I have the option not to, if I choose? *Fermé Figure* gave me the opportunity to practice this when I wanted, and it was empowering. I had to let go of the risk of others' reactions.

The Nod

The Nod is exactly what it sounds like, a small nod of your head, aimed at whoever you are choosing to greet. You can use it to acknowledge someone without saying anything to them, so it's a simple way to make brief eye contact, nod in acknowledgement of another person, and move on. I have found this tool invaluable in establishing a brief recognition, yet immediately moving my focus elsewhere, and avoiding further engagement. When I use it, I often think in my mind of the Sanskrit word *namaste,* which refers to a traditional Hindu greeting, in which I say to myself: *I honor your inner light.* Instead of treating encounters with others as opportunities to connect flirtatiously, I can see them as opportunities to briefly honor another person's positive essence, and then move on.

The One- and Two-Way Mirror

The One- and Two-Way Mirror are simple visualizations of a shiny mirror between you and the person in question. If they are staring at you, a one-way mirror facing out will bounce their gaze back to themselves. If you find yourself staring at them, a two-way mirror will do the same for you. This technique is bolstered when paired with the next one, The Breath.

The Breath

The Breath is what it sounds like: taking slow, deep breaths in and out while focusing all your attention on the sensations of your own body. The idea is to use your breath to deepen your sense of present-moment awareness, and shift your focus from a person or situation outside yourself to an internal focus or "gaze" within your mind and body.

Becoming Shimmeringly Present

This was a whimsical effort that ultimately proved to be my favorite, because I found it fun and it worked so well for me. It begins with using The Breath technique above, and when you feel centered and fairly calm, you then visualize all the cells in your body starting to shimmer and sparkle with the primal joy of being alive. It is an affirmation of the life force flowing in your body, and when practiced regularly, this technique tends to bring not only relief from being stared at or staring at another, but also a brightening of mood.

If you try these techniques or have found even better ones, please write to me at my blog at www.stacisprout.tumblr.com, I'd love to hear about it.

Appendix E:
What to Do If Your Boyfriend or Girlfriend Tells You They Are a Sex Addict

WHEN A FORMER BOYFRIEND TOLD ME he was a sex addict, it was a terrifying moment (for the details, see Chapter 11, "So I'm Dating a Sex Addict"). I wished I'd known what to ask to help me make sense of what he was saying, and what it might mean for me, but I didn't. I offer the following advice that I wished someone would have given me back then.

1. Make sure you have privacy and are in a safe place. If not, get there immediately.

2. Thank them for their honesty and tell them you hope they understand if you are shocked/surprised/concerned/upset by this news. (Often partners discover hidden evidence, as opposed to being told directly; that's a deceptive betrayal common to pre-recovery or early stages of recovery.)

3. Tell them you'd like to ask some questions so you can better understand them. You may want to get a pen and paper and write the answers down for exploring with a therapist later. You may be in shock. It may be hard to remember. If this seems overwhelming, make an appointment with a sex addiction specialist and have the conversation with a therapist present. See the Resources section at the end of this book for ideas on where to find someone.

4. Ask them the following questions, as calmly as you can, though if you are not numb you may feel like screaming or fleeing (as you move into fight-or-flight mode) or avoiding the whole thing (that's what I did, dissociated it, aka "freeze and float"). But if you are able to deal with it directly, you may feel more empowered. Hang in there, and remember,

333

you will get better information for yourself with a calm approach.

> › How long have you known you were a sex addict?

> › How did you figure it out?

> › Have you seen a therapist who gave you that label?

> › Are you now seeing a therapist?

> › Is your therapist a specialist in sex addiction? If not, do they have any additional training in that area?

> › Do you go to any 12-Step support groups or get other help? If so, how often, and which programs? Do you have a sponsor?

> › How long have you been getting this help?

> › How do you define your sobriety?

> › How long have you been sober from those behaviors?

5. Then tell them you will need to think about all of this and take some time to make sense of it, to decide what it means for you. Tell them you will need to talk with someone else to get help to sort this out, but you also want to respect their privacy, as sex addiction is a vulnerable thing to admit. Tell them the person or people you'd like to talk it over with (your therapist, those close to you that you can trust). Ask them how they feel about your sharing this information with these people.

6. Consider carefully whom you tell, and your intentions for telling. If you decide to work things through with the sex addict, some people you tell might not understand or support you, and it may be good to leave your options open for the future. However, getting support is your number one

priority, so you don't need permission to share something this significant with your support network.

7. Check your gut/intuition if you think the person is lying about any of their answers to the questions above. Deception, minimization, and blame-shifting are common with all addictions pre-recovery or in the early stages of recovery, and it might be worse with sex addiction due to the deep shame that's so often involved. Openness, calmness, and a lack of defensiveness are typically signs that someone is further along in their healing journey. You can learn a lot from tone of voice, quality of eye contact, and general mood during a conversation.

8. No matter how hurt or angry you might feel about what you hear, do not seek retaliation. If you post what you learned on Facebook or other social media, or send a group e-mail to everyone you know, or to the sex addict's family or work-place, it might feel satisfying in the moment, but such acts can perpetuate harmful patterns of betrayal and exploita-tion. If you feel protective and want to warn others, however, that's important to explore with safe support.

You will have to decide, based on what you learn, if it is right for you to continue your relationship. Finding a specialty therapist and/or sponsor with experience in navigating a relationship where sex addiction is present can be essential. Be graceful but firm: you get to make up your mind and don't have to commit to anything. Sex addiction is a real game changer, but its recovery can transform addicts into exceptional people, so discernment is key.

If you are engaged and the wedding is soon, depending on the answers above, you may need to cancel it until you can get more clarity. If your fiancé or fiancée is not in recovery of any kind, it may be best to postpone the wedding—no matter how sad this makes you and others—and get expert help immediately. You will most likely need it.

For more information, self-assessment quizzes, and a specialty therapist locator/directory, visit www.sexhelp.com. To find a 12-Step support group for partners of sex addicts, and for outstanding books for those betrayed by a sex addict, see the Resources section at the end of this book.

Appendix F:
Full Letter to My Father About
Covert Sexual Abuse

DEAR DAD,

I am writing because I realize that there are some things I need to say to you that I have been unable to say before now. I'm saying these things to you in a therapy setting so we both might have professional support to have the best chance of hearing each other, and because I would like you to consider what I have to say and, if you choose, to discuss this further in your therapy. I'm glad mom is here. I thank you both for your willingness to do this. I have been working on this letter actively in my therapy, and on some level for much, much longer. Might we say "The Serenity Prayer" together before I read further?

> God grant me the serenity to accept the things I cannot
> change,
> Courage to change the things I can,
> And wisdom to know the difference.

Thank you. I want to remind you that I love you. I am still learning what that means. Growing up I realized, even as a young child, that you and mom were emotionally very hurt, and it made you act in ways that were not your true selves. I loved you both and tried with my child's brain to figure out how to help you. I decided that I would try my best to be quiet and not do anything that would stress you out. I would be invisible, and that might bring you peace, or at least not make things worse for you. And for me. Because it was also true I was scared of you both and wanted to stay out of your way, for those times you got mad. But a big part of my being so "good" as a little girl was to try to help you, and to help you love me. I learned in our family that there were certain things one did not talk about.

337

But as an adult I have learned that avoiding talking about important things can actually hurt a relationship and create distance and even more stress. I believe that my words today are the most loving thing I can offer you.

I was always an extremely sensitive child. I was tested as gifted, and one of my gifts is this sensitivity. I have perceptions and feel emotions at levels that have overwhelmed me for most of my life. I have gravitated to addictions as a way of coping with my painful feelings. As you know I identify as a recovering food, sex, love, and money addict, and have been sober and in recovery for these addictions for many years. I have hated this sensitivity of mine, and have had to work hard to experience it as a gift from God, and something to protect and nurture instead of trying to cover up, stuff, or hate. I have made a lot of progress on this, and as a result have been going through tremendous pain—grieving and clearing out both present-day and past hurts. This has taken a lot of energy, time, and money. I go to therapy, massage therapy, physical therapy, grief support therapy, and chiropractic appointments regularly. I pay for all of this myself. I pray, journal, meditate, exercise, and try to eat well on a daily basis. I spend lots of time talking or being with supportive people who know me well and to whom I feel comfortable talking about my healing with. I go to 12-Step meetings and do lots of volunteer service work with others as well. It is a huge part of my life, just to stay sober and happy and not sink into addictions and depression. As you know, I have chosen not to take psychiatric medications, and though I have to do more in these other areas to compensate, this has been a good choice for me.

I remain grateful that you both led the way to recovery for me, especially mom, and that you are both willing to be here in therapy so that we now might pursue healing together. Few of my friends have parents willing to do this; I know how rare our family is, to have come from such dysfunction and be hanging in there seeking healing. You both have attempted to find healing with therapy several times in my life, and I am grateful for all your attempts. Particularly dad when I was suicidal and you came to therapy with Margaret, even though you hated her and did not trust her at all. You may have saved my life back then. I also remain deeply grateful for your letting me live at the mobile home rent and utility cost-free when I did bottom out on my addictions and despair, was suicidal again, and was unable to work. You gave me a car and your love, money and kindness, and again, that may have saved my life. Not to mention the fact that I wouldn't be alive without you, as my parents, and I am very grateful to be on this planet, thanks to you.

I believe you both are as sensitive as I am, or more so, and have struggled with addictions and "acting out" too as a way of coping with painful feelings no one helped you to deal with. I believe our whole family struggles with this too, in their own ways. I think it has been going on for generations on both sides of our family. And, I believe we are all doing our best to try to cope with our lives. That said, I have some things to say, and they may be painful for you to hear.

I was harmed as a child, which had a great impact on me. I have spent much of the last nineteen years attempting to heal from this harm, almost always going to therapy, and for the last nine, adding 12-Step recovery. I blocked out most of the first sixteen years of my life—no memories at all. My friends used to tease me about my inability to remember very significant events and I would laugh about it, but it was actually a symptom of severe post-traumatic stress disorder called dissociative amnesia, aka "trauma blocking." No one saw it or could diagnose it, because I suppressed the other symptoms in my attempt to seem "normal."

Some of my traumatic experiences came from sources we now

know about. Working in therapy has helped me recall and heal from much of the pain I endured. Yet there is still a great deal I do not consciously remember, even now. I don't know if you know this, but I have insomnia and nightmares almost nightly, and I believe this is a symptom of post-traumatic stress from hurts I am still not strong enough to "know" in my waking hours. Although I am intending to talk specifically about my relationship with you, Dad, for the majority of the rest of this letter, I do want to tell you something first that I believe is very significant about me: there was a lot more harm that happened to me in my childhood that I remember, but that I have not talked with you about. If you are interested in knowing more, and the timing is right, I will invite you to a therapy session with my therapist and we can talk further about it.

But for today, I will focus on the state of our relationship: what is true for me is that I have been very distant from you for quite a while. I used to spend more time with you a couple of years ago, but even then I kept some distance. I have struggled to be around you and mom because of your constant bickering, fighting, an undercurrent of tension and bitterness. I saw the same thing with Grandpa and Grandma Sprout, and of course much worse with Grandpa and Grandma Westby. This discomfort I felt at your inability as a couple to resolve your anger at each other caused me to avoid you. Both you and mom turned to me for support, and although I gave as much as I could, I had my own life to live and could not be your therapist. I am very grateful you have sought help, finally, and hope your relationship continues to improve. Nonetheless, damage has been done. Although I love you both, I am really sick of your conflicts, and I think I would be happy if I never had to hear about them again.

Dad, today I almost never call you directly, I do not ask to spend time with you, and I rarely go to your home. I see you occasionally at family events and we talk then, or we chat once in a while when you happen to answer mom's phone. I'm not sure if you noticed this, but for me this was a deliberate change that I made after you decided to make an amends to me, without any guidance. We went for a walk and you gave me a blanket apology for the ways you felt you had harmed me in my life.

I have been avoiding you since then because of how I felt after hearing your amends. Namely, angry, and deeply hurt. But I stuffed all these feelings, got busy, and didn't deal with it until now. I think now we are all stronger, and God has paved the way for this session.

After reflecting on why I felt so angry, I realized it was because I felt you did not truly understand what you were apologizing for. The rest of this letter is an attempt to clarify my perspective of how I've felt that my authentic sexuality was harmed by you. In my opinion, you have yet to grasp the meaning of your actions and the impact your harm has caused—and is still causing—me and others. You always protest that you did not sexually abuse me, and by this you mean you did not come into my room at night and touch me sexually. But what I am talking about here is called COVERT sexual abuse, not OVERT sexual abuse. A definition of covert sexual abuse is listed at the end of this letter.

My specific examples of ways I believe I was covertly sexually abused by you are: I believe you became sexually attracted to me as I developed from a pre-adolescent to a teenager, and I felt the unspoken energy of your sexual attraction. I have felt it on and off throughout my life. Just because you have denied it was there, that does not mean that I did not experience it. As you know, I am very sensitive to others' feelings, even if they are unspoken. Your unwanted sexual attention in our home when I turned about age 15 made this gift of sensitivity feel like a particularly cruel curse.

You took an unhealthy interest in how I dressed and would often make flirtatious, sexualized comments when I dressed in a way you found attractive, or when you happened to catch a glimpse of me naked or partially naked, for example saying "Hubba, hubba, ding, ding, baby you got everything" to me in a sing-song voice.

You took an unhealthy interest in my developing body and commented about how I looked often, criticizing my body shape and comparing my body unfavorably to Christi or saying it was "just like mom's" as if we were cattle on an auction block and you were the rancher. You acted as if my body was an object subject to your judgment and approval instead of a special miracle and wonderful part of me. At times you praised my body in ways that were inappropriate for a father to his daughter. I recall a comment you made about my breasts being the perfect size, when you said, "Anything bigger than a handful is a waste." And you sometimes talked with my friends and me about sex with graphic detail that made me feel uncomfortable, even though I never asked you questions about sex.

Your graphic sex talk in front of my friends made them feel uncomfortable, which was embarrassing for me—having the creepy dad who sits in the living room with his robe falling open to reveal his underwear, supposedly "teaching" his teenage daughter and her friends about sex. This was hypocritical; you had a horrible sex life with mom and yet you tried to teach us all about it as if you were an expert.

You frequently walked around the house in your underwear, sat with your underwear showing, and at least once answered the front door in your underwear.

You acted at times as if you were romantically attracted to me, gazing into my eyes and telling me how beautiful I was, comparing me to a movie star you'd had a crush on as a boy.

You sexualized my sister, commented on her body, appraised her beauty, and acted as if you were in love with her romantically. You treated her more as a spouse than a daughter at times, confiding in her and getting jealous of her friends.

Your anger, judgment, and frequent hateful behaviors toward mom were awful to witness. I felt that although you did not admit it, you actually despised women, and mom most of all. I suspect you fear women, especially ones you are intimate with or attracted to sexually, and only know how to relate to them as sexual objects, not as whole, complex, amazing human beings with whom you might learn and grow.

You brought pornography in our home, which I, as a curious kid, naturally found. This was more evidence to me of your lack of respect for women as whole people and your seeing them instead as sexual objects to be used for your pleasure. You left these toxic images easily available for me to view, both with a magazine and cable pornography channels. These images were harmful for me to see, and gave me many harmful lessons about sex, women, men, and power. I feel that your looking at pornography demonstrated your lack of faithfulness toward mom. Instead of directly addressing your sexual problems together, you passively pursued a quick sexual hit via watching other women, and men, exploit themselves sexually.

You also flirted with women besides mom in public, especially waitresses in restaurants. I experienced this also as your blatant infidelity to mom.

As a result of your actions and my experiences with you, I felt confused, angry, hurt, and most of all, shameful. I knew it was not right for a father to act sexually attracted to his daughter, and treat me in these ways, but I blamed myself, as if there was something wrong with my body and my developing sexuality. I absorbed your contempt and objectifying attitude toward my own body. I felt uncomfortable having my friends over and stopped inviting them, or if I did have friends over we avoided you as much as we could.

Your behavior also contributed to distance from Christi and I, fostering jealousy and competition for your unhealthy and toxic affection. Your behavior, and the pornography you brought into our home, taught me contempt for women and their sexuality, and yet also to value sex as a way to have power over men and superiority over other women. These were false lessons that proved very harmful to my development and later choices.

For example, I developed poor judgment in how to choose a boyfriend. I gravitated toward men who were also sexually sick, like you were, and who did not treat me, or women in general, with love and respect. I re-created relationships that reminded me of yours and mom's, and have endured much pain and unhappiness as a result. I flirted with men who were married or had girlfriends, and was emotionally and sexually unfaithful in all of my adult relationships before recovery. Despite your attempt to teach me to "wait to have sex until I was married," your other actions about sex gave me a much deeper, and more harmful, message. I did not learn to value healthy sexual boundaries and the principle of sexual faithfulness in a committed relationship. I harmed many people as a result, and myself most of all.

I now have learned that your sexual behavior toward me was actually your sickness, and not my fault. I have learned that your behavior toward me had a name, which was "covert incest" and that it was wrong and harmful. Although I take responsibility for the harmful choices I made in my life, and the effects my choices had on others, I also believe that your sickness and resulting actions contributed to my inability to make better choices.

It was natural for me to want to be loved by you in a consistently nonsexualized way, but I did not receive this. It was natural for me to develop into a beautiful, sensual, and sexual young woman, but my development was tainted by the shame I felt as a result of

344

your unwanted sexual attraction. I deserved to be treated with love, honor, and respect by my father. I deserved to be protected, rather than objectified, sexually, by you. I deserved to be taught that sex is natural and a powerful gift, and to have values instilled as to how to make healthy choices to preserve the beauty of this gift.

I also deserved the model of a mature, loving relationship between my parents. Seeing your lack of maturity and fighting with mom, as I mentioned earlier, has been a chronic source of discomfort and pain for me. Instead, much of what I have learned about intimacy has come through 12-Step recovery, therapy, my training as a therapist, and books.

Dad, I do not believe you have fully acknowledged the depth of your sickness in this area. I have experienced you minimizing this harm when I have attempted to explain, repeatedly over time, how painful and damaging your behavior was to me. You may wonder why I continue bringing it up, or why, since I have mostly removed myself from exposure to your sexual immaturity and further harm by you, this is a big deal. It's important to me for the following reasons:

I miss you and would like to be closer with you, but your lack of healing in this area prevents me from feeling safe to be around you. I know that sooner or later, even now, you will make a sexually immature comment, joke or flirtation and I will feel uncomfortable and faced with the choice to confront you and endure your likely defensiveness, minimization, making a joke, or denial; or I say nothing and feel unprotected. This is a key factor in why I avoid you. Even as recently as last month, when I called on your phone returning a call for mom, you answered the phone "Hey, Good-Looking." Such a way of greeting me is not acceptable to me! You may be okay with the status of our relationship, but I am not. I never try to organize family functions anymore, I avoid them at times so that I might avoid this dynamic, and I don't bring my friends around you.

I am not saying I am perfect in this area. Last year I sent out an e-mail to our family that caused you discomfort, using swear words as a joke. That was immature of me and I know that caused you and Christi discomfort, and I apologized for that. But I learned from that mistake, and I have not repeated the behavior.

Though I broke up with Ron, at some point I will have a long-term relationship, and I feel uncomfortable introducing a male friend or partner to you. I feel afraid you will say or do something that reveals your immaturity in this area. Although I can't control this, I feel concerned that it will occur. I don't want to have to coach him prior to meeting you that you are sexually immature and have acted this out with all women throughout my life, and that you may make a comment revealing your flirtation or sexual objectification of me, Christi, mom, women, or sex in general. But unless you change this, that's exactly what I'll do to prepare.

I feel protective of Christi and want you to work on healing so that she might experience a father who can be sexually appropriate and make a genuine living amends to her.

I feel protective of mom—though I have felt harmed by her in different ways and will be sharing my feelings with her in a different letter—and would like mom to experience your healing in this area, and your genuine amends.

Most of all, I feel protective of my niece and your granddaughter. Your behavior toward her is an important part of how she develops, and I will do everything in my power to prevent her from being subject to your sickness. I am grateful that although I did not learn much protectiveness from you or mom, I have learned enough from other sources to be protective of children. As long as you are unconscious about your behaviors, as you have demonstrated via your continued comments and your minimization with me, you will be unable to help acting out the same destructive cycle with the next generation.

346

As she grows up and her sensuality develops, I believe your inappropriateness will emerge with her even more. I want us to work on this directly now to prevent this from happening. And I want us to have a clear conversation now so that you will know what I am referring to if or when it happens again, because I intend to address it directly at that time. I do not want my niece to be confused or think it is her fault that you are acting strangely around her.

I'm also aware that your grandson/my nephew learns how to be a man in part from you. I do not want you passing along these behaviors to him.

I hope you can consider the things I have said and that you choose to pursue healing in these areas. That is your choice and I cannot control it. But until I can see evidence of this maturing in your sexuality, and the resulting ability to have boundaries in what you say, do, and how you handle your attractions, I will continue my distance from you. I'm sorry to say that even now I think about Thanksgiving and partially dread the occasion, because I fear you will make a comment that reveals your immaturity. I truly hope, for the sake of our relationship and because you deserve it, you become willing to work on this in your therapy.

For now, if we are together and I hear a comment or for any reason feel uncomfortable with your actions, I will do my best to address this directly in the moment. I would like help from your therapist today to discuss and perhaps role-play how I might respond to any comments I might feel uncomfortable about.

Thank you for being willing to listen to what I have said today. I will leave a copy of this letter with you and with your therapist for your chart, in case you wish to refer to it in the future. On the last page I have written down a book I request that you read, called *Silently Seduced*, to get a better idea of what I've been talking about today. If you do get and read this book, I request you let mom read it too, and afterward I would like us to have another therapy session to talk about it. I would like our family to heal this dynamic, and I believe we can. The generation before us did not do so, which I believe is why you did not learn healthy boundaries. I believe Grandpa and Grandma Sprout were sick in these areas, as were Grandpa and Grandma Westby, and the harm they caused you contributed to your actions. But I think we can do better now.

I am open for feedback if you want to respond.

Resources on Sex Addiction and Much More!

THE CONCEPT OF SEX ADDICTION remains relatively new, as does the concept of addiction itself. Alcoholics Anonymous (AA) was the first 12-Step program created to address recovery from the pain of any addiction. AA was launched in 1935, two years after Prohibition was repealed in America, after which one of its founders, Bill Wilson, was dubbed "the greatest social architect of our century" by British visionary Aldous Huxley. Since AA's inception to address compulsive drinking, additional 12-Step programs have sprung up using similar guiding principles to address a wide variety of other compulsions, for example, compulsive eating, gambling, and the compulsive incurring of unsecured debt. These support meetings are free and available worldwide in-person and electronically, both online and via telephone.

All 12-Step communities organize for one primary purpose: to gather and help each other get and stay sober from whatever addiction they are focused on. To reach this goal, experienced members help newcomers "work the steps," or explore a series of twelve self-reflection exercises with the support of a sponsor, who acts as a guide along the journey to sobriety. The programs are not religious, but the self-reflection involved in the twelve steps invites members to acknowledge their addiction (Step One) and self-define a caring "higher power" (Steps Two and Three) that will inspire and guide their subsequent recovery work. Atheists and agnostics are welcome in 12-Step programs; for them, a "higher power" is defined in non-theistic terms. One of my favorite translations of "God" from atheists in the program is using the acronym G.O.D. to mean "Gratitude Over Drama." I also like "Great Out Doors."

In the late 1970s, several fellowships were founded to address compulsive sexual behavior, also known as sex addiction. Like AA's creation after the end of Prohibition, the 12-Step programs for sex addiction followed on the heels of other major societal paradigm shifts: the sexual revolution of the 1960s and the widespread availability of hard-core pornography in the early 1970s. I find these synchronicities curious: was society seeking to balance out the extremes of drinking from the Roaring Twenties and objectified, nonrelational sex in the pornographized 1970s with the subsequent birth of 12-Step fellowships for alcoholism and sex addiction soon thereafter?

As a therapeutic concept, sex addiction was introduced to the public in 1983 via a book titled *The Sexual Addiction* by Patrick Carnes (later retitled to the more palatable *Out of the Shadows: Understanding Sexual Addiction*). Many more resources have become available since then, but the ever-growing global, anonymous access to sexually explicit media and liaisons promotes opportunities for compulsive sex on a daily basis. At the same time, avenues for healing are also exploding, offering new methods and technologies for rapid treatment that health care professionals thirty years ago could barely have imagined. Thanks to Dr. Carnes and many others, there are more resources than ever for healing from sex addiction!

Looking for Professional Help?

IF YOU ARE INTERESTED in finding a CSAT or getting certified as a sex addiction therapist, I recommend the resources at the International Institute for Trauma and Addiction (www.iitap.com).

If you are a health care professional interested in a more general training on "problematic sexual behaviors" that includes the basics of assessing and treating such behaviors, see the Society for the Advancement of Sexual Health (www.sash.net).

If you are looking for a trained Lifespan Integration therapist for help with healing trauma, or help in getting trained in the Lifespan Integration technique, visit www.lifespanintegration.com.

There are many other types of healing modalities and trainings out there, with more being added all the time, and I celebrate the growing awareness of sexual addiction recovery and trauma healing in all its forms!

12-Step Programs for Sexual Addiction

Support sites for those struggling with their own sexual or relationship addiction.

Sex Addicts Anonymous (SAA): 713-869-4902,
    www.saa-recovery.org

Sex and Love Addicts Anonymous (SLAA): www.slaafws.org

Sexual Compulsives Anonymous (SCA): 800-977-4325,
    www.sca-recovery.org

Sexual Recovery Anonymous (SRA): www.sexualrecovery.org

Support for people whose lives have been affected by someone else's sexual or relationship addiction.

Codependents of Sex Addicts (COSA): 866-899-2672, www.cosa-recovery.org

CoSex and Love Addicts Anonymous Connecticut (COSLAA): 860-456-0032, www.coslaa.org

S-Anon: 615-833-3152, www.sanon.org

Support for couples affected by addiction, often with a sex addiction focus.

Recovering Couples Anonymous (RCA): 877-663-2317, www.recovering-couples.org

Books by Topic

Emotional Incest

Silently Seduced: When Parents Make their Children Partners, Kenneth M. Adams, Ph.D.

The Betrayal Bond: Breaking Free of Exploitive Relationships, Patrick Carnes, Ph.D.

The Emotional Incest Syndrome: What to Do When a Parent's Love Rules Your Life, Dr. Patricia Love, with Jo Robinson

When He's Married to Mom: How to Help Mother-Enmeshed Men Open Their Hearts to True Love and Commitment, Kenneth Adams, Ph.D., and Alexander P. Morgan

Trauma Healing

The Body Keeps the Score: Brain, Mind, and Body in the Healing of Trauma, Bessel van der Kolk, M.D.

More information about dissociation: http://morethananidea.ca/aboutdissociation/what-is-dissociation/

Healing Trauma: Guided Imagery for Posttraumatic Stress, Belleruth Naparstek

Invisible Heroes: Survivors of Trauma and How They Heal, Belleruth Naparstek and Robert C. Scaer

The Courage to Heal: A Guide for Women Survivors of Child Sexual Abuse, Ellen Bass and Laura Davis

The Sexual Healing Journey: A Guide For Survivors of Sexual Abuse, Wendy Maltz

MaleSurvivor (www.malesurvivor.org)

Moving Beyond: Healing the Trauma of Physical and Sexual Abuse Through ThetaHealing, Judy Dragon

The Success and Strategies of Lifespan Integration, Catherine Thorpe, M.A.

Nonviolent Communication: A Language of Life by Marshall B. Rosenberg

Working with Children with Sexual Behavior Problems, Eliana Gil and Jennifer A. Shaw

Trauma and Recovery: The Aftermath of Violence—From Domestic Abuse to Political Terror, Judith L. Herman

Mindsight: The New Science of Personal Transformation, Daniel J. Siegel, M.D.

Trauma Into Truth: Gutsy Healing and Why It's Worth It, Rythea Lee

Women, Sex, and Love Addiction

Escape from Intimacy: Untangling the "Love" Addictions: Sex, Romance, Relationships, Anne Wilson Schaef

Facing Love Addiction: Giving Yourself the Power to Change the Way You Love, Pia Mellody, with Andrea Wells Miller and J. Keith Miller

No Stones: Women Redeemed from Sexual Addiction, Marnie C. Ferree

Ready to Heal: Breaking Free of Addictive Relationships, Kelly McDaniel

Women, Sex, and Addiction: A Search for Love and Power, Charlotte Davis Kasl

Is It Love or Is It Addiction: The book that changed the way we think about romance and intimacy, Brenda Schaeffer

Codependency and Other Recovery Resources

About Codependency, Channing Bete Company

Codependent No More, Melody Beattie

Emotional Intelligence, Daniel Goleman

Books by Topic

Feeding the Hungry Heart, Geneen Roth

Forgive Your Parents, Heal Yourself: How Understanding Your Painful Family Legacy Can Transform Your Life, Barry Grosskopf

Healing the Shame That Binds You, John Bradshaw

How Al-Anon Works for Families and Friends of Alcoholics, Al-Anon Family Groups

How to Get Out of Debt, Stay Out of Debt, and Live Prosperously, Jerrold Mundis

Earn What You Deserve: How to Stop Underearning & Start Thriving, Jerrold Mundis

It Will Never Happen to Me! Children of Alcoholics: As Youngsters—Adolescents—Adults, Claudia Black

My Fluorescent God, Joe Guppy

Social Intelligence: The New Science of Human Relationships, Daniel Goleman

When Society Becomes An Addict, Anne Wilson Schaef

Partners of Sex Addicts

Deceived: Facing Sexual Betrayal, Lies, and Secrets, Claudia Black, Ph.D.

Facing Heartbreak: Steps to Recovery for Partners of Sex Addicts, Stefanie Carnes, Ph.D., Mari A. Lee, LMFT, and Anthony D. Rodriguez, LCSW

Intimate Treason: Healing the Trauma for Partners Confronting Sex Addiction, Claudia Black, Ph.D., and Cara Tripodi, LCSW

Mending a Shattered Heart: A Guide for Partners of Sex Addicts, Stefanie Carnes, Ph.D.

Wondrous Sexuality

Aphrodite's Daughters: Women's Sexual Stories and the Journey of the Soul, Jalaja Bonheim

From the Living Room to the Bedroom: The Modern Couple's Guide to Sexual Abundance and Lasting Intimacy, Drs. Bill and Ginger Bercaw

Healthy Sex.com (www.healthysex.com) and everything by Wendy Maltz, especially the CERTS model of healthy sex (Consent, Equality, Respect, Trust, and Safety)

If the Buddha Dated: A Handbook for Finding Love on a Spiritual Path, Charlotte Kasl

Intimacy and Desire: Awaken the Passion in Your Relationship, Dr. David Schnarch

Mirror of Intimacy: Daily Reflections on Emotional and Erotic Intelligence, Alexandra Katehakis and Tom Bliss

Promiscuities: The Secret Struggle for Womanhood, Naomi Wolf

The Genderbread Person v2.0 (http://itspronouncedmetrosexual. com/2012/03/the-genderbread-person-v2-0/). This website presents a brilliant new model for considering gender identity, expression, biology, and attractions beyond the binary concept of gender I grew up with. I'm so excited about the transformation of gender that has emerged, and looking forward to learning more.

The Heart and Soul of Sex: Exploring the Sexual Mysteries, Gina Ogden, Ph.D.

The New Rules of Marriage: What You Need to Know to Make Love Work, Terrence Real

The Return of Desire: A Guide to Rediscovering Your Sexual Passion, Gina Ogden, Ph.D.

Vagina, Naomi Wolf

Women Who Love Sex: Ordinary Women Describe Their Paths to Pleasure, Intimacy, and Ecstasy, Gina Ogden, Ph.D.

Inspirational

Anastasia, Vladimir Megré, and the entire Ringing Cedars Series

Daring Greatly: How the Courage to Be Vulnerable Transforms the Way We Live, Love, Parent, and Lead, Brené Brown

Goddesses In Everywoman: A New Psychology of Women, Jean Shinoda Bolen, M.D.

Guided Meditations, Explorations, and Healings, Stephen Levine

Inanna: Queen of Heaven and Earth, Her Stories and Hymns From Sumer, Diane Wolkstein and Samuel Noah Kramer

Kinship with All Life, J. Allen Boone

Night, Elie Wiesel

The Celestine Prophesy: An Adventure, James Redfield

Meeting Jesus Again For the First Time: The Historical Jesus and the Heart of Contemporary Faith, Marcus J. Borg

The Power of Now, Eckhart Tolle

The Reluctant Shaman: A Woman's First Encounters with the Unseen Spirits of the Earth, Kay Cordell Whitaker

The Shack, Wm. P. Young

Truth or Dare: Encounters with Power, Authority, and Mystery, Starhawk

About the Author

STACI SPROUT is a licensed psychotherapist, author and publisher with twenty years of experience as a therapist and social worker in a variety of settings from community mental health and hospitals to private clinical practice. Staci is a Certified Sex Addiction Therapist (CSAT), and since 2006 has dedicated her practice to helping individuals, groups and couples in recovery from sex and relationship addictions. She conducts trainings on sexual ethics for professionals and is an engaging retreat and conference speaker, sharing the story of her recovery from childhood trauma and multiple addictions with warmth and clarity. She lives near Seattle, Washington, with her husband, who is also in recovery.

About the Author

For publicity, book signings, and speaking engagements concerning *Naked In Public: A Memoir of Recovery from Sex Addiction and Other Temporary Insanities,* please direct inquiries to:

recontextmedia@gmail.com

For more information about this book or its author, visit:

www.stacisprout.com,
www.facebook.com/staci.sprout,
www.stacisprout.tumblr.com, and
www.twitter.com/stacisprout

If you wish to reach the author directly, please contact Recontext Media and we will forward your request. Both the author and publisher appreciate hearing from you and learning about your experience of the book. Recontext Media cannot guarantee that every correspondence can be answered, but all will be forwarded.

CPSIA information can be obtained
at www.ICGtesting.com
Printed in the USA
FSOW04n1851271215
14753FS